THE GREAT SCHOOL DEBATE
Choice, Vouchers, and Charters

Thomas L. Good
Jennifer S. Braden
University of Arizona

LEA LAWRENCE ERLBAUM ASSOCIATES, PUBLISHERS
2000   Mahwah, New Jersey   London

Lawrence Erlbaum Associates, Inc., Publishers
10 Industrial Avenue
Mahwah, New Jersey 07430-2262

Cover design by Kathryn Houghtaling Lacey

Library of Congress Cataloging-in-Publication Data

Good, Thomas L., 1943–
    The great school debate : choice, vouchers, and charters / Thomas L. Good,
Jennifer S. Braden.
        p. cm.
    Includes bibliographical references and index.
        ISBN 0-8058-3691-8 (cloth : acid-free paper)—
0-8058-3551-2 (paper : acid-free paper)
        1. Privatization in education—United States. 2. School
choice—United States. 3. Educational vouchers—United States.
4. Charter schools—United States. 5. Education—United
States—Evaluation. I. Braden, Jennifer S. II. Title.

LB2806.36.G66 2000
379.3'2'0973—dc21   99-056827
                                                                CIP

Books published by Lawrence Erlbaum Associates are printed
on acid-free paper, and their bindings are chosen for strength
and durability

Printed in the United States of America
10 9 8 7 6 5 4 3 2

Brief Contents

Contents

Preface

It is indisputable that most Americans are concerned with the quality of their schools. The controversy about school quality in the 1990s is but the latest chapter in an intense and ongoing debate that spans the second half of the 20th century. Beginning with the launching of Sputnik and moving through a series of "crisis" reports over the next four decades, citizens have periodically been told that America's public schools are failing and that this failure threatens national security. Frequently, these critics point to low test scores to support their claims.

Other critics, including many influential policymakers, acknowledge the crucial historical role played by our public schools but contend that educational needs in the 21st century demand dramatically new forms of schooling. Ironically, many of these same policymakers, while calling for new standards and goals, insist that schools be held publicly accountable through the use of old standardized tests that are not aligned with the new goals they advocate. Still other critics contend that although most U.S. schools are productive, crisis situations abound in inner-city schools. There are those who assert that equality of opportunity, the core ideal of American democracy, is being threatened as more and more children are educated in separate racial and socioeconomic enclaves rather than in common educational settings. Furthermore, there are arguments about who should control education reform. Some argue that the business community and career preparation should pull the reform engine; others strongly argue that the design of the school curriculum must flow from the needs of citizenship and the general principles of democracy.

In addition to the debate about the quality of our public schools, there is also strong concern regarding the breadth and direction of its curriculum. Do Americans want their schools to focus primarily on academic goals (as in Japan or Singapore) or do they want them to develop students' social, emotional, and physical skills as well? Should schools continue to deal with broad social issues such as drugs, violence, intolerance, and malnutrition that have been neglected by the broader society?

This book attempts to frame and extend these debates in the following manner. In chapters 1 and 2, we systematically examine the quality of public schools as seen through the major reform efforts of the past 50 years. We then analyze why these reforms have fallen short of their goal. In chapter 3, we examine the claim, so frequently put forth by the media, that the academic achievement of today's students is deteriorating.

In chapter 4, we examine one of the outgrowths of recent school reform, the call for more choice for American students, often in the form of vouchers and privatized schools. We show how school choice is not new but has been spreading in many public schools systems over the past 25 years in the form of alternative and magnet (theme) schools with open enrollment plans. We also review available evidence regarding the effects of moving education from the public to the private sector.

In chapters 5 through 7, we reach the core of our book, the debate over charter schools. We examine both the logic and the legal foundations behind the charter school movement and then review the emerging research base on the effects of this movement. We systematically review available evidence regarding such things as rationales, innovation, special education, student achievement, and parent–student satisfaction.

Finally, in chapter 8, we examine the highly politicized nature of contemporary educational debate and call for bipartisan support for education rather than maneuvering for political gain. Should we fail to do this, public education, historically a positive, stabilizing force in American life, may deteriorate due to inadequate and biased funding. We end with a general call for increased support of and funding for educational research, particularly in inner-city schools.

ACKNOWLEDGMENTS

We would like to acknowledge some of the many people who contributed to the preparation of this book. Sharon Nicholas assisted with typing dictated drafts of certain chapters and provided useful feedback throughout the process. Jere Brophy read some of the early chapters and provided substantive feedback along with considerable information concerning the charter school movement in Michigan and elsewhere. Mary McCaslin helped us conceptualize two of the chapters and provided extensive editorial suggestions. Marion Pickens provided information on Arizona charter schools and a better understanding of the legislative perspective on school reform. Chris Kirkpatrick provided beneficial editorial feedback and was instrumental in the preparation of the indexes. Others who read and critiqued specific chapters or the entire manuscript include David Berliner, George García, DeWayne Mason, Tom Payzant, F. Howard Nelson, and Nancy Winitzky. We are especially appreciative of the support of our editor, Lane Akers, whose continuing support for the book was instrumental in bringing it out in a timely fashion.

—*Thomas L. Good*
—*Jennifer S. Braden*

Chapter 1

American Education: How Good Is It and Who Should Control It?

As a new century begins, it is important to consider changes that are occurring in our environment, economy, and culture and to consider what those changes hold for the quality of our personal lives. Will Americans live longer and enjoy healthier lives? Will tomorrow's workforce spend fewer hours at work and experience a higher quality of life; or as some predict, will the children of the 1990s find it difficult to achieve the same quality of life enjoyed by their parents? What will the American economy be like in 2025 or 2050? What will the quality of day-to-day life be for citizens 25 or 50 years from now? In the future, will American economic, military, and political power continue to set the standard for the world? Most readers in considering these questions are apt to start their predictions with two words: It depends. Citizens have a long list of "it depends" statements, but most will include education as one key building block for the future: "It depends on whether American education can keep pace with a rapidly changing world."

Citizens value high-quality education but are confused about how to define it and are in conflict about the quality of today's public schools. Some (especially parents) are reasonably satisfied with American schools, but many policymakers are convinced that the present system of schooling is so flawed that it can be saved only by bold, aggressive experiments. In particular, many critics call for new, experimental forms of schooling, such as voucher plans (public funds to subsidize private school education), and charter schools (public funds to establish schools under a contract with the state).

Indeed, some citizens are so critical of today's public schools that they are willing to allow state monies to be spent in private religious schools. That some Americans want dramatic changes in public schooling is easy to document. For example, front-page stories in newspapers across the country included "Florida to Allow Student Vouchers"[1] and "Florida to Take Voucher Plunge"[2] and described New York City's raging debate about the need for vouchers to improve student learning.

New York Mayor Rudolph Giuliani, City Council Speaker Peter Vallone, and Governor George Pataki have asserted that New York City public schools are in a state of emergency. Mayor Giuliani, who has stated that the city school system should be "blown up," has been a particularly strong advocate of vouchers. In contrast, New York Schools' Chancellor Rudy Crew has been a strong opponent of vouchers, to the point of threatening to resign if a voucher plan were approved.[3]

Charter schools are flourishing, as many citizens and policymakers have provided considerable political clout to this movement. We explain the development of charter schools and voucher plans later in the book. We mention these new reforms here to make it clear that school reform is not academic or political rhetoric. Charter schools and voucher plans have a visible and growing presence in American education. A sweeping debate is in progress across America about the quality, form, and control of public education that may change the face of public education of the future.

This book frames the current debate about the quality of American education. Next, it summarizes the debate on American schools—how good are our schools and who should control the curriculum and reform efforts? Third, the book provides a comprehensive review of modern alternatives that are being proposed to replace, or at least supplement in important ways, the American public school system. Here, we examine the arguments for choice generally and voucher plans and charter schools specifically. In this regard, the book addresses various questions including: What is the rationale for charter schools and voucher plans? Who attends these schools? How effective have they been? How can they be altered in ways to make them even more effective?

The first part of the book frames the modern issue of school reform by addressing the history of reform. What is the tradition of reform in American schools? Who has led past reform efforts? How effective have these school reforms been and what specific improvements have occurred? To what extent have past reforms and experiments in education been driven by solid ideas or only by simple faddism with no supporting data? These are important issues because if we do not attend to the lessons of history we are doomed to repeat past failures. This chapter discusses the case for and against public schools and profiles some of the major participants in the debate.

EDUCATING YOUTH:
CONSENSUS AND CONFLICT

The development of youth's knowledge, skills, and attitudes has always been important to this country's success. Today, however, American youth and their education are becoming even more important to the country's economic security. By 2025, one of five Americans will be 65 years old or older and by 2040, one of four Americans will be 65 or older. Baby boomers are rapidly approaching the age of 65, and America's future economic success will be in the hands of today's youth to an unprecedented extent. At present, there are 3.2 workers supporting every retiree; however, after baby boomers retire, that ratio will decrease markedly to 1.8 workers for each retiree.[4] Further, there are social and moral reasons,[5] as well as economic ones, for educating youth well. Most citizens accept the premise that good education provides a fundamental cornerstone for a productive democracy.

At various points in our history Americans have fought vigorously over the funding of education. In notable contrast, current polls consistently illustrate that the majority of Americans are willing to support increased spending for improving the quality of schools. Yet, despite the obvious importance of education, there is virtually no consensus on such questions as: How good is American education? How can it be improved? How can improvements be demonstrated? There is a clear indication that our society places a high value on formal education as well as a clear controversy over the quality of our schools.

Current controversy in education centers on three fundamental issues: the *quality* of American schools (is the system adequate?); who will *control* public education (federal or state government, local school districts, parents); and how do we best *design* schooling in the 21st century (market forces vs. governmental control). We review the first two sources of controversy in the sections that follow. The third issue is addressed indirectly here, but we return to it in more detail in later chapters that describe the choices offered by voucher plans and charter schools.

THE QUALITY OF AMERICAN EDUCATION

Controversy surrounding the quality of American schools focuses on one central question: Can public schools properly educate our students for the 21st century? There are supporters and detractors of public schools at every discernable level of this issue. Policymakers and educators express diverse opinions including that (a) in general, American schools are doing a reasonably good job and with strategic investments would be even better; (b) some American public schools are world class and some are among the worst in the world; (c) in general, American schools are inferior; and (d) it is time to abandon the public school system. Clearly, we have a confusing and wide array of opinions about public education.

The Case Against the Common Public School

Some citizens and many policymakers have expressed deep disappointment about the performance of public schools. Although many will grant the conclusion that the common public school once served our democratic society well, they argue that as we move further into an information-driven society we need schools that are fundamentally different from those we and our parents attended. Many Americans have concluded that public schools have outlived their usefulness.

However, within the camp of those who believe that public schools are failing there are different explanations for why this is the case, and often the explanations are contradictory. For example, many Americans believe that schools are failing to produce a sufficient number of students who demonstrate adequate academic knowledge and an ability to use that knowledge to solve problems. Many of these citizens are satisfied with the school curriculum and the tests used to measure it but feel that students and teachers simply aren't doing well enough. That is, they argue that students' school achievement is unacceptably low in terms of both how American students performed in earlier times and how they compare today with students in other countries. These critics argue that American schools simply are not challenging students to work hard enough and that policies of social promotion and a curriculum filled with permissive choice have undermined students' ability to undertake difficult academic challenges.

In contrast, others contend that the current common public education system is outdated and unable to prepare students for the demands of the 21st century. These critics argue that public schooling needs to be radically transformed and that new forms of schooling, new approaches to learning, and new subject matter are needed. Thus, those who attack public schools include citizens and policymakers both who argue for a return to the basics and who argue for new curricula.

Critics of public schools claim that the present system is too languid and resistant to change. Thus, proponents generally see competition in the form of alternative school choice as a necessary imperative to inject American schools with the vigor and enthusiasm needed to yield important innovation or to pursue with renewed vigor the basic curriculum already in place.

Public school critics tend to agree on two issues. First, schools have become bloated with high-paid and often unnecessary administrators, and the cost of nonacademic programs and supervision has reached unacceptable levels of expenditure. Second, current enactments of schooling result in too few dollars of funding being spent in support of classroom teachers. These critics have indicated a willingness to pay for school funding but only if additional resources are spent on instructional services and opportunities for students.

Others contend that American education has become too uniform and promotes a curriculum and instruction they characterize as "one size fits all." Given that the school system largely represents a single approach to education, many students are poorly served is an argument policymakers frequently use when decrying the inadequacy of the American curriculum for dealing with bright and talented students.

Still other citizens are critical of the American public school system for political reasons dealing with privatization. Privatization has become a popular philosophy that argues for shrinking government on the premise that market forces can solve domestic social problems more reliably than the government can and at less cost. Presently, the political pressure for privatizing education comes primarily in the form of increasing educational choice (e.g., the freedom for families to send their children to educational settings other than the one public school within their attendance zone).

Other individuals promote market forces as a good way to make schools more competitive, even though they do not necessarily support privatization beliefs. That is, some critics argue for more choice because they believe in market forces and competition. They think that if schools have to compete for students, the process of competition will stimulate innovation in schools and increase their responsiveness to community needs. Given the opportunity to choose or to define a school program, parents, principals, teachers, and students will be empowered, and such market forces will lead to schooling that is both more efficient and more responsive. Whether this improvement takes place in state-supported or private schools is not a key issue for these critics.

In the past, many politicians have proclaimed an educational crisis so pervasive as to suggest that poor education is a threat to the economic and military well-being of the country. Additionally, some critics claim that strategies often invoked as solutions in the past are inadequate for addressing present problems (e.g., attracting better teachers, aligning the curriculum, spending more). However, to further complicate the problem, as noted earlier, critics of public education today define the problem differently. Some believe that the curriculum is inadequate or has moved too far away from basic subject matter, whereas an equal proportion of critics argue just the opposite! Still other critics place the cause of the decline on low performance standards and lack of hard work, a charge sometimes directed at teachers but at other times at students, parents, or administrators.

Thus, a range of arguments has been expressed against the public school including (a) the basic curriculum is poorly taught; (b) the wrong curriculum is taught; (c) parent and student interests are lost in the large (and expensive) bureaucracy; (d) motivation and hard work in schools is insufficient; (e) government supported schooling does not encourage innovative practice; (f) privatized and market orientation will encourage administrators, teachers, students, and parents to work harder.

The Case for the Common Public School

The common public school has become an institution that serves all children. It provides a free and appropriate public education for students regardless of their abilities or disabilities. The common public school is a national institution that forms the basis for education in the United States. The Center for Educational Policy has argued that public schools fulfill various needs:

Historically, schools have prepared students to be good citizens in four ways: (a) teaching students about the role of government in the United States; (b) upholding civic values by teaching students to be good citizens and good neighbors; (c) equipping students with the civic skills they need to be effective participants in a representative democracy; and (d) promoting tolerance and respect for diverse peoples and different points of view.[6]

Additionally, the public school system provides a safety net for school reform efforts. For example, some would agree that the common public school is the reason that charter or private schools may exist. Public schools provide charter and private schools with the flexibility to limit their student body by age, ability, or special goals or interests. They provide charter schools with a well-established safety net so they have the option to fail midyear. And, in some cases, they provide sponsorship to the charter school. Ultimately, the public school system is responsible for all students regardless of the school they attend. For example, a student who is referred for special education services but attends a private school is the responsibility of the public school system if the private school cannot or will not provide the needed services.

Those who advocate for the public school claim that, in general, schools are doing well and that when they are inadequate it is often because of inadequate funding. Advocates note that the quality of education is more likely to be improved by direct investments than by beliefs in "pie in the sky" theories like marketplace competition. For example, if the goal is to improve the quality of teachers, why not increase funding for salaries so that more well-qualified people enter the teaching field? Advocates question the wisdom and the economics of duplicating school buildings and library resources among other things. They argue that rather than funding 25,000 new school libraries, wouldn't it be wiser to improve the quality of existing public school libraries at a fraction of the cost? If, in fact, school bureaucracies have become bloated, expensive, and insensitive to parents and students, why not enact legislation to handle these abuses rather than hiring even more directors and school administrators (for charter schools) with the hope that they will be more responsible to students? Changing the public school system through duplication (e.g., charters) means that even more money will be spent on administrators and facilities and less on children and classroom instruction.

Many argue that the way to make public schools more innovative, effective, and responsive to consumers is to make them compete more—let parents choose their school. Some see the competition argument as specious. For example, faced with new competition it is possible in many school locations that administrators who must recruit students will spend disproportionate amounts of money for newspaper ads and slick brochures, not for teacher salaries.

Some strongly argue that investments in charters, vouchers, and private education guarantee that there will be less money for public education.[7] If the problem of poor public education, when it occurs, is largely because of insufficient resources, then investments in alternative education will guarantee that more public schools will fail. Such investments are seen as a serious self-fulfilling prophecy: If significant amounts of resources are removed from public education, the system will decline rapidly.

Many advocates support the common public school because they believe that it is the common school system that fuels a successful democracy. Common experiences lead to shared rituals and trust that in turn allow us to accept events like a change in presidential or congressional power without military intervention—the common school has taught us that there will be another day, another election. Benjamin Barber has argued that public schools are important not because they serve the public but because they define and shape the country as a public.[8] He asserted:

> The *public* in public schools stands for plurality and diversity. America is not a private club defined by one group's historical hegemony .... What we share in common is precisely our respect for difference: that is the secret to our strength as a nation, and it is the key to democratic education.[9]

Neil Postman made a similar argument for public schools this way:

> It *creates* a public. And in creating the right kind of public, the schools contribute toward strengthening the spiritual basis of the American Creed. That is how Jefferson understood it, how Horace Mann understood it, how John Dewey understood it.[10]

Public school advocates also value the concept of diverse students sharing common experiences. Public schools allow for more opportunities (and choice), such as chess club, band, sports, and a range of extracurricular activities seldom available in charter schools. Given the many choices allowed in public schools, some advocates wonder if much of the motivation for charter schools and vouchers is directed toward issues other than improving student experiences.

Some politicians, although they reject vouchers, support public charter schools because they believe they can flourish in ways that do not erode the "publicness" of schooling. Other politicians find it difficult to separate charter schools and voucher plans because both involve selection and privilege. Chapters 4 and 5 address these issues systematically.

In summary, the case for the public school has various aspects including (a) many public schools do a good job of educating students; (b) parents of school-age children are generally supportive, especially in non-inner-city settings; (c) those who attack public schools largely do so because of political interest or for reasons of personal gain; (d) given the enormous investments already made in public schools, retaining the current system is better and less expensive than replacing or duplicating it; (e) the public school is the vital force that unifies Americans in ways necessary for maintaining a democracy.

THE CALL FOR CHARTER SCHOOLS
AND VOUCHER PLANS

Some citizens and their elected policymakers feel that public education has lost its competitive edge and contend that we can only revitalize American education through school choice as represented in voucher programs and charter schools. *Vouchers* are educational subsidies that students and parents can use to attend the school of their choice, including private schools. Voucher supporters, in general, believe in less governmental control and that the private sector uses resources more imaginatively and efficiently than does government. In contrast, *charter schools* are public schools that are educational experiments that operate under a contract between a state representative and an individual or group of individuals. The charter specifies the conditions under which the school is permitted to operate. In general, charter schools allow for more flexibility in spending, in hiring teachers, and in the curriculum than is the case for regular public schools. (Detailed information on vouchers, how charters vary, and the various solutions they propose is presented in chapters 4 and 5.)

Despite their claims about a crisis in public education, some citizens feel strongly that the only solution is to improve public education, because it is the only way to educate citizens if they are to play cooperative and responsible roles in a democracy. Thus, to those Americans, vouchers are seen as unacceptable choices, because they provide public funds to private schools, including private religious schools. In contrast, they find charter schools attractive, because they allow for increased and needed choices within the public school system. Yet, other citizens feel that public charter schools function, for all practical purposes, as private schools; hence, the creation of autonomous public charter schools takes away from the common core of shared public schooling for American youth.

Other citizens assert that vouchers are important because they provide students economic access to schools that are already functioning well, especially private religious schools in inner-city settings. They ask, Why deny children access to schools that appear to have reasonable educational effects? Citizens contend that they must have the right to choose where their children go to school and that they are unwilling to go to a poor school just because it is a public school. Chester Finn has argued that critics of charter schools pay too much attention to issues of desegregation to the neglect of the quality of a child's education.[11] Yet others argue that it is important to attend to both issues and that we do not have to engage in dichotomous thinking.

CONTROL OF PUBLIC SCHOOLS

Much of the controversy brewing over public education is found in the debate over who should have ownership or control of public schools. Arguments are made for control at the federal, state, local, and parental levels.

Many Americans feel that the federal government is best left out of education. Citizens and policymakers argue that issues of assigned curriculum and assessment of student mastery are best done at the local level. Some believe that less federal involvement in education virtually guarantees that the quality of education will improve, because parents and citizens are involved in day-to-day decisions about education. Others strongly believe that the federal government must be involved in education if for no other reason than to set the moral imperative of equitable funding. Advocates of the federal government's role in education assert that states vary widely in the support provided to the educational needs of children and that without the presence of the federal government (and its discretionary funds that can be denied to states) the variability in state funding would be even greater.

States and local school districts also fight over control. Many state lawmakers believe that the state has a fundamental responsibility to assure that local school boards treat their varied constituencies fairly. Yet other state legislators believe that too many educational decisions are made at both the federal and state levels and that local school boards should have more power.

Recent events help sharpen the distinctions in the fight for control of education. President Bill Clinton argued the need for an extra $400 million to support after-school programs but only for schools that do not practice social promotion (allowing students to pass to the next grade level even though they have not mastered all material assigned to the present grade level). Clearly, this discretionary use of public money is a powerful attempt by the federal government to push state governments and local school districts to crack down on social promotion.

An example of state control is the New York State legislature's recent mandate of a statewide test. Many local school districts complain that their values and standards are being bypassed and that they know better than the state how to define curriculum goals and to measure student learning. Anemona Hartocollis contended that hundreds of private and many traditional public schools in New York State "are fighting a new state decision to abolish home grown and sometimes idiosyncratic graduation requirements like portfolios and oral examinations and to require every high school student in the state to take tough new Regents' Exams as a condition of graduation." She also noted "the dissident schools include a handful of affluent, high-performing suburban schools districts, including Scarsdale, Bronxsville, Mamaroneck, and Chappaqua."[12] These schools historically have not awarded Regents' diplomas but rather have relied on standards such as the SAT, Advanced Placement tests, and tests written by their own classroom teachers.

Similarly, many parents complain that local school districts are insensitive to the unique learning needs of students (especially their own) and argue for more power to influence school policies and especially the right to choose the school their children attend (i.e., not be restricted to attendance boundaries). Some parents are voting with their feet by selecting charter schools or engaging in home schooling (teaching their own children). In contrast, those who believe in federal, state, or local control bemoan the potential abuse that may occur (e.g., the teaching of racial hatred) if parents are not accountable to some group.

Varied Stakeholders in the Debate on Public Education

Controversy over the public school system has many hues, and we acknowledge the complex mix of those who believe in or do not believe in public schools. Many criticize public schools because they want a stronger academic curriculum (more independent student work and more choice in terms of projects, etc.). Some want schools to primarily address the basic curriculum and argue that allowing student choices in topics to study waters down high standards. Some who actively participate in the conflict may do so for reasons that have nothing to do with improving students' education. For example, advocates of reform may support charters because they believe charter schools will allow students who have similar characteristics and values to be educated apart from students who differ. Public school advocates may support the current system primarily because they believe that radical changes in schooling will increase costs and consequently raise taxes. Such citizens may prefer change but support the status quo because they prefer lower taxes. Similarly, there is variation between citizen groups (e.g., Democrats, Republicans) as well as within groups. For example, some supporters of public schools and public charter schools strongly support the call for higher standards (such as a more rigorous curriculum, introducing subject areas like statistics and measurement at the elementary school level).

Political Interests

Although some partisans in the debate are best distinguished by their primary interest in the quality of education (how effective are public schools?) and some because of their philosophical beliefs about the publicness of education, others, as mentioned, are better described by their political interests. There can be no doubt about political interest in educational issues. A recent study that surveyed state legislators in all states found that the number 1 issue for lawmakers of both genders is education.[13]

Citizens' interest in public education is not new, and thus, it is not surprising that both President Clinton and Senator Bob Dole had strong education reform platforms in the 1996 presidential election. Clinton, and Democrats generally, supported charter schools, whereas Dole, and Republicans generally, supported vouchers. Both political parties supported the argument that American public schools need to be reformed and called for more parent choice in educating their children.

These political tendencies continued in the November 1998 elections. Democrats were more likely to support charter schools, and more Republicans favored voucher plans. Further, in his State of the Union address, on January 20, 1999, President Clinton attempted to motivate the country about educational issues and said, "we must do better. Each year the national government invests more than $15 billion in our public schools. I believe we must change the way we invest that money, to support what works and to stop supporting what doesn't."[14] Among his recommendations were (a) all schools must end social promotion; (b) all states and school districts must turn around their worst performing schools or shut them down; (c) all states and school districts must be held responsible for the quality of their teachers; (d) parents must be empowered with more information and more choices; (e) all states and school districts must adopt and implement discipline policies; (f) 5,000 classrooms must be built because of decaying schools and to help facilitate smaller classes.

President Clinton argued strongly for charter schools: "And parents should have more choice in selecting their public schools. When I became President, there was one independent, public charter school in all of America. With our support, there are 1,100 today. My budget assures that early in the next century, there will be 3,000."[15]

In response to President Clinton's remarks, Congressman Steve Largent, Republican of Oklahoma, suggested that Republicans believe in market principles like competition and hard work and that for too long the federal government has dictated how our children are taught:

> One of our priorities is to give control of our schools to local communities. We want the most important election affecting your children's education to be the one that decides who sits on the school board, not who you send to Washington. Parents deserve the opportunity to choose the best school, with the best curriculum, best teachers, and safest environment for their children.[16]

Clearly, Republican and Democrat responses to school reform vary in terms of the desirability of federal versus local control. Both positions embrace the importance of education, but they argue about the form and control of public education. And the education agenda continues into the future. Leading candidates for the presidential election in 2000 already have stated their positions on education.

The political debate on public schools has so permeated the culture that even popular writers use the political saliency of educational issues in their writing. For example, Richard North Patterson's most recent book, *No Safe Place*,[17] has two presidential contenders debating the quality of the public schools and public school reform such as vouchers and charter schools.

> Like most parents you don't want your own kids going to schools that are overcrowded, under funded, and unsafe ... I support school vouchers to help parents send their kids wherever they can ... you oppose them ... I support charters for public schools, free of the rules that protect bad teachers and students who deal in drugs and violence ... you oppose them ... I support higher standards for teachers ... you oppose them.[18]

One ugly contention is that policymakers can glibly play politics with education because the constituents with the greatest need have little political power. Barber explained the continuing (and exaggerated) assault on American children and their schools as largely driven because students are politically invisible.[19] However, some politicians seem to consider the moral consequences of educational funding. For example, some politicians, although they reject vouchers, support public charter schools, because they believe charter schools can flourish in ways that do not erode the "publicness" of schooling.

Business Interests

Politicians are interested in education because of constituents' interests. American business has also expressed considerable interest in education. Since the publication of *A Nation at Risk* in 1983, there have been a growing number of school–business partnerships. Some educators have decried the presence of these influences; whereas others have noted their useful financial contributions to public education. Businesses' motivation for educational involvement is varied. Some, no doubt, are interested because improving public education is for the common good; whereas, for others the interest is economic—to make it easier and cheaper, to recruit talented employees.

Michael Bazeley of the *San Jose Mercury News* noted:

> The story's been told in Silicon Valley so many times it is near mythic proportions. A large, high-tech firm pulls out all the stops to lure a hot-shot executive here from an out-of-state company. But the deal collapses when the candidate gets spooked about sending his kids to California's beleaguered public schools.[20]

Bazeley, on the basis of a small poll of about 1,000 citizens found that 65% of parents reported that the schools attended by their children are doing a very good job. Further, only 7% of parents thought schools were doing a poor job as opposed to 20% of the public at large. Bazeley asserted that it is not parents but corporate leaders who complain the loudest and contend that the poor quality of public schools has hurt their businesses. He suggested that many members of the high-tech industry use their considerable political and financial clout in the educational debate.

However, as is the case with citizens and their elected leaders, the business community has mixed views about how to improve education. As a specific example of interest in public education, in 1993 Walter H. Annenberg created a stir in the educational community when he contributed $500 million to help reform public schools. By making this gift, the largest ever made to public education, Annenberg expressed his strong belief that public schools are a good investment. Those who believe in school choice and vouchers were not far behind in their philanthropy. On June 9, 1998, several business leaders pledged to raise $200 million to support a national voucher program that would afford the opportunity for at least 50,000 inner-city public school children to enroll in private or parochial schools. The motivation for this generous contribution, according to Jacques Steinberg writing in *The New York Times*, was to "prod failing public schools into improving by subjecting them to market forces."[21] This group of business leaders, referred to as the Children's Scholarship Fund, reported that they have $140 million in pledges. Commenting on the Children's Scholarship Fund, Theodore J. Forstmann, a businessman who contributed $50 million noted, "competition makes you better ... if you have a totally free marketplace in anything and you don't compete you go broke. If you do compete you prosper."[22]

By April 21, 1999, the group had virtually made good on its $200 million pledge when it announced that $170 million in scholarships had been awarded to allow 40,000 children from low-income homes to attend private schools. Mr. Forstmann reported that 1,236,360 students had applied for scholarships that ranged from $600 to $1,600 a year for 4 years. Since the average cost of attending a parochial school is $2,500, parents were willing to make up the difference themselves so their children could attend a private school. Mr. Forstmann interpreted the high number of applications as "indicating a deep satisfaction among parents with the [private school] education their children are getting."[23]

However, it seems that the gifts from the children's scholarship fund were motivated by beliefs of privatization and competition as much as by the nature of the educational program. For example, Hartocollis wrote, "Mr. Forstmann said he had no interest in promoting vouchers or Catholic schools, only in challenging what he called the government's monopoly in education. 'We need a competitive environment,' he said."[24]

These two massive gifts reflect a distinct business interest in education; however, the motivation behind these gifts is different. Annenberg's gift was to strengthen the public school system. The Children's Scholarship Fund was to challenge the public educational system. Both groups were voting with their pocketbooks by investing in their preferred form of education.

Identifying the explicit motivation for supporting or attacking public education is difficult. As a case in point, one of Mr. Forstmann's large cofounding donators to the Children's Scholarship Fund was Mr. Walton (of the Walmart fortune), who happens to own stocks in a for-profit corporation that manages charter and noncharter public schools. (Does Walton want citizens to spend their voucher monies in his schools?) Big businesses' interest in education is more than empty rhetoric; they are investing vast amounts of money in education. Businesses' support for education (including higher education) increased from $850 million to $4.25 billion from 1985 to 1994.[25] Many of these gifts from businesses come with strings attached—donors expect certain privileges or access. For example, in the spring of 1998, the University of Connecticut, Storrs Campus, accepted $19 million from Pfizer to build a research laboratory in which the university will receive 20% of the space and Pfizer 80%.[26]

However, corporations' "generosity" should be understood in light of the business communities' decreasing burden for local property taxes, which directly support local schools. Corporate America's share of local property taxes has dropped from about 45% in 1957 to 16% in 1990. Businesses presently have interest in investing in education; however, unlike the 1950s when they had little voice in how their dollars were spent, now they demand an active role for their financial support.

Media's Role

Since at least 1950, the media has been a harsh critic of American schools. Public anxiety about and criticism toward the media remains high in the wake of several firings of media persons in the summer of

1998 (of individuals who rushed to print without getting a story correct or in some cases accepting fake data, or manufacturing erroneous information themselves). However, even before this public outcry, educators complained that the press was hostile toward and grossly misleading in its representation of American schools as of "poor quality."[27] Indeed, some contended that the media in the 1980s and early 1990s presented youth, students' school performance, and the schools they attend in sweepingly stereotypic, negative, and misleading ways. The media, by stressing negative news about American students, teachers, and schools, helped to fuel politicians' claims about the decline of American schools. The authors of the 1997 *Phi Delta Kappa\Gallup Poll* concluded that "the low grades given the nation's public schools are primarily media-induced. Whereas people learn first hand about their children's schools, they learn about the nation's schools primarily from the media."[28]

Many educational writers endeavor to gather and interpret news as fairly as possible. Still, in some cases other motives may influence the objectivity of reporting. It is obvious to newspaper owners and those who write articles and editorials that if all schools had to compete vigorously to obtain students, it would certainly enhance advertising budgets and profits. Even if newspapers were predisposed to give free space for schools to sell themselves, competition between schools is good for the newspaper business. For instance, parents motivated to buy papers to determine which schools are good certainly adds to the perceived value and profits of newspapers. In contrast, there is less profit incentive for reporting good things that happen in public schools.

In the mid-1990s, some educational researchers began a counterattack and noted that the media's reporting systematically underreported students' accomplishments.[29] These scholars also illustrated the wide variation in student performance in American schools.[30] This counterattack has had some influence on media reporting. Recent essays in distinguished popular publications have started to write about the state of American education in more complex and balanced ways.[31]

Some journalists not only have described the rich but perplexing diversity of American schools but also have concluded that much of ineffective education is not due to a bloated administrative staff or teachers who do not work hard enough but to inadequate funding. Sarah Mosle, in a 1996 article in *The New Republic,* wrote, "To insist that educators perform miracles in dilapidated and overcrowded schools, with few supplies, and with support in communities that are being destroyed by poverty and violence, is *not* idealism."[32] Peter Schrag, writing in a 1997 issue of the *Atlantic Monthly* noted that, in part, media pay less attention to the positive contributions of schools because good news weakens the voucher case for conservatives and liberals' argument for more money.[33] He wrote:

> Ideologically inspired lamentations about the parlous state of American education masks the much more complex truth ... A growing number of people in the name of world class standards, would abandon through vouchers, privatization, and other means, the idea of the common school altogether. Before we do that, we'd better be sure that things are really as bad as we assume. The dumbest thing we could do is scrap what we're doing right."[34]

Brent Staples, writing in a *New York Times Magazine* article, asserted, "On the whole, American schools are far better than most critics wish to admit, particularly at the high end, where they easily rival the best Japan and Western Europe have to offer."[35] Staples continued by noting that at the low end in inner-city schools there are acute problems. Still, with these and other exceptions noted, the press, in general, remain negative about the quality of schools.

Parents' and Citizens' Positions

Despite some citizens' concerns about the quality of their schools, various contemporary polls consistently suggest that a majority of Americans are willing to pay additional money for education if they can be convinced that the quality of education can be improved.[36] However, defining, assessing, and improving the quality of American education has been both an active and an elusive goal throughout the second half of the 20th century. School officials face a major Catch-22. To enhance funding they must assure quality, but demonstrating quality in educational settings has been an intractable task in part because what constitutes quality is rarely well-defined.

Despite the constant assault by politicians, the business community, and the media on the quality of American education, citizens are generally positive about their schools, and parents are especially positive. Gerald Bracey has studied parent support for public education for many years and has noted that there is substantial evidence that parents are consistently supportive of local schools (as opposed to schools in general).[37] Still, given that over 1 million parents applied for the scholarship program we described previously, it is obvious that some parents are interested in alternatives to the schools their children attend. Some parents even have sufficient concerns about public education to engage in the practice of home schooling, as we mentioned. But parents have varied motivations for maintaining or attacking the public school system. In many cases, those self-interests also serve the interests of public school personnel. Parents benefit when increased funds provide new services and equipment for their children. Similarly, parents who are dissatisfied with the extant system benefit to the extent that more options are created. Hence, given their political or educational goals, parents' reports about the quality of public schools may be exaggerated both positively and negatively.

Colleges of Education and Certifying Groups' Interests

Those who educate teachers (colleges of education) and who provide them with certification also have an agenda in the debate. Many simply want to train the best teachers they can, but some teacher educators want a crisis to resolve. Bracey put the case this way: "The marked claims of ideologies are, unfortunately, abetted by the many in the university community who have invested heavily in the idea of school failure, staking their reputations and their grant applications on a condition of crisis."[38] After all, if there is a crisis, teacher educators can claim fees for consulting to solve the crisis. Many teacher educators view their role as advocate to new visions of schooling, and a crisis provides a platform for "new visions."

In addition, some teacher educators are more attuned to the needs of state or federal agencies than to those of the public schools. For example, the late David Clark claimed, "The American common school is an endangered species; the WIMPS in education will not defend it. They are afraid of losing their money or access to the corridors of power."[39]

SHARPENING THE DEBATE
OVER PUBLIC EDUCATION

Advocates for reform often speak in general ways and avoid addressing tough questions. Some time ago, Larry Cremin argued:

> I would maintain that the questions we need to raise about education are among the most important questions that can be raised in our soci-

ety, particularly at this juncture in its history. What knowledge should 'we the people' hold in common? What values? What skills? What sensibilities? When we ask such questions, we are getting at the heart of the kind of society we want to live in and the kind of society we want our children to live in. We are getting at the heart of the kind of public we would like to bring into being and the qualities we would like that public to display. We are getting at the heart of the kind of community we need for our multifarious individualities to flourish."[40]

Twenty-five years later these questions still remain largely unaddressed. Given the lack of consensus about both the goals and quality of education, it is not surprising that strategies for improving the quality of education are markedly varied—ranging from investing more in public schools to eliminating the current public school system—and are offered by a range of individuals from politicians to businessmen to educators to parents. We wrote this book to focus the current debate and to bring specific arguments and evidence to this critical discussion.

A SYNOPSIS

In the section that follows we lay out our plan for the rest of the book. However, before doing so, we feel it useful to put our cards on the table and to discuss how we react to the complex, confusing, and conflicting arguments about the quality of our schools and how they can be improved.

In contrast to the many critics and advocates who generalize about American education, we find it difficult to do so, given the tremendous range in how schools function. We find it hard to define the average quality of schooling. We have A-level schools and we have F-level schools. Other writers also have alluded to the enormous variation in American schools, but we feel that most have grossly overestimated or, the more common problem, grossly underestimated the quality of American schooling.[41]

Much educational reform fails because it is designed too generally. If the quality and problems of schooling vary sharply—and they do—it follows that varied solutions are needed. However, reform movements are never differentiated. They routinely define problems in simple terms and offer simple solutions. As a case in point, one general reform solution widely recommended now is the need to reduce class size. We concur that reduction in class size is generally a good idea. But reduction in class size is more important in some contexts (at certain grade levels, for certain subjects, and for certain goals) than in others. Moreover, reducing class size in some schools or classes may only waste scarce resources (e.g., in schools that have inadequate teachers or school facilities). Uninspired teachers are apt to teach a class of 30, 20, or 10 in similar ways.

Ironically, after 50 years of intense school reform efforts, there is at best scant agreement on the central purposes of American schools. Despite the considerable attention that has been directed at choice (charter schools, vouchers) and at issues concerning the quality of education, there isn't even rudimentary agreement on goals. In addition to the spate of policy documents on general reform and school quality (e.g., A Nation at Risk), there have been thousands of proposals written by applicants who seek charter school status. Yet, such proposals have done little to clarify the fundamental goals they pursue.

Given that the problems of schooling are poorly defined, the proposed solutions are overly general, and the relationship between solutions and purposes are rarely made explicit, it is not surprising that the effects of charter schools (and other forms of choice—vouchers, privatization) are problematic. We argue (and present evidence to support our beliefs) that investments in charter schools haven't led to widespread innovation in educational programs nor to better student achievement. Indeed, many of these schools represent irresponsible and wasteful uses of public funds, and in some cases, the charter school experiment has had harmful effects on students.

Despite our assessment of the general effects of charter schools, there is some knowledge that can be gained form the present investment. For example, there are schools that are providing special niches that seem to compliment, and even extend, the range of students that public schools can serve well. Further, we can identify ways for strengthening charter school legislation that lead to more innovation in classroom instruction. Ironically, one of the several arguments we make invokes the rhetoric used by charter school advocates who want public schools to be more competitive. Namely, if charter schools are to become more innovative, we argue that the process for obtaining a charter needs to become more competitive.

Our somewhat optimistic conclusion that under certain conditions school choice can have some positive consequences for public education is limited to the public charter school movement. Our endorsement of public schools and to a lesser extent of the potential of charter schools is not out of blind allegiance to public schools. Indeed, in the book we identify many problems of public schools, including recommendations that some public schools closed. We do not support the widespread use of vouchers and tax credits that use substantial amounts of public monies to support private and religious education. Later in the book we clarify why we believe the use of public monies for private education will harm public education in ways that are detrimental to the majority of Americans.

In addition to providing suggestions for improving charter schools and charter school legislation, we also provide some general recommendations for improving American schools. These comments are designed for educators, policymakers, and parents.

Plan for the Book

This chapter explores the present political, philosophical, and economic issues that surround the debate on: How good are public schools? Citizens bring multiple agendas to the discussion, and given possible vested interests, it is prudent to seek out evidence rather than to rely on rhetoric alone. Having set the stage in chapter 1, the remainder of the book brings needed evidence to the debate in order to frame problems and to evaluate proposed solutions.

Chapter 2 examines the history of various educational crises asserted since 1950. A number of prestigious reports purported to have described the state of American education. However, these reports describe the problem in different ways, and what constitutes problems with American education has changed from decade to decade. After reviewing this parade of crises in American education, we frame the modern debate on the quality of American education—what can we say, as we enter the 21st century, about the quality of our schools and students?

Chapter 3 examines the evidence relevant to the claim that currently American education is in a state of crisis and only radical reform will save it. We primarily review evidence on student performance in the last decade and note that student progress on various measures continues to be reasonably high and that on some performance measures American students' achievements are at notable levels. The evidence reviewed in chapter 3 makes it clear that the educational system per se does not face a crisis even though it is the case that in some school districts and in some states student performance is sufficiently low to merit major reform efforts. We conclude chapter 3 by noting that although performance on average is adequate, there are several reasons why one still might want to reform American schools (e.g., the sorts of skills needed in the 21st century may call for different types of education).

Chapter 4 reviews the current debate calling for reform in American schools. We examine recent legislation and court rulings that allow for the expenditure of state funds to support vouchers and the expenditure of state dollars on private religious schools. It is important that we also examine the logic behind the choice movement. What are the arguments on why choice and market plans (vouchers, charter schools) will out perform traditional public schools? Further, we examine the effects of large-scale voucher programs that have been implemented in Cleveland and Milwaukee. On the basis of the evidence, we reach two major conclusions. First, vouchers and advocates of choice have achieved a major political victory. Voucher plans are in place, and this foothold will guarantee, at least in the short run, that more schools will implement them (e.g., Florida has passed enabling legislation for voucher plans in low-achieving schools). Second, vouchers have not secured an educational victory. There is no evidence that voucher plans have improved students academic learning. Hence, low achievement still continues for many students despite their enrollment in voucher plan schools.

Chapter 5 explores both the laws and the visions that fuel the development of charter schools and answers the following questions: Why were they created? How do they vary from state to state?

Chapter 6 reviews the formal research that is available for describing what charter schools actually do and how they affect student learning. We review evidence describing (a) rationales for charter schools, (b) innovation, (c) special education, (d) demographics, (e) parent and student satisfaction, (f) parent involvement, (g) relationships between charter and noncharter public schools, and (h) student achievement.

We end chapter 6 by assigning grades to the various activities and goals that charter schools address. The charter school aspects that we assigned formal grades to include parent involvment, curriculum innovation, innovation in organization, choice, and demographic factors. The grades we assign range from G+ to U. At this time, we see the promise of charter schools as more illusionary than demonstrated.

Chapter 7 turns to an analysis of anecdotal evidence. Here we consider newspaper articles and other anectotal reports. We report some of the stories behind the formal evaluations that illustrate some of the excesses and abuses that have occurred in charter schools (e.g., pending law suits regarding denial of special education services, the selling of charters to the highest bidder—not to the applicant with the best educational plan). We note that the abuses that have occurred in some charters schools could have been prevented by more adequate legislation and more active supervision. However, we also spotlight several instances illustrating where charter schools provide important educational services to students who were pushed out of public schools.

Chapter 7, building on the formal evidence, anecdotal reports, and case analyses presented in previous chapters, makes a series of policy and research recommendations for citizens, legislators, parents, and teachers. These recommendations deal with the critical tension between the need for creative innovation and experimentation along with the rights of individual students and parents.

Chapter 8 starts by examining literature on privatization, the growing belief—especially among conservative Republicans—that most public industries (schools, hospitals, prisons) are better managed by the private sector. We note that privatization in institutions generally has not brought new creative plans. Hence, we argue that, like vouchers and charter schools, privatization is not a panacea and that if we are to reform public schools we must be cognizant of reform "mistakes" made in 20th century schools. The chapter presents arguments for the necessity of funding educational research and for how we can design and support better research plans and strategies that will yield thoughtful experimentation so that we have the necessary information for the improvement of American schools.

Endnotes

1. Bragg, R. (1999, April 28). Florida to allows student vouchers. *The New York Times,* p. A1.
2. Kallestad, B. (1999, April 28). Florida is first to take school voucher plunge. *The Arizona Daily Star,* p. A1.
3. Editorial. (1999, April 27). The schools in New York City: Abolish the board. *The New York Times,* p. A30.
4. Joint Economic Committee. (1995, June 28). Medicare: Boom and bust. *Economic Update.* Congress of the United States.
5. Good, T. L. (Ed.). (1996). This issue: Talking "truth to power" [Special issue]. *Educational Researcher, 25*(8).
6. Center of Educational Policy. (1999). Public schools and citizenship [Online]. Available: http://www.ctredpol.org/pubs/pubschool_citizen.html
7. Bowen, R. (1999, January 13). Charter schools, then what? *The New York Times,* p. A25.

8. Barber, B. R. (1997). Public schooling: Education for democracy. In J. I. Goodlad & T. J. McMannon (Eds.), *The public purpose of education and schooling* (pp. 21–32). San Francisco, CA: Jossey-Bass.

9. Ibid., p. 29.

10. Postman, N. (1995). *The end of education: Redefining the value of school.* New York: Knopf, p. 18.

11. Finn, C. (1997). The politics of change. In D. Ravitch & J. P. Viteritti (Eds.), *New schools for a new century* (pp. 226–250). New Haven, CT: Yale University Press.

12. Hartocollis, A. (1999, January 29). Statewide tests draw some local outcries: Schools fighting new Regents' exams. *The New York Times,* p. A15.

13. Howe-Eerhovek, S. (1999, February 4). Record for women in Washington legislature. *The New York Times,* p. A14.

14. President's State of the Union Address. (1999, January 20). The text of the President's state of the union address to Congress. *The New York Times,* p. A22.

15. Ibid.

16. Reply from the Republican Party (1999, January 20). Republicans call for tax and education efforts to benefit families. *The New York Times,* p. A23.

17. Patterson, R. N. (1998). *No safe place.* New York: Knopf.

18. Ibid., p. 404.

19. Barber, B. R. (1997). Public schooling: Education for democracy. In J. I. Goodlad and T. J. McMannon (Eds.), The public purpose of education and schooling (pp. 21–32). San Francisco, CA: Jossey Bass.

20. Bazeley, M. (1998, June 21). Taking schools to task. *San Jose Mercury News,* p. 1A.

21. Steinberg, J. (1998, June 10). Voucher program for inner-city children. *The New York Times,* p. A27.

22. Ibid.

23. Hartocollis, A. (1999, April 21). Private school choice plan draws a million aid-seekers. *The New York Times,* p. A1.

24. Ibid., p. A25.

25. Hartocollis, A. (1999, April 21). Private school choice plan draws a million aid-seekers. *The New York Times,* pp. A1, A25.

26. Ibid.

27. Berliner, D., & Biddle, B. (1998). The lamentable alliance between the media and school critics. In G. Maeroff (Ed.), *Imaging education: Media and schools in America* (pp. 26–45). New York: Teachers College Press.
   Cuban, L. (1998). The media and polls on education–over the years. In G. Maeroff (Ed.), *Imaging education: Media and schools in America* (pp. 69–82). New York: Teachers College Press.
   Ogle, L., & Dabbs, P. (1998). The media's mixed record in reporting test results. In G. Maeroff (Ed.), *Imaging education: Media and schools in America* (pp. 85–100). New York: Teachers College Press.
   Wadsworth, D. (1998). Do media shape public perceptions of America's schools? In G. Maeroff (Ed.), *Imaging education: Media and schools in America* (pp. 59–68). New York: Teachers College Press.

28. Rose, L. C., Gallup, A. M., & Elam, S. M. (1997). The 29th annual Phi Delta Kappa/Gallup poll: Public's attitudes toward the public schools. *Phi Delta Kappan, 79*, 41–56.
29. Maeroff, G. (1998). *Imaging education: Media and schools in America*. New York: Teachers College Press.
30. Bracey, G. (1994). First world, third world, all right here at home. *Phi Delta Kappan, 75*, 649–651.
Bracey, G. (1996). International comparisons and the condition of American education. *Educational Researcher, 25*, 5–11.
Berliner, D., & Biddle, B. (1995). *The manufactured crisis: Myth, fraud and the attack on America's public schools*. New York: Addison-Wesley.
Berliner, D. (1996). Uninvited comments from an uninvited guest. *Educational Researcher, 25*, 47–50.
Rose, M. (1995). *The promise of public education in America: Possible lives*. Boston: Houghlin Mifflin.
31. Applebome, P. (1996, March 24). Can the schools stand and deliver? *The New York Times*, p. 4E.
Mosle, S. (1996, June). What we talk about when we talk about education. *The New Republic*, 27–36.
Schrag, P. (1997, October). The near-myth of our failing schools. *Atlantic Monthly*, 72–80.
32. Mosle, S. (1996, June). What we talk about when we talk about education. *The New Republic*, 36.
33. Schrag, P. (1997, October). The near-myth of our failing schools. *Atlantic Monthly*, 72.
34. Ibid., p. 80.
35. Staples, B. (1998, January). The new politics of education casts Blacks in a starring role. *The New York Times Magazine*, pp. 35, 49–51.
36. Applebome, P. (1997, September 14) Scold war: Yelling at the little red menace. *The New York Times*, pp. D1, D5.
37. Bracey, G. (1997). *The truth about America's schools: The Bracey reports, 1991–1997*. Bloomington, IN: Phi Delta Kappa Educational Foundation.
38. Ibid., p. 153.
39. Ibid., p. 153.
40. Cremin. L. A. (1975, September). Public education and the education of the public. *Teachers College Record, 77*, 11.
41. Good, T. L., Sabers, D. L., & Nichols, S. L. (1999). Underestimating youth's commitment to schools and society: Toward a more differentiated view. *Social Psychology of Education, 3*, 1–39.

Chapter 2

Crisis in Public Education: Past and Present

Public schools are under attack. However, charges that public schools are inadequate are not new. Politicians have frequently argued that an acute crisis exists in American education. Historically crises centered on the low quality of public education have been found to be overblown. Therefore, it is important to understand if today's politicians are simply crying wolf (once again) for political purposes. In chapter 3 we address evidence to determine whether our schools are in crisis; here we review historical cries of crisis in American schools.

Throughout the 20th century, American educators have enthusiastically endorsed a particular school reform only to discard it within a few years. Further, the history of reform is not a linear trail of refinement and growth. Some arguments made in the 1950s returned virtually unaltered in the 1990s. Once an "innovative" school reform is deemed obsolete, it is not abandoned in any final way. Typically, a rejected reform is placed on a shelf for a while and then repackaged, given a new label (e.g., progressive education becomes open education), and presented as a new and needed reform. Usually this process of recycling takes a few decades, but there are instances where educational fads are rapidly reversed. For example, roughly a decade ago the California Board of Education abruptly abandoned phonics as an approach to reading instruction and mandated whole language instruction as "the" approach. Recently, the California legislature assumed an opposite position of advocacy and asserted the need for phonics-based reading instruction. When yesterday's fad is replaced by today's fad, it is often rejected with strong emotion. Bill Lucia, the executive director of the California Board of Education, commenting on the whole language mandate stated, "We performed a heinous experiment."[1]

Our historical analysis of educational faddism is not intended as a defense of public schools. Further, we do not suggest that public schools cannot or should not be reformed simply because past attempts have failed to do so. However, before we engage the present school debate—the need for voucher plans and charter schools—it is important to acknowledge that the productivity of American schools has been the subject of continual argument, reform, and on occassion experimentation. We believe that a failure to understand the history of reform contributes to a tendency to underestimate the difficulty of change and an inability to recognize the complexity of teaching and learning in social settings. A review of past reform efforts should help us to define problems of schooling more clearly and thus help us to see how choice, voucher, and charter plans fit into the current debate on education.

AMERICAN SCHOOLS UNDER ATTACK: A BRIEF HISTORICAL REVIEW

The typical reform pattern in U.S. education has been to posit a general problem and then provide a reform movement to solve it. Unfortunately, such reform efforts are poorly defined, and accordingly, when implemented in schools, are diffuse. A fundamental issue in the reform of American education is the repeated failure of reformers to precisely delineate problems and particular strategies needed to address them. Herbert Kliebard, who studied progressive education, noted:

> The more I studied this the more it seemed to me that the term encompassed such a broad range, not just of different, but of contradictory ideas on education as to be meaningless. In the end, I came to believe that the term was not only vacuous but mischievous. It was not just the word "progressive" that I thought was inappropriate, but the implication that something deserving a single name existed and that something could be identified and defined if only we tried.[2]

Sputnik: The Math–Science Crisis

The first acute, modern crisis in American schooling was claimed with the Soviet's launching of Sputnik. To understand this crisis, it is useful to examine both pre-Sputnik and post-Sputnik solutions to schooling and society.

Pre-Sputnik. World War I was a divisive event in American life. Before American troops were committed to the war, while our troops were there, and even after they returned home, there was considerable angst and debate about involvement in a "foreign" war. Hence, despite the alarming military events in Europe in the 1930s, our commitment to the preparation of war materials was delayed as American politicians and citizens were reluctant to become involved in another foreign war.[3] December 7, 1941, and the Japanese infamous bombing of Pearl Harbor, ended the debate, and Americans were committed to another world war. In early 1942, when the intense mobilization of the war effort took place, it was far from certain that Americans would win the war.

The moral, intellectual, industrial, and educational capacity of the American culture was demonstrated in the ability of our country to compete in World War II. Americans entered the war grudgingly—and behind, in terms of available weapons and the like—however, students who attended American schools of the 1920s and 1930s demonstrated both the creative capacity and the will to work diligently on important tasks and ultimately to win the war.

Sputnik. The Soviet's launching of Sputnik in October 1957 touched off a wave of concern about the adequacy of math and science instruction in American schools. Critics argued that the public schools of the 1940s and 1950s had lost their intellectual rigor. This belief led to intense scrutiny of existing schooling. It was believed that concerns could be addressed by a change in mathematics curriculum. This curriculum change, in time, became known as *new math*.

Post-Sputnik. Anxiety about the Soviets' military capability and their superiority in space exploration touched off a great concern for recruiting talented math and science teachers, and arguments about how to reform the curriculum. New math advocates asserted that the mathematics and science curriculum should become more formalized, more abstract, more rigorous, and that students should be exposed to mathematics based on set theory. Unfortunately, these enthusiastic recommendations were advanced by advocates with no empirical evidence that such practices would enhance students' mathematical performance. Professor Kline, a critic of new math, wrote against the theory that math knowledge should be as abstract as possible. He contended:

> Students are asked to learn operations with sets and the notion of subset, finite and infinite sets, the null set (which is not empty because it contains the empty set), and lots of other notations which are abstract and in fact rather remote from the heart and essence of arithmetic. Yet on this abstract basis, students are required to learn arithmetic. The whole theory of sets should be eliminated. On the elementary and high school levels it is a waste of time.[4]

In contrast to new math proponents, Kline argued that mathematics should be presented and learned in a way that helped students understand the physical world. He recommended starting with real-world problems that cause students to investigate a particular mathematic topic rather than an abstract thought. He argued that at times the reasoning and arguments called for in new math were so abstract that even he began to lose track of what he knew about mathematics:

> There are other differences between the modern mathematics curricula and what I and others would recommend. The modern curricula insists on precise definitions of practically every word they use and, by actual count, the first two years of the school mathematics study group curriculum asks students to learn about 700 precise definitions. This is pure pedantry. The common understandings which students have acquired through experience are good enough and formal definitions are usually not needed. After reading the formal definition of a triangle, I had to think hard to be sure that it really expressed what I knew a triangle to be. Another point of issue is symbolism. Because symbolism has made mathematics more effective many naive "mathematicians" now seem to think that the more symbols they introduce the better the mathematics. What they have done is to make a vice out of a virtue.[5]

New math emerged and disappeared very quickly. It is instructive to note that those American scientists and mathematicians who "won" the Sputnik space challenge in the 1960s were products of an earlier school system that had emphasized a traditional form of mathematics teaching. Apparently, exposure to this presumably outdated curriculum (old math) did not prevent scientists and engineers educated in the 1940s and 1950s from making notable contributions to our successful space program in the 1960s. It appears that the Sputnik crisis was overblown, at least in terms of proof that American schools had deteriorated notably.

Critics of new math also questioned whether its proponents were motivated because of educational beliefs or for reasons of political power. One professor of physics suggested that new math simply created uncertainty and confusion about mathematics teaching and allowed the "in" mathematics crowd to get grants and status.[6]

> In many ways the new math movement has the character of the children's crusade of the middle ages. It is recognized as such by many responsible educators, but it is difficult to stop because of the very large and tightly knit web of vested interest preying on the mathematical unsophistication of the press, the public, and the foundations themselves. Under these circumstances, I urge administrators to forget the prestige of the sponsors and view with restraint and enthusiasm anything which does not really make sense to them, rather than be Sputnik-panicked into the hysterical adoption of new programs.[7]

New math, like progressive education before it, came and went without any consensus about how it should be defined, implemented, or evaluated.

Individualized and Humanistic Education

During and after the Sputnik crisis many educators began to develop individualized plans for education, and some of these plans provided not only individual packets of materials but also began to integrate aspects of computer-assisted learning. Considerable time and monies were spent by professional curriculum developers and teachers individualizing curriculum. These individualized programs took many different forms in the 1960s and early 1970s (e.g., Individually Guided Education, Individually Prescribed Instruction Plan).[8]

These approaches were designed to allow students to move at their own pace—students with rocket science potential could study independently and not be held back by students who took longer to learn. Some schools implemented individualized plans, and learning stations that allowed students to move from one set of activities to another became popular in many classrooms.

However, the majority of classrooms were unfazed by the individualization revolution. Negative reactions to individualized programs quickly followed. Critics argued that students should not learn material in isolation and posited a need for more open, humanistic education.

Thus, the interest in individualized education in the 1960s was followed in the 1970s with a concern for humanistic education (giving students more freedom to make their own choices about curriculum topics to study and attention to personal feelings as well as cognitions), and considerable enthusiasm was expressed for making schools open in terms of both architecture and curriculum plans.[9] Open education was demonstrably costly. Existing school buildings were remodeled to accommodate open-plan teaching, and many new schools were built using open-space architectural designs. As enthusiasm for open education diminished, many open-space schools were remodeled to allow for traditional instruction.

Defining open education proved to be an arduous task. As can be seen in Table 2.1, some generally common dimensions were argued to be representative of open education. Although some of the ideas were interesting, the notions about open education tended to be presented as general shibboleths devoid of context. For example, there was no discussion about contextual issues—should high schools be more open than elementary schools, or do some subjects or intellectual pursuits demand more structure than others? As can be seen in Table 2.1, those advocating open environments wanted students to have more control over the types of activities studied, the scheduling of educational events, and even the evaluation of learning. In open programs, teachers' basic role was redefined as guides and facilitators rather than presenters of subject-matter material.

Widespread humanistic approaches and enthusiasm for open education had a short duration (roughly 1970–1980). The open education curriculum can be fairly credited with having the effect of adding more electives to the curriculum and encouraging instructional styles other than lecture. However, in time, many criticized these reforms on the grounds that they lowered standards by offering a cafeteria-style approach to the curriculum—it was argued that given the chance to choose, many students chose only "desserts," ignoring the core subjects.[10] Other critics compared the reform achieved by the open education movement to shopping malls where students roamed aimlessly in the curriculum and languished without structure and adult "guidance."[11]

TABLE 2.1

Key Differences Between Open and Traditional Education

Variable	Open	Traditional
1. Initiation of teacher-student interaction	Student	Teacher
2. Space	Flexible	Fixed
3. Student activities	Wide range	Narrow range
4. Source of activity	Students' spontaneous interests	Teacher or school prescribed
5. Use of time	Flexible	Fixed
6. Teacher focus	Individual student	Large or whole group
7. Content and topics	Wide range	Narrow range
8. Student–student interaction	Unrestricted	Restricted

Note. Adapted from information provided by Katz, L. (1972). *Developmental stages of preschool teachers.* Urbana, IL: ERIC Clearinghouse on Early Childhood Education.

The movement rapidly dissipated for a variety of reasons (e.g., teacher stress associated with team teaching 90 students in an open space, the noise and movement that teachers had to deal with that bothered some teachers and students who were easily distracted, and lack of any supporting empirical data to demonstrate enhanced student outcomes). Open education took many forms and consequently had vastly different effects on students' affective, cognitive, and social development. Included in open education classrooms were exciting, effective, innovative teaching as well as some of the worst manifestations of traditional teaching and innovative teaching that was ineffective.[12]

A Nation at Risk

Following the open education movement, in 1983, the National Commission of Excellence in Education boldly asserted in *A Nation at Risk* an imperative for educational reform. The authors of the document wasted no time in getting to their point:

> Our nation is at risk. Our once unchallenged preeminence in commerce, industry, science, technology and innovation is being overtaken by competitors throughout the world .... If an unfriendly foreign power had attempted to impose on America the mediocre educational performance that exists today, we might well have viewed it as an act of war. As it stands, we have allowed this to happen to ourselves. We have even squandered the gains in student achievement made in the wake of the Sputnik challenge.[13]

Given the shocking claims about the poor quality of American schools, critics argued that the public schools of the 1960s and 1970s (the products of open and humanistic education) had lost their intellectual rigor. Some have argued that the National Commission of Excellence in Education's *A Nation at Risk* was the most important educational report from this century. Even though the report was directed at American schools, it has been translated into various languages including Arabic, Greek, and Japanese. Tommy Tomlinson's writing in 1986, 3 years after the publication of the report, noted that over 500,000 copies of the report were distributed by various school organizations. He wrote:

> The report has sparked a degree of debate and discussion of educational matters unsurpassed since Sputnik. Within a few months after the release of the report the *New York Times* had run almost fifty articles in which the name of the commission was specifically cited; the *Washington Post* printed over forty articles. *Time, Newsweek, U.S. News and World Report*, and *Better Homes and Gardens*, among many other magazines, in company with a myriad of newspapers, news broadcasts, columnists, and pundits had described, discussed, and debated the conclusions and implications of the Report."[14]

The authors of *A Nation at Risk's*[15] prescription for improving schooling involved various recommendations including longer school days, longer school years, and more homework. Essentially these recommendations called for more of the same type of school experiences. *A Nation at Risk* suggested that American schools were adequately focused in terms of curriculum and instruction but that students and teachers needed to work harder. Although there were other recommendations in the report (more school–business partnerships, one-half year of computer science), the core recommendation was that youth and teachers needed to renew their commitments to school work. Although less publicized by the media, the report called for the recruitment of better teachers and suggested increased compensation to attract more qualified teachers. A synopsis of *A Nation at Risk*'s recommendations is presented in Table 2.2.

TABLE 2.2
Five Major Recommendations From *A Nation at Risk*

Recommendation A: Content

We recommend that State and local high school graduation requirements be strengthened and that, at a minimum, all students seeking a diploma be required to lay the foundations in the Five New Basics by taking the following curriculum during their 4 years of high school: (a) 4 years of English; (b) 3 years of mathematics; (c) 3 years of science; (d) 3 years of social studies; and (e) one-half-year of computer science. For the college-bound, 2 years of foreign language in high school are strongly recommended in addition to those taken earlier.

Recommendation B: Standards and expectations

We recommend that schools, colleges, and universities adopt more rigorous and measurable standards, and higher expectations, for academic performance and student conduct, and that 4-year colleges and universities raise their requirements for admission. This will help students do their best educationally with challenging materials in an environment that supports learning and authentic accomplishment.

Recommendation C: Time

We recommend that significantly more time be devoted to learning the New Basics. This will require more effective use of the existing school day, a longer school day, or a lengthened school year.

Recommendation D: Teaching

This recommendation consists of seven parts. Each is intended to improve the preparation of teachers or to make teaching a more rewarding and respected profession. Each of the seven stands on its own and should not be considered solely as an implementing recommendation.

Recommendation E: Leadership and fiscal support

We recommend that citizens across the Nation hold educators and elected officials responsible for providing the leadership necessary to achieve these reforms, and that citizens provide the fiscal support and stability required to bring about the reforms we propose.

Note. From National Commission for Excellence in Education. (1983, April). *A nation at risk: The imperatives for educational reform.* Washington, DC: U.S. Department of Education.

In their analysis of indicators of risk and problems of American education, the Commission reported numerous issues. Some of their concerns follow:

- The amount of homework for high school seniors had decreased and grades had risen as average student achievement declined. Secondary school curricula no longer had a core purpose—a cafeteria-style curriculum was in place in which deserts and appetizers were often mistaken for main courses.
- Average achievement of college graduates was lower than in the 1970s.
- Business and military leaders complained that they were required to spend vast amounts of money on costly remedial education programs.
- In 13 states, 50% or more of the units required for high school graduation could be electives chosen by the student. Given this freedom to choose the substance of half or more of their education, many students opted for less demanding personal service courses, such as bachelor living.
- In England and other industrialized countries, it was not unusual for academic high school students to spend 8 hours a day at school, 220 days per year. In the United States, by contrast, the typical school day lasted 6 hours and the school year was 180 days. A study of the school week in the United States found that some schools provided students only 17 hours of academic instruction during the week and the average school provided about 22.
- A California study of individual classrooms found that because of poor management of classroom time, some elementary students received only one-fifth of the instruction others received in reading comprehension.

It is also important to comment on what the report did not address. Despite the numerous earlier attacks on American education that had questioned the premises, goals, structures, and inequities of American schools,[16] there was no basic argument against the general extant purpose of American education. For example, the Sputnik–new math crisis called for radical change in the math curriculum. The individualized movement called for more flexibility in the pacing of curricular material, and the open movement called for more student choice in assignments and more opportunity for students to work together. In contrast, *A Nation at Risk* basically called for more of the same (the report wanted students to take more core courses but, except for computer science, recommended courses that were already in the curriculum). In essence, *A Nation at Risk* recommended that curriculum breadth and student choice of subject matter (that had been introduced by the open education movement) be curtailed.

The report did not differentiate among types of schools or discuss varied student performance across school districts; it emphasized the general inadequacies of student performances in American schools. This undifferentiated report went forward despite notable accounts that students in many urban settings were failing, and despite knowledge of inequitable school funding across school districts and the deleterious state of many school buildings.[17] Clearly, *A Nation at Risk* ignored some issues that could be characterized as fundamental problems of American education and essentially issued prescriptions to work harder, keep pace, and, of course, overtake Japanese youth.

A Nation at Risk had some notable influences on American education. Specifically, it stimulated many of the schools who had abandoned a core curriculum to embrace it. It was also successful in encouraging states to beef up graduation requirements (take more math) and to address the laissez-faire curriculum in some "shopping mall" high schools (i.e., to offer fewer electives).

It is instructive to see that we have overtaken (at least temporarily) the Japanese and the rest of the world in economic productivity. Those business women, bankers, scientists, and managers who contributed to the economic revival in the 1990s were composed of many students who had been educated in American public schools labeled by *A Nation at Risk* as so poor as to constitute a threat to our national economic security. Students educated in the public schools of the 1950s, 1960s, 1970s, and 1980s seem to have built a society that is more productive than that of any other nation. Indeed, as we enter the 21st century, in many ways we are the envy of the world.

Prisoners of Time

The passage of time apparently did not correct the problem with American schools. Eleven years later, the sequel to *A Nation at Risk—Prisoners of Time*[18] provided a similarly scathing critique of American schooling. American education was still in crisis, it claimed, but in roughly a decade the solution for solving the crisis took a new form. Now, more of the same was not being called for (e.g., longer school days) but rather structural changes were demanded (e.g., longer school periods) to provide students with extended time for inquiry and discussion. This report consistently recommended a more active role for American students in the learning process. It called for flexible use of time and resources (e.g., team teaching[19]), and more thematic and integrated approaches to subject-matter instruction (e.g., interdisciplinary inquiry). The key recommendations from the *Prisoners of Time* report appear in Table 2.3.

Prisoners of Time drew on some of its predecessors' reports but ignored many previous recommendations and added many of its own (like the open education movement it stressed flexible use of time and team teaching, and like *A Nation at Risk* but unlike open educators, it asserted the need for more basic subject-matter instruction). A core suggestion was that the general answer for American education was more subject-matter achievement (especially more integrative or thematic approaches to subject-matter mastery). Authors of *Prisoners of*

TABLE 2.3
Eight Recommendations From the *Prisoners of Time* Report

1. Reinvent schools around learning, not time. We recommend a commitment to bring every child in the United States to world-class standards in core academic areas.

2. Fix the design flaw: Use time in new and better ways. We recommend that state and local boards work with schools to redesign education so that time becomes a factor supporting learning, not a boundary marking its limits.

3. Establish an Academic Day. We recommend that schools provide additional academic time by reclaiming the school day for academic instruction.

4. Keep schools open longer to meet the needs of children and communities. We recommend that schools respond to the needs of today's students by remaining open longer during the day and that some schools in every district remain open throughout the year.

5. Give teachers the time they need. We recommend that teachers be provided with the professional time and opportunities they need to do their jobs.

6. Invest in technology. We recommend that schools seize on the promise of new technologies to increase productivity, enhance student achievement, and expand learning time.

7. Develop local action plans to transform schools. We recommend that every district convene local leaders to develop action plans that offer different school options and encourage parents, students, and teachers to choose among them.

8. Share the responsibility. Finger pointing and evasion must end. We recommend that all of our people shoulder their individual responsibilities to transform learning in America.

Note. From National Education Commission on Education and Learning. (1994, April). *Prisoners of time.* Washington, DC: U.S. Government Printing Office.

Time informed Americans that their high school students received considerably less instruction in basic core subject areas than did Japanese, Chinese, or German students. Thus, ipso facto, the authors of *Prisoners of Time* concluded that our schools needed to spend more time on basic subject areas, especially using thematic and interdisciplinary approaches. In this respect, the authors of *Prisoners of Time* wanted to finish the job started by *A Nation at Risk*; namely to largely restrict the curriculum to core subjects.

In particular, *Prisoners of Time* asserted that in terms of hours spent on basic math, science, and history, there were notable differences between American students and students elsewhere. The report noted that American students spent only 1,460 hours on core subjects; whereas in Japan students spent 3,170 hours in basic subject-matter instruction, in France 3,280 hours, and in Germany 3,528 hours. The commission concluded that these differences were alarming and argued for more time spent on subject-matter instruction.

Although it is instructive to note the differences in time allocated to core subjects across countries, it does not necessarily imply that American classrooms should double the amount of time spent on math. In contrast, it can plausibly be argued that in a system that has diverse goals, the present allocation of instructional time is appropriate in many schools, some schools need only a moderate adjustment, and some schools need major shifts in time allocation. Despite this wide variation, the report writers chose to argue for a general crisis. Many newspapers reported that increasing time spent on core subjects was a good idea for all schools. For example, an editorial, "Wasted Days," that appeared in *The Arizona Daily Star* enthusiastically endorsed the commission's report. The editorial included the following quote from the report: "The traditional school day must now fit in a whole set of requirements for what has been called the 'new work of the schools'—education about personal safety, consumer affairs, AIDS, conservation and energy, family life and driver's training."[20]

A general prescription—increasing the amount of time spent studying core subjects—as a cure-all for American education seems absurd. Its equivalent would be for a doctor to prescribe aspirin for all patients (including those suffering from diabetes and lung cancer)! The observation that schools attempt to do too much is hardly new.[21] Further, in a pluralistic society it is no accident that schools attempt to address some social problems. Thomas Good commented on the indiscriminate cry to increase school time on core subject matter this way:

If the curriculum includes some study of family life, it is because some political constituency and citizens thought this content would improve the curriculum. Perhaps educators and citizens were concerned because children were having children and children were killing children. They may have thought that information about family life and personal safety might allow sixth graders to make it to high school so that they could receive extra instruction in history. Were these citizens and policy makers wrong?[22]

The authors of *Prisoners of Time*, as with *A Nation at Risk*, ignored societal factors that might affect the performance of youth. Largely ignored in the recent report were issues of poverty, abuse and violence,[23] inadequate physical plants,[24] and recognition that students are social beings as well as subject-matter learners.[25] Although thematic approaches and interdisciplinary study were advocated as the essence of reform, no evidence was presented to show that the use of these recommended strategies related to improvements in students' achievement, thinking skills, or interests. Further, the authors failed to ask vital contextual questions. For example, should time allocations be shifted radically in American high schools in order, for example, to allow more study of history? If so, in which schools, urban, suburban, affluent, poor?

Goals 2000

"Goals 2000," started during the Bush administration and ended during the Clinton presidency, is a report that articulated educational goals for American schools to achieve by the year 2000. This policy debate both preceded and endured to the *Prisoners of Time* publication. Goals for the year 2000 are presented in Table 2.4.

"Goals 2000" provided another good example of the vagueness of educational goals. One goal asserted that American youth will be number 1 in math and science in the year 2000. It would be nice to lead the world in science, but how would we know when we became number 1?

Does this world class status imply gender equality or racial equality in access to advanced mathematics and science courses in high school, or does it mean that the mean performance level will be enhanced on some particular measure of mathematical and science performance? What

TABLE 2.4
National Education Goals

By the year 2000:

1. School Readiness: All children in America will start school ready to learn.

2. School Completion: The high school graduation rate will increase to at least 90 percent.

3. Student Achievement and Citizenship: American students will leave grades four, eight, and twelve having demonstrated competency in challenging subject matter—including English, Mathematics, Science, Foreign Languages, Civics and Government, Economics, Arts, History, and Geography—[and leave school] prepared for responsible citizenship, further learning, and productive employment.

4. Teacher Education and Professional Development: The nation's teaching force will have access to programs for the continued improvement of their professional skills and the opportunity to acquire the knowledge and skills needed to ... prepare ... students for the next century.

5. Mathematics and Science: U.S. students will be first in the world in science and mathematics achievement.

6. Adult Literacy and Lifelong Learning: Every adult American will be literate and will possess the knowledge and skills necessary to compete in a global economy and exercise the rights and responsibilities of citizenship.

7. Safe, disciplined, and alcohol- and drug-free schools: Every school in America will be free of drugs, violence, and the unauthorized presence of firearms and alcohol and will offer a disciplined environment conducive to learning.

8. Parental Participation: Every school will promote partnerships that will increase parental involvement and participation in promoting the social, emotional, and academic growth of children.

Note. From Public Law 103-227, Goals 2000: Educate America Act (1994).

are the assumptions about the variation that will be associated with these improvements? Do we care what happens to the other 70% of our students if 30% raise the national average in mathematics performance to unprecedented heights? Or is it the case that policy makers really only care about the top 1% of American youth: America as represented by the best of the best?"[26]

If our students outperformed all other countries' students on math and science tests, but our eminence as the leader in rocket science engineering slipped, would we feel better about student performance and the quality of our schools?

Equally laudable is the goal that high school graduation rates will increase to at least 90%. However, the report is silent on what sorts of funds, resources, or changes in practice would bring about this notable improvement. It should be understood that at present the average dropout rate in large inner-city urban areas is roughly 51%, although in some cities it is substantially higher. Certainly "Goals 2000" statements were high, but one thing is certain—they will not be accomplished by the year 2000 or anytime soon. Asserting higher standards does not automatically lead to greater effort and enhanced performance. Despite the frequent mention of "Goals 2000" in the popular press and educational journals, its impact on the curriculum can not be found, nor unfortunately its impact on dropout rates!

Politicians' Education Summit

In 1996 at the National Education Summit,[27] President Clinton, most of the state governors, and prominent business leaders from each state participated in their own "analysis" of American education and proceeded to make policy recommendations. Apparently, government and business leaders were no longer content to rely on educational commissions to analyze problems: They wanted direct involvement in shaping American education. The National Education Summit resulted in several recommendations for American education, two of the most salient ones being the need for enhanced technology and higher standards.

The goals articulated at the National Education Summit differ from those expressed in "Goals 2000". Within a few years the problems and solutions for American education had again changed in important ways. It seems unlikely to us that high school graduation will be impacted favorably simply with the provision of higher standards and enhanced technology.

Also missing from the summit analyses were contextual issues in education, such as inequitable funding and deteriorating conditions of schools. Even though extensive reports were available on these topics from the Government Accounting Office,[28] any recognition that research support for linking technology to students' learning gains was virtually non-existent,[29] as well as any awareness that the call for higher standards was vague if not vacuous.[30] Although earlier reports had called for more recognition of and support for teachers, summit leaders expressed no interest in improving the working conditions of teachers.

In summary, the nature of the problems with American education has varied across reports. Policy critiques of American education have focused principally on inadequate student achievement, not on needed resources (equipment, research, curriculum, or teacher recruitment, etc.) for improving achievement. Policymakers' affective stance was clear: They were upset with the performance of American schools, but the precise basis for their dissatisfaction remained unstated.

Subject-Matter Standards

The 1980s and 1990s also saw considerable activity designed to reform subject-matter curriculum as professional societies such as the National Council of Mathematics Teachers (NCMT, a group composed of college level, high school, and to a lesser extent middle and elementary school teachers interested in mathematics and science) developed new visions of curriculum and new instructional theories describing how students should learn the curriculum. After NCMT's initial work, many other professional societies followed their lead and developed their own curriculum standards.[31] The thinking involved in these subject-matter discussions within the various professions also influenced the thinking and recommendations of those who wrote *Prisoners of Time*. Thus, the recommendations from professional societies and those of *Prisoners of Time* overlapped considerably.

An Example: Chemistry. As a case in point, the American Chemical Society in its publication entitled "Chemistry and the National Science Education Standards" called for less focus on content knowledge and skills and more inquiry-based learning. Further, the report called for less teacher-centered instruction and more student-centered learning, for students to work in teams and not alone, and for less single-discipline focus (e.g., physics, chemistry) and more focus on interdisciplinary courses that cut across related subject-matter areas.

We find these suggestions problematic. First, these subject-matter recommendations are presented in a blatantly dichotomous fashion and in many respects they provide a déjà vu reminder of the open classroom movement (e.g., teacher as guide not presenter, knowledge rests in the learner, and so forth). The various subject-matter reports have assumed that schools have a common instructional problem and thus common solutions are recommended. See Table 2.5 for an example of

TABLE 2.5
Recommendations From Subject-Matter Study Groups

Teaching Emphasis for Beginning Teachers		
	Less of This	*More of This*
	Lecturing as the primary teaching mode	Teaching through inquiry
	Using cookbook labs	Labs requiring students to solve problems
	Algorithmic worksheets	Using chemistry to solve real-world problems
	Relying on target students	Involving all students in the lesson
	Asking primarily knowledge-level questions	Asking primarily higher cognitive-level questions
	Test or exams with only multiple-choice questions	Test or exams with a variety of questions: multiple-choice, short-answer, problems

Changing Emphasis in Lesson Plans		
	Less Emphasis On	*More Emphasis On*
	Lesson plans that present content only and rely on students' ability to recall facts	Planning an inquiry-based science program
	The "sage on the stage" approach, where the activities are all centered on the teacher	Teachers who present lessons that guide and facilitate student learning
	Lessons that lead to cumulative exams, although the lessons themselves are never evaluated	Plans that include an ongoing assessment of teaching and learning
	Set blocks of time and lessons that require all students to learn at the same rate	Plans that allow for providing students enough time, space, and resources to learn the science

(Continues)

TABLE 2.5 (Continued)

Changing Emphasis in Lesson Plans		
	Less Emphasis On	*More Emphasis On*
	Plans that have students working alone or in unrelated groups	Lessons that incorporate cooperative learning and collaboration among students

Changing Emphasis in Teaching Standards		
	Less Emphasis On	*More Emphasis On*
	Transmission of teaching knowledge and skills by lectures	Inquiry into teaching and learning
	Learning science by lecture and reading	Learning science through investigation and inquiry
	Separation of science and teaching knowledge	Integration of science and teaching knowledge
	Separation of theory and practice	Integration of theory and practice in school settings
	Individual learning	Collegial and collaborative learning
	Fragmented, one-shot sessions	Long-term coherent plans
	Courses and workshops alone	A variety of professional development activities
	Reliance on external experiences	Mix of internal and external expertise
	Staff developers as educators	Staff developers as facilitators, consultants, and planners
	Teacher as technician	Teacher as intellectual reflective practitioner
	Teacher as consumer of knowledge about teaching	Teacher as producer of knowledge about teaching

(Continues)

TABLE 2.5 (Continued)

Changing Emphasis in Teaching Standards		
	Less Emphasis On	*More Emphasis On*
	Teacher as follower	Teacher as leader
	Teacher as an individual based in the classroom	Teacher as a member of a collegial professional community
	Teacher as target of change	Teacher as source and facilitator of change

Changing Emphasis		
	Less Emphasis On	*More Emphasis On*
	Assessing what is easily measured	Assessing what is most highly valued
	Assessing discrete knowledge	Assessing rich, well-structured knowledge
	Assessing scientific knowledge	Assessing scientific understanding and reasoning
	Assessing to learn what students do not know	Assessing to learn what students understand
	Assessing only achievement	Assessing achievement and opportunity to learn
	End-of-term assessments by teachers	Students engaged in ongoing assessment of their work and that of others
	Development of external assessments by measurement experts alone	Teachers involved in the development of external assessments

Note. Tables reprinted with permission. National Research Council. (1996). *National science education standards*. Washington, DC: National Academy Press.

what the American Chemical Society believes should be emphasized or deemphasized in American education. For many reasons, the sweeping reforms proposed by subject-matter groups remind us of the new math movement. In particular, this movement stands largely on theory (and some would contend that the reform advice is given as much for political as for educational reasons).

As can be seen in Table 2.5, the report prescribed desired reform by noting what we need more of and less of in teaching and learning. For example, the report asserted the need for more collegial and less individual work. Such dichotomous suggestions that focus on the cosmetic form of instruction and ignore quality (how the form is implemented) will do little to improve classroom learning. In most cases, appropriate education requires an integration of strategies rather than an exclusive focus on one strategy. It seems important to have both individual and collegial learning, the assessment of scientific knowledge and of scientific understanding and reasoning, an assessment of what students do not know as well as what students know. Leaving aside our judgment, it should be noted that there is considerable theory to support the recommendations made by various subject-matter groups but scant empirical evidence. In many ways, these proclamations about good practice are reminiscent of earlier recommendations for new math. Lacking empirical data, enactments of these recommended teaching strategies may produce an increase, no change, or even a decline in student performance.

Some of these recommendations are undoubtedly sound in specific contexts. That is, in some schools teachers do not challenge students sufficiently or engage them in scientific and mathematical reasoning. However, in other contexts teachers do provide sufficient emphasis on understanding and reasoning. In this case, it would not be good practice to encourage these teachers to increase the amount of time they spend on reasoning and application exercises because it would reduce the number of new concepts to which students are exposed.[32]

Reform changes in curriculum and teaching proposed by subject matter groups are vastly inconsistent with the assertions presented in *A Nation at Risk*. New proposals have argued the need to alter in important ways the subject-matter content taught in American schools.

CIRCULARITY OF REFORM

Since at least the mid 1950s, American education has been described as being in crisis by politicians and the media. However, the "problem" of American education has varied from decade to decade. At times, mathematics was too abstract, not abstract enough, too practical, not socially relevant. Classrooms in one decade were too structured but in a few more years viewed as lacking in structure. The policy recommendations for reform varied markedly from report to report. As a group, the reform writings on American schools (from 1950 through the year 2000) were strikingly inconsistent.

An especially informative example of the circularity of educational faddism is the recurrence of an emphasis on progressive education. As we mentioned early in the chapter, enthusiasm for open education was at its apogee in the early 1970s; however, open education was essentially a reenactment of progressive education that had been championed by John Dewey and others in the 1920s and 1930s. Dan Reschly and Darrell Sabers demonstrated the similarity of the open education movement with the previously tried and discarded progressive education movement.[33] They found that open education attitudes were correlated +.80 with progressive education attitudes! Reschly and Sabers reminded us that progressive education rose and then declined only to appear again as open education:

> Progressive education's demise after about 1947 was surprisingly abrupt. The original movement, dating back roughly to 1920, was the foremost educational movement in America for two and one-half decades. The progressive approach and Dewey's ideas were widely acclaimed in classroom teacher organizations, college and university departments of education, and even among prominent social critics .... Despite the great interest in progressive education (often with little or incomplete understanding) there was a serious problem: implementation.[34]

Open education, the reenactment of progressive education, emerged in the early 1970s with much fanfare but quickly faded in large measure because of definitional and implementation issues and no consensus on what outcomes of schooling were most important.[35] Similarly, the new math of the 1960s has become NCMT's new math of the 1990s.

We do not discuss the theme of faddism in education reform to be cynical or to suggest that reform is not possible. However, we want to state strongly that reform in American education has largely been a rush from one panacea to another. Such faddism must be halted if meaningful reform is to occur.

The history of reform has illustrated that simple calls for reform have been poorly defined. Hence, as we turn to later chapters that frame the reform arguments presented by choice, voucher, and charter school advocates, it is instructive to see if the reformers avoid the past mistakes identified in this chapter.[36]

We have reviewed the problem descriptions and recommended solutions of various educational policy reports. We have reviewed several major reports calling for the reform of American education. An examination of these reports has revealed that, as a group, the opinion of reform advocates about the problems of American education were as wide and diverse as typical citizens' beliefs. Recommendations not only varied widely but they also often presented flatly contradictory assertions.

We now turn to the current controversy about the crisis of public education. Are current schools performing so poorly that we need to radically reform them by creating new alternatives in the form of charter schools and voucher programs? What evidence do we have about the quality of education in American schools?

Endnotes

1. California returns to phonics to help kids read better. (1998, December 11) *The Arizona Daily Star*, p. 1.
2. Kliebard, H. (1986). *The struggle for the American curriculum: 1893–1958*. New York: Routledge, p. IX.
3. Goodwin, D. K. (1994). *No ordinary time*. New York: Simon & Schuster.
4. Moise, E. E., Clanadra, A., Davis, R. B., Kline, M., & Bacon, H. M. (1965). *Five views of the "new math."* Washington, DC: Council for Basic Education. (ERIC Document Reproduction Service No. ED 001 370), p. 14.
5. Ibid., p. 16.
6. Ibid.
7. Ibid., p. 9.
8. Good, T., Biddle, B., & Brophy, J. (1975). *Teachers make a difference*. New York: Holt, Rinehart & Winston.
9. Barth, R. (1970). When children enjoy school: Some lessons from Great Britain. *Childhood Education, 46*, 195–200.
10. Powell, A. G., Farrar, E., & Cohen, D. (1985). *The shopping mall high school: Winners and losers in the educational marketplace*. Boston, MA: Houghton Mifflin.
11. National Commission on Excellence in Education. (1983, April). *A nation at risk: The imperative for education reform*. Washington, DC: U.S. Department of Education, National Commission for Excellence in Education.
12. Good, T., Biddle, B., & Brophy, J. (1975). *Teachers make a difference*. New York: Holt, Rinehart & Winston.
13. National Commission on Excellence in Education. (1983, April). *A nation at risk: The imperative for education reform*. Washington, DC: U.S. Department of Education, National Commission for Excellence in Education.

14. Tomlinson, T. M. (1986). A nation at risk: Background for a working paper. In T. M. Tomlinson & H. J. Walberg (Eds.), *Academic work and educational excellence: Raising student productivity* (p. 4). Berkeley, CA:McCutchan.

15. National Commission for Excellence in Education (1983, April). *A nation at risk: The imperatives for educational reform*. Washington, DC: U.S. Department of Education, National Commission for Excellence in Education.

16. Silberman, C. (1970). *Crisis in the classroom: The remaking of American education*. New York: Random House.

17. Kozol, J. (1967). *Death at an early age*. Boston: Houghton Mifflin.

18. National Education Commission on Time and Learning. (1994, April). *Prisoners of time*. Washington, DC: U.S. Government Printing Office.

19. Team teaching was highly recommended in the 1970s when open education was being widely recommended; again we see the tendency for something that is popular to decline in interest only to resurface some years later.

20. Editorial (1994, May 7). Wasted days. *The Arizona Daily Star*, p. 18A.

21. Good, T., Biddle, B., & Brophy, J. (1975). *Teachers make a difference*. New York: Holt, Rinehart & Winston.

22. Good, T. (1996). Teaching effects and teacher evaluation. In J. Sikula, T. Buttery, & E. Guyton (Eds.), *Handbook of research on teacher education* (2nd ed., pp. 617–666). New York: Simon and Schuster Macmillan.

23. Taylor, A. (1996). Conditions for American children, youth, and families: Are we "world class"? *Educational Researcher, 25*, 10–12.

24. Natriello, G. (1996). Diverting attention from conditions in American schools. *Educational Researcher, 25*(8), 7–9.

25. McCaslin, M. (1996). The problem of problem representation: The summit's conception of student. *Educational Researcher, 25*, 13–15.

26. Good, T. L. (1996). Educational researchers comment on the education summit and other policy proclamations from 1983–1996. *Educational Researcher, 25*(8), 6.

27. National Education Summit. (1996, March) [OnLine]. Available: http://www.summit96.ibm.com

28. U.S. General Accounting Office (1995a). *School facilities: Conditions of America's schools*. Washington, DC: U.S. Government Printing Office.
U.S. General Accounting Office. (1995b). *School facilities: America's schools not designed or equipped for the 21st Century*. Washington, DC: U.S. Government Printing Office.

29. Mergendoller, J. (1996). Moving from technological possibility to richer student learning: Revitalized infrastructure and reconstructed pedagogy. *Educational Researcher, 25*(8), 43–46.

30. Sabers, D., & Sabers, D. (1996). Conceptualizing, measuring, and implementing higher (or hire) standards. *Educational Researcher, 25*(8), 19–21.

31. Good, T. L., & Brophy, J. (2000). *Looking in classrooms* (8th ed). New York: Longman.

32. Ibid.

33. Reschly, D., & Sabers, D. (1974, June). Open education: Have we been there before? *Phi Delta Kappan*, 675–677.

34. Ibid., p. 676.

35. See chapter 7 in Good, T. L., & Brophy, J. (2000). *Looking in classrooms* (8th ed.), New York: Longman.
36. There were many reform reports issued during the 1950 to 2000 era that have not been reviewed in this chapter. However, these policy documents show the same issues that we have raised here, conflicting opinions about the problem of American education and what to do about it. However, we think that the reports we have choosen here are most of the major ones and are representative of the general issues and problems.

Chapter 3

Student Performance in American Schools: An Empirical Report Card

Chapter 2 reviewed various policy recommendations associated with previous crises in education. Problems of American education, and their solutions, appeared akin to fashion fads, changing form quickly from one season to another. The current "crisis" is based on the assumption of a growing gap between current and past performance of students' achievement in schools as well as a lowered performance by contemporary American students compared internationally. In this chapter, we examine the relevant evidence. Do we need major school reform—charter schools and vouchers—to address a major and continuing erosion of student performance?

To assess the level of students' performance in contemporary American schools, we review results from standardized achievement tests allowing historical comparisons (how do today's students compare with those of the 1970s or 1980s?) and international data (how do American students' performance compare with other countries' students'?). To supplement our analyses we also consider data describing students' recent performance on advanced placement tests for college credit as well as current data addressing graduation rates, college enrollments, and the charges of grade inflation and social promotion. Finally, we analyze citizens' perceptions about the quality of public schools and their beliefs that American schools must be about more than subject-matter achievement.

STUDENT ACHIEVEMENT

Despite dramatic and frequent newspaper headlines that announce a decline in the quality of American schools—most notably falling student scores on standardized achievement tests—this decline cannot be demonstrated with strong empirical data. Although it is true that in some American schools (especially in some inner-city schools) students are performing abysmally, more generally, our schools appear not to be in crisis. Several educational researchers have made this point clearly, most notably Gerald Bracey, and David Berliner and Bruce Biddle.

Decline in American Schools Over Time?

Gerald Bracey has argued for some time that the charge that students today perform less well on academic tests than those in the past is largely a myth (an extensive summary of his varied works on the topic can be found in his book *The Truth About America's Schools*[1]). Similarly, Berliner and Biddle, in their book *The Manufactured Crisis*, have extensively reviewed the literature related to student achievement in American schools over the past 30 years and also concluded that the charge that student achievement has fallen is a myth. They examined various sources for comparing student test performance over time including: the Scholastic Aptitude Test, the American College Testing program, the Preliminary Scholastic Aptitude Test, the National Assessment of Educational Progress, the Commercial Test of Achievement, and the Graduate Record Examination.

After an extensive review of these data sources, Berliner and Biddle reached two conclusions. First, participation in America's higher education has increased notably over time—progressively more Americans from all ethnic groups have been attracted to higher education programs. Second, "moreover, despite this expansion, today's college seniors seem to know, on average, either as much or a bit more than the seniors of earlier years."[2] So, the argument that today's students, as a group, are less knowledgeable than those of 10, 20, or 30 years ago is groundless.

These same data sources have been reviewed independently by other researchers. Jeffrey Henig, in his book *Rethinking School Choice*, presented conclusions similar to those of Berliner and Biddle.[3] Henig noted that SAT scores did decline in the mid-1960s through the late

1970s, and this fact provides a data point about which many policymakers and the media expressed considerable alarm. However, since the late 1970s, verbal scores have stabilized and math scores have started to improve. Moreover, he noted that data from the National Assessment of Educational Progress (NAEP), a test that many American students take at both the elementary and the high school levels, have provided additional encouragement. In particular, science achievement increased for both elementary and secondary students and for all ethnic groups over the last decade. Mathematics scores also increased for all age groups. Seventeen-year-olds have registered improvements in science achievement between 1982 and 1994; and in fact, in all comparisons, 1994 scores were higher than 1982 scores.

Some have decried the erosion of the American high school curriculum. However, Henig noted that a comparison of courses taken by 1982 graduates with those taken by 1987 graduates indicated that high school seniors in 1987 took many more courses in computer sciences, foreign languages, math, and science than was the case for seniors in 1982. Interestingly, he noted that such gains occurred both in public and private schools but were greater both proportionately and in absolute terms in public schools. The need for a review of curriculum in private schools is warranted given these recent research findings.

New Evidence

There are also new data beyond those documented by Berliner, Biddle, Bracey, Henig, to suggest that students' performance levels have risen. The Center on Educational Policy, using data provided by the U.S. Department of Education, illustrated that since 1987 American students have continued to take more rigorous course work. As Fig. 3.1 shows, from 1982 to 1994 the number of American students completing core academic curriculum has increased in all ethnic groups. Further, data released by the Center on Educational Policy documented that (a) fewer students from all ethnic groups dropped out of school in 1996 than was the case in 1972 and 1983, (b) more students from all ethnic groups went to college in 1997 than was the case in 1972 and 1985, and (c) students' math achievement for 17-year-old students increased in all ethnic groups from 1982 to 1994.

Based on reports provided by the Center of Education Policy, fewer White, Black, and Hispanic students in the 1990s dropped out of school than in the 1970s and 1980s. This is instructive per se, but the

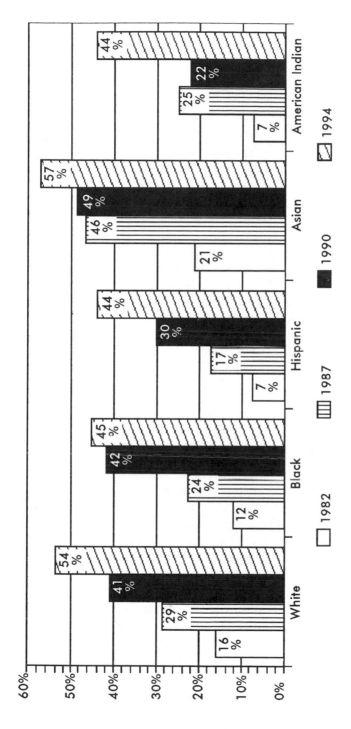

FIG. 3.1. Percentage of High School Graduates Completing a Core Curriculum by Race/Ethnicity, 1982, 1987, 1990, and 1994. The core curriculum consists of 4 years of English, and 3 years each of social studies, science, and mathematics. (Source: U.S. Department of Education, National Center for Education Statistics, *The Condition of Education 1996*.

finding takes on an added dimension when considered in light of a 1997 *Phi Delta Kappa/Gallup Poll* finding that a majority of Americans believe that dropout rates are higher than they were 25 years ago and are increasing![4] Such a discrepancy between fact and fancy is sufficiently large to again suggest that media make it possible for citizens to hold exaggerated beliefs about school failure. Further, data comparing the percentage of high school graduates enrolled in college for the fall after graduation illustrated that compared to 1972 and 1985 a higher percentage of students were enrolled in college in 1997 (1997 enrollments in college: White 67%, Hispanic 66%, and Black 60%). Hence, college populations are becoming both larger and more diverse.

Stable Student Performance: New Data.   Richard Rothstein recently reviewed earlier studies conducted with the Iowa Test of Basic Skills (ITBS) and produced data to illustrate the continuing stability of student achievement.[5] The ITBS is important because it is the only widely used achievement test that has comparable scores over a long time period (1955 to the present). Rothstein's review illustrated that students' performance increased from 1955 to roughly 1965 and then dropped for a decade. Since then they have moved back to record levels, with current students showing solid performance on the exam. Hence, there is solid evidence that achievement in American schools, on average, appears about as good as always despite the fact that American schools are educating more students, including a higher percentage of low-income students, than ever before.

State Variability in Students' NAEP Performance.   Given that states and local communities are primarily responsible for funding public education, one wonders why so much is made of how American students, on average, compare with German, Scandinavian, or Chinese students? If one could argue that educational goals, resources, and standards were constant or even somewhat similar across the country, it might make some sense to pursue the comparative questions by aggregating information across the country as a whole. However, extensive analyses of extant data have provided striking evidence that there is notable variation in curriculum, standards, and resources from state to state. Given this discrepancy, it might make more sense to compare how students from individual states fare in comparison to, say, German youth rather than talking about the country as a whole. As an example, state composite scores on the National Assessment of Educational

Progress (NAEP) in math and science produced wide variation among states. In science, students in Maine, North Dakota, Montana, and Wisconsin scored notably high, whereas in the District of Columbia, Louisiana, Mississippi, Hawaii, and California, students scored notably low. In fact, if we could drop these five low-scoring states, the country would be well on its way to being number one in science!

One fundamental way to look at students' academic achievement across states is presented in Table 3.1. This table provides information about the percentage of fourth and eighth graders who scored at proficient, basic, or below basic levels on the 1996 NAEP mathematics assessment. The table also provides information about the per pupil funding provided by each state. Variation in students' performance (and money spent on education) across states is notable. For example, in Connecticut 75% of the students fell in the proficient or basic level whereas in Louisiana only 44% of the students fell in this same range, with 56% of the students falling in the below basic level. We also remind readers that although scores on NAEP assessment showed wide state variation, in general, they are increasing. These new data further extended the conclusions reached earlier by other scholars. The performance of American students continues to increase. The most recent NAEP achievement tests were in 1998 and in this year, the subject surveyed was reading. Again the trend of increasing scores was evident.

State Spending and NAEP Achievement Scores. How does one explain the variation in student performance from state to state? Biddle explored the relationships between child poverty rates, state spending for education, and students' 1996 NAEP mathematics performance.[6] He reported that differences in state funding and students NAEP performance were correlated +.43 (states spending more money on education had higher student performance). Further, there was an amazingly strong correlation (-.70) between state child poverty rates and state NAEP performance (high poverty rates were associated with low NAEP results).

In a related effort to determine the relationship of state funding for education, we calculated the relation between students' 1996 NAEP mathematics performance as well as reading and science performance with average state spending per pupil. Our findings showed a substantial correlation between resources and performance. Higher funding levels were associated with higher levels of achievement. The correlations between adjusted state spending for education and students'

TABLE 3.1

Percentage of Students Falling at Proficient, Basic, and Below Basic Levels on the 1996 National Assessment of Educational Progress Mathematics Exam at Fourth- and Eighth-Grade Levels

STATE	Fourth Graders' Math Performance			Eighth Graders' Math Scores Performance			State Per Pupil Expenditure
	Proficient	Basic	Below Basic	Proficient	Basic	Below Basic	
Alabama	11	37	52	12	33	55	$5,052
Alaska	21	44	35	30	38	32	$6,601
Arizona	15	42	43	18	39	43	$4,683
Arkansas	13	41	46	13	39	48	$5,244
California	11	35	54	17	34	49	$4,789
Colorado	22	45	33	25	42	33	$4,941
Connecticut	31	44	25	31	39	30	$7,289
Delaware	16	38	46	19	36	45	$7,228
Florida	15	40	45	17	37	46	$5,606
Georgia	13	40	47	16	35	49	$5,248
Hawaii	16	37	47	16	35	49	$5,387
Idaho	*	*	*	*	*	*	$4,732
Illinois	*	*	*	*	*	*	$5,553
Indiana	24	48	28	24	44	32	$6,264
Iowa	22	52	26	31	47	22	$6,504
Kansas	*	*	*	*	*	*	$6,145
Kentucky	16	44	40	16	40	44	$5,583
Louisiana	8	36	56	7	31	62	$5,167

(Continues)

TABLE 3.1 (Continued)

STATE	Fourth Graders' Math Scores			Eighth Graders' Math Scores			State Per Pupil Expenditure
	Proficient	Basic	Below Basic	Proficient	Basic	Below Basic	
Maine	27	48	25	31	46	23	$6,295
Maryland	22	37	41	24	33	43	$6,708
Massachusetts	24	47	29	28	40	32	$6,201
Michigan	23	45	32	28	39	33	$6,689
Minnesota	29	47	24	34	41	25	$6,112
Mississippi	8	34	58	7	29	64	$4,633
Missouri	20	46	34	22	42	36	$5,169
Montana	22	49	29	32	43	25	$6,411
Nebraska	24	46	30	31	45	24	$6,762
Nevada	14	43	43	*	*	*	$5,359
New Hampshire	*	*	*	*	*	*	$5,942
New Jersey	25	43	32	*	*	*	$8,436
New Mexico	13	38	49	14	37	49	$5,047
New York	20	44	36	22	39	39	$7,635
North Carolina	21	43	36	20	36	44	$5,346
North Dakota	24	51	25	33	44	23	$5,689
Ohio	*	*	*	*	*	*	$5,916
Oklahoma	*	*	*	*	*	*	$5,445
Oregon	21	44	35	26	41	33	$6,248

(Continues)

TABLE 3.1 (Continued)

STATE	Fourth Graders' Math Scores			Eighth Graders' Math Scores			State Per Pupil Expenditure
	Proficient	Basic	Below Basic	Proficient	Basic	Below Basic	
Pennsylvania	20	48	32	*	*	*	$7,092
Rhode Island	17	44	39	20	40	40	$6,468
South Carolina	12	36	52	14	34	52	$5,428
South Dakota	*	*	*	*	*	*	$5,222
Tennessee	17	41	42	15	38	47	$4,747
Texas	25	44	31	21	38	41	$5,889
Utah	23	43	31	24	46	30	$3,985
Vermont	23	44	33	27	45	28	$6,512
Virginia	19	43	38	21	37	42	$5,923
Washington	21	46	33	26	41	33	$5,417
West Virginia	19	44	37	14	40	46	$6,784
Wisconsin	27	47	26	32	43	25	$7,097
Wyoming	19	45	36	22	46	32	$6,590
U.S. AVERAGES	20	42	38	23	38	39	$5,906

Note: *indicates state does not participate in national assessment, survey, or data collection. All figures are in percentages.
Adapted from Education Week. (1999). *State-to-State data comparisons: All students achieving at high levels* [Online]. Available: http://www.edweek.org/htbin/qc99_state_compr.pl and Education Week. (1999). *Resources: Adequacy* [Online]. Available: http://www.edweek.org/ sreports/ qc99/states/indicators/in-L5.htm

performance on various 1996 NAEP tests can be seen in Table 3.2. In all comparisons the percentage of students scoring at the proficient level (the highest performance level) on a NAEP test were positively correlated with state spending (higher spending was associated with a higher percentage of students in the higher performance level). In contrast, in all comparisons the percentage of students scoring at the below basic level (the lowest performance level) on a NAEP test were negatively correlated with state spending (higher spending was associated with a lower percentage of students at the below basic level). These results are notable—more funding is related to a higher percentage of high-performing students, less funding with a higher percent-

TABLE 3.2

Correlations of Adjusted State per Pupil Spending with Percentage of Students Scoring at the Proficient or Below Basic Levels on Various NAEP Tests in 1996, 1998[a]

Level	Subject	Correlation With State Per Pupil Spending	
		1996	*1998*
Proficient	Fourth-grade reading	+.478*	+.562*
	Fourth-grade math	+.548*	
	Eighth grade reading		+.536
	Eighth-grade math	+.533*	
	Eighth-grade science	+.477*	
Below basic	Fourth-grade reading	-.460*	+.540*
	Fourth-grade math	-.495*	
	Eighth-grade reading		+.434*
	Eighth-grade math	-.478*	
	Eighth-grade science	-.426*	

Note. *significant at the $p = .01$ level.
[a]All grade levels and subjects are not measured each year. All data available for 1996 and 1998 are presented here.
Adapted from Education Week. (1999). *State-to-state data comparison: All Students achieving at high levels* [Online]. Available: http://www.edweek.org/htbin/qc99_state_compr.pL and Education Week. (1999). *Resources: Adequacy* [Online]. Available: http://www.edweek.org/sreports/qc99/states/indicators/in-t5.htm

age of low-performing students. As can also be seen in Table 3.2, average state spending and students' 1998 performance in reading were also highly correlated.

It is interesting that some have tried to discredit recent increases in the NAEP 1998 reading results by noting that the percentages of students excluded from the test in some states were higher than in previous testing. For example, in Kentucky 10% of students did not participate in testing as opposed to 4% in 1994.[7] However, if one wants to consider minor differences in samples (which is a legitimate issue) then it is important to consider the number of students in 1970, when American achievement scores were at their apogee in terms of the number of special education students that were excluded from classrooms (before the Individuals with Disabilities Education Act of 1975) and hence not counted on such measures as these.

Variation in State SAT Performance. Variation, of course, is present in every type of academic measure used for assessing student performance. We compared student performance on the SAT at two points in time, 1987 and 1997, and included only states where at least 30% of students in the state took the SAT. Our comparisons yielded two conclusions. First, general verbal performance has essentially stayed the same—two points less in 1997 than in 1987. In contrast, in math average performance in 1997 was significantly greater than in 1987—today's students scored 13 points higher! What is also important about these data is the fact that many more American students took the test in 1997 than in 1987. These data indicated not only state-to-state variance (e.g., compare 1997 verbal performance in Oregon [525] to Hawaii [483]), but also indicated that student performance on a measure valued by many Americans has stayed stable or increased over time.

Clearly, there are many complex factors other than money that create variation in students' educational performance across states. Further, it is clear that money can be spent on many things. Still, these data have provided a strong basis for concluding that reasonable levels of funding are a necessary, if not singular, condition for educational performance. For example, if students are to use computers effectively they must have contemporary computers, and if students are to do well on advanced placement tests, the schools must have sufficient resources to provide advanced courses.

Grade Inflation. Another damaging charge against the public school system is the accusation of grade inflation—a claim that public schools give away unearned, higher grades. If this is the case, there is very little motivation for students to work, especially on tasks requiring thinking and sustained effort. Various policy groups have claimed that social promotion is rampant, that it erodes achievement, and that it must be curbed. As a case in point, President Bill Clinton on January 7, 1999, brought additional attention to the putative practice of social promotion when he proposed a large ($400 million) increase for after-school programs, but only for schools that had explicit policies ending social promotion.

The possibility that reports of monolithic social promotion practices are misleading is provided in a recent study that provided provocative information about the level of grades students actually receive.[8] This study explored the grading practices in one large urban school district and noted that the distribution of grades students received was markedly lower than what was commonly reported by the media. For example, as shown in Table 3.3, the majority of students' grades were below 80%. The table also shows that the average grade for all subjects ranged from 70.9% to 72.3%. Failure rates were substantial (e.g., 36.8% of seventh graders failed science), and in all comparisons (i.e., by grade and subject area), more students were failing (below 70%) than were receiving grades above 80%. These data suggest that a universal charge of grade inflation is untenable.

It seems important for policymakers to collect data (e.g., grades actually given, observed attendance rates) before making sweeping judgments about schooling. We believe that if comprehensive data were collected there would be enormous variation in assigned grades, school absentee rates, and so on, just as existing data show enormous differences in schools' resources and in student performance.

In the past, some educators not only have demonstrated empirically that teachers have assigned low grades but also have lamented the likelihood that assigned grades may be too low. Doris Entwisle and Alec Hayduk, writing in 1978, compared grades (1 = A to 4 = D) assigned in first-grade classes in disadvantaged and advantaged neighborhoods.[9] They reported that "differences between average first marks in the two schools were enormous. In reading, the average first mark was 1.77 (a little over a B) in the middle-class school. The average first mark in the working-class school was 3.15 (between a D and a C). Even at the end of first grade the average reading

TABLE 3.3
The Assignment of Grades in Middle Schools in One Large Urban School District

Course Grades	Grade 6				Grade 7				Grade 8			
	Eng	Math	Sci	SS	Eng	Math	Sci	SS	Eng	Math	Sci	SS
Above 80	21.8	21.6	23.9	25.4	23.2	21.7	21.0	22.3	24.7	21.0	22.6	24.8
In 70s	46.8	40.7	45.8	39.8	45.6	42.7	42.2	41.4	46.2	47.7	44.5	44.8
Below 70 (Failing)	31.3	37.5	30.3	34.7	31.2	35.6	36.8	36.4	29.0	31.1	32.9	30.0
Average Grade	71.6	71.1	72.0	71.9	71.7	71.2	70.9	71.1	72.3	71.6	71.4	72.1

*Subject abbreviations: Eng = English; Math = Mathematics; Sci = Science; SS = Social Studies.

Note. From Jordan, W. J., Plank, S. B., Partland, J. M., & Legters, N. E. (in preparation). *Report card grades in disadvantaged urban middle schools: School, teacher, and student influences on course failures.*

mark in the working-class school was almost a full unit below that in the middle-class school (2.59 vs. 1.73). Most working-class children got D's and C's in first grade, whereas middle-class children got A's and B's."[10] Further, they reported four serious grading problems in first-grade classrooms in the working-class school. First, students received contradictory evaluations[11] (students in these classrooms received considerable praise and support from teachers, but their formal marks were low). Second, students were evaluated on performances over which they lacked control. Third, students were unable to predict the relationship between their work and its evaluation by their teacher. Fourth, the students in the working-class classrooms were seemingly being asked to meet unattainable standards.

Grade inflation, as any issue, will likely exist in some schools but not in others. Labeling problems as rampant without data creates artificial issues that take time away from defining real problems and addressing them. We return to this theme later in the book.

Student Success on Advanced Placement Tests. The enrollment of high school students entering college in the fall of 1997 was record setting in terms of ethnic diversity, academic preparation, academic aspiration, and earned college credit. Indeed, their average SAT scores were at the highest level in 26 years—since 1971. Importantly, the number of minority students taking the test was up substantially. A decade ago only 22% of students taking the SAT were minority. Now, minority students comprise 32% of high school graduates taking the SAT.[12]

High school students have also made notable progress in terms of the number of students both taking and passing advanced placement tests for college credit. This should be good news to Americans as advanced credit placement lowers the time and cost of a college education for students and also provides a proxy exam to illustrate that students' learning in high schools has been productive and successful.

In slightly less than a decade (between 1987 and 1996), the number of advanced placement exams taken by American high school students more than doubled. Specifically, the number of students taking advanced placement exams has grown from 364,804 to 824,329. The College Board reported that more than 100,000 graduates of the high school class of 1996 started college with academic credits—this represents about one-fifth of college freshman. According to the College

Board extrapolations, the news is going to get even better. The president of the College Board predicts better performance for the high school graduates in the year 2000. He estimates that 300,000 high school students will enter college with academic credit. Not only has the number of students taking advanced subject placement tests increased in all subject areas (the only exception is French), but also the number of women and ethnic minority students has increased substantially in the past decade as can be seen in Tables 3.4 and 3.5.

Also, as with all measures, student variation in advanced placement tests show marked differences across states. For example, in Ohio in 1998, 30,274 students took advanced placement tests as compared with Missouri, where only 7,745 students took advanced placement tests.[13]

College Admission. In 1999, college admissions were reported to be at an all-time high, with a record 14.8 million students enrolled in 4-year, higher education institutions.[14] Indeed, Bronner reported "the college application season that just ended was the most competitive in the nation's history. A roaring economy, a population boom, an in-

TABLE 3.4

Advanced Placement Exams for College Credit 1987–1996 by Gender and Ethnicity

	Number of Candidates		Number of Exams	
	1987	*1996*	*1987*	*1996*
American Indian	643	2,491	813	3,535
Asian	21,101	58,778	32,770	107,470
Black	8,141	22,373	10,443	31,554
Mexican American	3,854	12,018	4,886	27,874
Puerto Rican	1,279	3,527	1,719	4,954
Other Hispanic	4,499	18,476	6,212	26,924
White	175,556	345,189	245,413	535,055
Male	129,126	235,607	188,800	386,061
Female	129,858	289,465	175,681	438,268

Note. College Board Press Release. (August 1996). *Almost one-fifth of students entering four-year colleges are eligible for credit through advanced placement* [Online]. Available: http:www.collegeboard.org/press/arch 9697/960822c.html

TABLE 3.5
Advanced Placement Exams for College Credit 1987–1996
by Content Area and Gender

College-Level Areas	Number of Examinations		Percentage of Men and Women			
			1987		1996	
	1987	1996	Male	Female	Male	Female
Art History	2,241	5,990	35	65	36	64
Art: Studio	2,310	8,536	40	60	44	56
Biology	28,124	64,651	49	51	45	55
Calculus AB	47,124	102,029	59	41	53	47
Calculus BC	11,260	20,823	69	31	63	37
Chemistry	15,809	37,462	69	31	58	42
Computer Science	8,368	11,065	84	16	84	16
Economics	n/a	23,277	n/a	n/a	59	41
English Language & Comp.	18,985	58,094	42	58	39	61
English Literature & Comp.	82,543	148,131	41	59	37	63
European History	19,642	38,887	56	44	49	51
French Language	7,946	11,987	32	68	31	69
French Literature	1,728	1,385	31	69	29	71
German Language	2,160	2,941	50	50	47	53
Government & Politics	9,175	45,319	58	42	50	50
Latin	2,545	4,405	56	44	51	49
Music Listening & Literature	353	n/a	48	42	n/a	n/a

(Continues)

TABLE 3.5 (Continued)

	Number of Examinations		Percentage of Men and Women			
			1987		1996	
			Male	Female	Male	Female
Music Theory	775	2,743	52	47	50	50
Physics B	5,814	18,664	76	24	65	35
Physics Mechanics	4,200	11,072	83	17	74	26
Physics Elec. & Magnetism	2,497	5,662	85	15	78	22
Psychology	n/a	14,308	n/a	n/a	35	65
Spanish Language	12,718	40,886	39	61	36	64
Spanish Literature	2,346	5,415	39	61	32	68
U.S. History	76,141	140,597	52	48	47	53
TOTAL	364,804	824,329	52	48	47	53

Note. College Board Press Release. (August, 1996) *Almost one-fifth of students entering four-year colleges are eligible for credit through advanced placement* [Online]. Available: http://www.collegeboard.org/press/arch9697/960822c.html

creasingly sophisticated education industry, and a growing belief that college is necessary for success have raised the stakes for acceptance to the nation's better colleges."[15] This increased competition for admission into the country's top colleges was attributed to several factors, including record high SAT scores, increased numbers of students taking advanced placement tests, and more top students applying to a wider variety of schools. As one example, "Tufts University in Medford, Mass., said it had turned away one third of the valedictorians who applied and a number of applicants with perfect 1,600 S.A.T. scores. The college received 13,500 applications for 1,200 spots."[16] Although some citizens decry the decreasing achievement of the nation's students, this deficit does not seem to be apparent in the college admission process!

TIMSS International Achievement Data. Available evidence has demonstrated that American student performance in the 1990s is not lower than that of American students in the 1970s and 1980s. What about international comparisons? Do verifiable data show any decline in performance of American students relative to those in other countries?

The Third International Mathematics and Science Study (TIMSS) of the 1990s, like its predecessors in the 1960s and 1980s, was sponsored by the International Association for the Evaluation of Educational Achievement. It is the largest and most comprehensive international comparison of education ever achieved. This report produced data that American high school seniors fared relatively poorly in international comparisons of science and math. Laurence Ogle and Patricia Dabbs reported:

> The largest study of its kind, TIMSS tested more than 500,000 mostly 13 year-olds worldwide, generating math and science scores from 41 countries. Overall, the United States scored slightly above the international average in science and slightly below the average in mathematics. Japanese, French, and Canadian students scored significantly higher than U.S. students in math, but American students scored about the same (3 points higher) on the science test as both German and Canadian students, and significantly higher than French students. In sum, the results indicated that American students scored near the middle of the international pack.[17]

Although noting that TIMSS was more accurately covered by reporters than were previous education reports, Ogle and Dabbs said that there were still major reporting glitches typically because of three basic reasons: "They ignored the data, they reported them erroneously, or they failed to ask the right questions."[18] They noted that an editorial in the *Chicago Sun-Times* declared a crisis because U.S. students were outperformed by students in Bulgaria. What the report failed to mention was that Bulgaria ranked fifth out of 41 countries in science and hence scored better than most countries.[19]

Like many research reports, the TIMSS was seized on by political leaders to advocate their beliefs. The late Al Shanker, former president of the American Federation of Teachers, asserted that America was average because it had not adopted tough standards like those of high-scoring countries. However, subsequent analyses provided mixed data—some higher scoring countries had standards but other high scoring countries did not. Hence, standards per se had no predictable impact on student achievement.

President Clinton noted the TIMSS data claims in his State of the Union Address on January 20, 1999. He reported:

> Our children are doing better. SAT scores are up. Math scores have risen in nearly all grades. But there is a problem: While our fourth graders out-perform their peers in other countries in math and science, our eighth graders are around average, and our twelfth graders rank near the bottom.[20]

Implications of TIMSS Results. If we temporarily suspend judgment on the validity of the test, what are the implications of the data? The authors of the TIMSS report offered seven explanations or suggestions for explaining the less than desirable performance of American students and schools.[21]

1. The fragmented math and science curriculum in American schools.
2. Students learning rules and applying them automatically rather than understanding the logic for such rules.
3. The absence of rigorous academic standards.
4. The belief that academic success is determined mainly by family background, not by hard work.
5. The overwhelming demands placed on teachers without adequate professional development or resources, especially time.
6. The low status assigned teachers in America.
7. Inequitable school funding and school practices such as tracking some students into less challenging curricula.

Since the TIMSS recommendations provided by the press are typically second- or third-hand, and thus, are often mediated sharply in ways that make it difficult to recognize the original recommendations, it is useful to directly quote from Professor Harold Stevenson, who recently prepared a commissioned synthesis and reflection piece on the TIMSS study.

> Attracting and retaining good teachers also depends on the status accorded them by the society in which they live. The U.S. public does not appear to be willing to support a professional status for teachers equivalent to that of professionals in other fields, such as law, engineering, and medicine. This is evident in their compensation, prestige in society, and in such a simple activity as being interrupted by others in the flow of

their lessons, something that was rare in Germany and inconceivable in Japan.[22]

Consistent with arguments by many educators and social scientists since at least the early 1960s, Stevenson's report acknowledged that demographics and the level of school finance play an important role in achievement results:

> Demographic factors are also obviously involved in students' academic achievement. Children attending poorly supported schools in impoverished or inner-city schools do not perform as well as those in affluent areas where funds are readily available to provide technology, laboratory and library facilities or other types of equipment and supplies needed for lessons in various subjects. As long as the financial support of education depends strongly on real estate taxes, inequities are bound to continue in the quality of education provided students in different locations.[23]

This argument is of course consistent with the data we presented earlier that showed a strong relationship between the quality of NAEP performance and state funding.

Stevenson's report recognized that what happens in schools is also an important determinant of achievement:

> Moreover, American students in different tracks enroll in different mathematics and science curricula. For example, the mathematics taught to vocational school students is different from that provided for those preparing to enter college. This is not the case in Japan, for example. Calculus is required of all high school students, regardless of their track, but the version taught to vocational school students is less rigorous in its proofs than is the calculus taught to students in the academic high schools.[24]

Although some of the recommendations that come from the TIMSS study can be found in previous policy reports (see chapter 2), the recognition of needed resources and the effects of poverty on educational progress is a relatively new emphasis. Scholars have often lamented the deleterious effects of inadequate resources on academic performance, but since the early 1970s, recognition of inadequate resources has been largely missing from policy documents. If one accepts the TIMSS finding that American students do not perform well enough, it is important to see that those associated with the study see these data of use not as an indicant of American schools but as an important commentary on societal support for schools.

Challenges to the Validity of the International Study.

Many have faulted the TIMSS findings on various grounds including the extent to which representative samples of each country were included in the testing. Indeed, attacks on the study have been so numerous that Commissioner Pascal Forgione (whose office sponsored TIMSS testing) attempted to defend the study in a published article.[25] Some have found his defense to be inadequate. For example, Bracey, reacting to Forgione's article,[26] criticized Forgione's suggestion that TIMSS data allowed for a comparison of our 12th-grade students against 12th-grade students in other countries. Bracey illustrated that in actuality in many countries, American 12th-grade students were compared with 13th- or 14th-grade students. Further, he noted that our 12th graders were compared with international students in their third year of study in a curriculum highly concentrated on math and science. Bracey reported that some countries only tested students in programs concentrated on science and mathematics and that in Norway and Sweden students had studied physics for 3 years before taking the TIMSS test. He noted that at least 23% of the items on the Advanced Mathematics test assumed that a student had taken a calculus course.

Apparent differences in international achievement can be explained in part by differences in content coverage. If students cover more course material (and other factors are similar) they would be expected to score higher on an exam that covers the additional material. Tom Good, Doug Grouws, and Terrill Beckerman[27] demonstrated this in a mathematics study comparing American classrooms in which students were making better than expected achievement gains with those classes in which students' achievement levels were lower than expected. One of the factors associated with the more effective mathematics classrooms (as measured by standardized tests) was pace of instruction. Indeed, the pace of mathematics instruction (i.e., the amount of mathematical material covered) correlated highly (.49) with students' subsequent exam performance.

Berliner and Biddle[28] noted that this same logic was applied to international comparisons by Ian Westbury. At the time data for the second international math study were collected (1980 to 1982), in Japan eighth-grade students were required to take algebra; in contrast,

American eighth-grade students could be found in four different types of math classes. When the comparison focused on American eighth-grade students who were actually taking algebra with Japanese students taking algebra, the putative advantage disappeared. Indeed, American students who actually took algebra performed better than Japanese students.

Given Stevenson's recognition that even students in tracked vocational schools in Japan are taught calculus, it doesn't make sense to compare Japanese students, all of whom have learned calculus, to students who have not taken calculus. Students are not going to do well on test items about material they did not cover.

Hence, two major conclusions can be reached about international comparisons. First, many of the differences in student performance can be explained by the fact that at the 12th grade level (where U.S. students perform the poorest), our students are being compared with older students and students who have been exposed to a more specialized curriculum. Second, the major policy recommendation—if one accepts the validity of the findings—is to increase resources (including well-qualified teachers) in those locations in which American students perform least well. When adequate resources are provided we find that American students do well in international comparisons.[29] Further, as we argue in the sections that follow, American schools are expected to do more than just teach subject matter.

Beauty Is in the Eye of the Beholder. During President Clinton's 1998 trip to China, he participated in a call-in radio program in Shanghai. A question about future educational changes between the United States and China prompted a discussion between President Clinton and the mayor, Mr. Xu. At one point, Mr. Xu noted the need for Chinese teachers to consider aspects of the American teaching system in order to foster greater individuality in students. "In Chinese education we talk about the filling of information into the student, whereas in the United States they try to make students more able. They try to teach you how to have the ability to do things. So Chinese are very good at tests, but not necessarily when it comes to scientific research."[30] Interestingly, on the same day, in Chinese newspapers the mayor of Shanghai commented that high test scores do not necessarily relate to high creativity and research productivity. Alternately, on the same day, the headline for the Tucson, Arizona, paper was "Student Test Scores Edging Up."[31] This article expressed the opinion (and considerable worry) that U.S. students' scores on standardized tests still remained too low.

Although some might argue that Mr. Xu was simply being polite to his American guest, there is some evidence to show that some country's educational policy is moving to emulate certain practices of American education. A report from the Ministry of Education in Singapore also suggested the need for thinking about broader ways of evaluating education. Even though Singapore has routinely been one of the top countries in mathematics since international testing began, it is instructive to note that they also are looking for at least some degree of ability to use information. The report noted that actions are being taken to reduce the curriculum load on students to free up time for more collaborative learning, more self-directed research, more independent investigations to develop process skills, thinking skills, and communication skills.[32] Further, the report argued:

> Our education system should not be judged solely by the number of A's our students get in major national examinations nor by the high standing of our students in international comparisons of science and mathematics achievement. Equally important is the quality of the people the education system produces—their integrity and character; their attitude towards work, their ability to be team-players, and their sense of responsibility and commitment to society. In short, an education that encompasses a balanced development of the whole personality—moral, cognitive, physical, social, and aesthetic".[33]

Our review of student performance in terms of comparison with American students in the past and international students currently has provided no solid data to support a claim of a crisis in American education. Although there may be reasons for refining or even radically changing public schools, a decline in student performance as assessed by conventional tests is not one of them.

CITIZENS' PERCEPTIONS OF SCHOOLS

Many policymakers and much of the media have asserted that we presently face a crisis in education. Interestingly and importantly, the views of citizens, as distinct from business leaders and government policymakers, are much more supportive of public schools.

The 1998 *Phi Delta Kappa/Gallup Poll* of the public's attitude toward public schools indicated that citizens continued to believe in the efficacy of public schools and that parents continued to be extraordinarily supportive of local public schools.[34] For example, when asked to respond to the question, "Students are often given the grades A, B, C, D, and Fail to denote the quality of their work. Suppose the public schools themselves, in this community, were graded in the same way. What grade would you give the public schools here—A, B, C, D, or Fail?" Forty-six percent of citizens assigned the grades of A and B whereas, 9% assigned the grade of D and 5% a failing grade. In contrast, in looking at data from citizens who actually have students in schools, the assigned percentages for A and B were 52%, and for D, 9% and 4% for fail. One of the educative factors associated with this poll is that it has been conducted annually for a number of years (i.e., since 1974 the poll has asked citizens to grade from A to F the public schools in their communities; since 1981 people have been asked to grade from A to F the nation's public schools; and since 1985, parents have been asked to grade the public school attended by their oldest child). Two general conclusions have been reached by those who conduct the poll. First, over time citizens consistently have given higher scores to schools with which they are more closely associated. That is, public school parents, when asked to rate the school their oldest child attends, gave the school higher grades than were given to schools in the community as a whole or to schools nationally. Parents who did not have children in school gave community schools considerably higher grades than they gave to the nation's schools in general. The pollsters have reached a second generalization:

> The differences are impressive. Over the last nine years the differences between the percentage of A's and B's given to the nation's public schools and to the local schools have averaged about 23 points. Even more startling is the difference between the percentage of A's and B's parents give to the school their oldest child attends and the percentage of A's and B's given to the nation's schools. Here the difference over the last nine years has averaged 47 percentage points.

> Taken together, these items suggest a second generalization: The low grades given the nation's public schools were primarily media-induced. Whereas people learned first hand about their *children's* schools, they learned about the *nation's* schools primarily from the media.[35]

Larry Cuban noted that the public has been consistent in its attitudes toward school and school issues for a long time and that the public's perceptions about what constitutes good schooling has been stable. He wrote, "it is public officials, policy experts, and media leaders' value-driven agendas for exerting influence and attracting audiences that have, albeit unintentionally, created roller coaster cycles and the myth of mercurial public opinion."[36]

Despite the rhetoric from government comparisons (*Prisoners of Time*, the National Education Summit) and the media's tending to emphasize bad news on schooling, citizens still support public schools, especially the ones they are served by. We suspect that citizens would be even more supportive of others' public schools (i.e., other than the ones attended by their children) if they were aware of the data reviewed here.

Parents' Perceptions of Social Promotion

The authors of a 1999 Public Agenda report were particularly chagrined at parents' inability to understand the pervasiveness of social promotion. "Yet another sign of parents' lack of knowledge is their underestimation of the pervasiveness of social promotion."[37] It is instructive to note that the authors of the Public Agenda report (and President Clinton) decried the ills of social promotions but did not define the problem (how do we know social promotion is pervasive) and failed to provide data that grade retention is better than social promotion. Indeed, existing data suggested that grade retention per se appears worse than social promotion per se. Research showed that at-risk students who were promoted achieved at the same or higher levels than their counterparts who were retained. In addition, studies of students who dropped out of school showed that retention increased the probability of dropping out by 20% to 30%.[38]

Like most issues in education, problems of grade inflation and social promotion are poorly defined. Poor definitions lead to poor and generalized solutions that offer simple dichotomies—either grade retention or social promotion—whereas in actuality many students benefit from social promotion as do others from retention (depending on the age of the student, the type of academic problem, and the range and quality of options available in the school, etc.).

A 1999 Public Agenda poll reported in *Education Week* indicated that parents' satisfaction with the schools their children attend continued to be very high. For example, 76% of parents reported that the schools their children attended were doing either a good or an excellent job, and 80% reported that their children's teachers know their subject matter very well. Further, the parent data suggested that things are getting better, as more than 60% reported that students in today's schools are learning harder material at a faster pace than when parents were in school. Authors of the report raised questions about whether parents had the qualifications to make such favorable decisions. (One wonders why the authors of the poll asked the question if they did not feel that parents had sufficient knowledge to answer the question.)

Parents as Scapegoats

At one point in time, Americans had an external enemy to use as a focus for rallying and mobilizing citizens, policymakers, and industrialists in the common goal of defending against an outside threat. However, the publication of *A Nation at Risk* clearly changed the rhetoric from external to internal sources of threat to our security (i.e., the American school system). As Peter Applebome noted, with the collapse of the Soviet Union and much of its immediate military threat, American schools became increasingly the common enemy around which society unites.[39]

Others, however, have claimed that American parents have become part of the internal problem, and that parents, like schools, have become scapegoats for the frustrations and ills of the American society. Mary McCaslin and Helen Infanti argued that parents as a group have increasingly received criticism from educators, policymakers, media, and researchers suggesting that too many are unwilling to spend the time to be effective parents.[40] They noted that among the many definitions of effectiveness, two common elements are often referred to, children's compliance with civil authority and school success. McCaslin and Infanti contended:

> Educators also have been put in combative positions with parents, and increasingly legislators, who challenge curriculum, content, and methods (e.g., bilingual education, reading methods, mathematics standards). Unlike the extant public school, the promise of charter schools is to harness parent's involvement in such matters. The swelling interest in charter schools suggests that parents who do want to participate rather than only volunteer in schools may take their competence and commitments elsewhere.[41]

Other scholars also have asserted that both conservatives and liberals have been involved in what essentially amounts to a war against parents. Indeed, at one point President Bush was sufficiently enraged by parent surveys that the U.S. Department of Education began a campaign to convince parents that they should have higher expectations for their children's achievement and for the performance of American public schools. Given that schools and parents are both under attack, it is possible that charter schools may provide a location for at least some forms of school–parent coalitions to flourish. There is some indication that the short-term response to public criticism of schools by educators is to blame parents as well as other external factors. In time, these two groups may become better coordinated allies.

SCHOOLS ARE MORE THAN SUBJECT-MATTER MASTERY

For some time scholars have argued that schools are expected to do more than help students acquire subject-matter knowledge. Further, we have known for some time that educators are aware of citizens' diverse expectations for schools and that they respond to these multiple roles. Hence, many contend that assessments of subject-matter achievement alone, even if conducted in a technically valid way, are too limited to evaluate the effectiveness of American schools. Berliner and Biddle questioned the value of comparing our school system with others using only very limited aggregate achievement scores, especially when the goals of American education are more diverse than in other countries. They put their case for "different visions" this way:

> We begin by noting that countries vary greatly in their notions about childhood and how to conduct education. This sounds like a truism, but it is also a fact that generates serious problems for comparative studies of achievement. For example, countries in continental Europe have traditionally used stiff national exams to sort out students at the end of primary or junior-high education, and only those who pass such exams are allowed to enter specialized high schools, *gymnasia*, that prepare them for university entrance. Many Asian countries also use such examinations today, but the United States does not. Does it make any sense, then, to compare the average, national achievements of high school students in mathematics, science, or literature from countries with such disparate systems of education?

> The issue becomes crucial when one ponders the unique values reflected in American education. To begin with, Americans think that children should have a wide variety of experiences. Our middle-class neighbors seem to agree that their children should participate in orga-

nized sports such as Little League, basketball, and soccer; engage in after-school activities such as piano lessons and dance; watch a good deal of TV; spend weekends in leisure pursuits; have their own cars and begin to date while in high school and so forth. This means, of course, that many American parents do *not* favor an educational system that assigns vast amounts of homework or that encourages students to become high-achieving drudges. By comparison then, American teenagers probably have more nonacademic interests and a wider knowledge base than do students from countries that stress narrow academic concerns.

As a nation, we apparently also believe that it's worthwhile for young people to gain work experience and to learn how to handle their own money. Thus, we promote employment for our teenagers; as a result, our young people are more economically active than is the youth of comparable nations—Japan, for example. (Given some of the critics' desires to promote growth in the nation's economy, why have they so consistently ignored this potential strength of America's young people?)

Again, Americans like their children to be creative, to be spontaneous, to be socially responsible and friendly, and to challenge unreasonable authority. Visitors to our country often comment with pleasure on these qualities in America's young people. But if school experiences in this country are designed to promote these qualities, it may also be that the schools downplay stress on the subservient conformity that generates high levels of subject-matter achievement in some other countries.

Americans are also profoundly committed to breadth of education. Primary students in our country not only study the three Rs, but they also paint, play musical instruments, debate, and compete in chess tournaments in their schools. American high schools offer a huge range of courses, and students are encouraged to sample these courses as electives and to participate in a host of extracurricular activities. This commitment to breadth shows up also in the concept of a four-year, liberal-arts undergraduate education, a concept unique to the United States; students elsewhere begin their professional training as doctors, lawyers, or licensed psychologists when they *enter* the university at age 18. Our system works well because students stay in school longer than they do in other countries. By comparison then, at any given age, American students are likely to be more broadly educated than are students elsewhere though they may not yet have as much detailed knowledge of specific academic subjects. They will acquire this knowledge over time, of course; and they should, on average, end up with a knowledge base that is uniquely broad as well as deep.[42]

There are data to support assertions that American students have commitments other then just school work. Bracey, using TIMSS data comparing 12th graders in various countries, concluded that 55% of American students work more than 3 hours a day. In other countries, the percentage of students working 3 hours a day is notably less; Australia, 25%; Canada, 39%; Iceland, 26%; Netherlands, 26%; New Zealand, 27%; and Norway, 27%. Bracey also reported that in 17 of 20 cases, the relationship between academic performance and work is linear. That is, the more hours worked, the lower the score; however, in America, the relationship was found to be curvilinear. Interestingly, those U.S. students who work up to 14 hours a week scored 506 (a score that is above the international average for all students); however, those who worked 24 to 35 hours a week scored 474, and those who worked more than 35 hours a week scored 448. In contrast, those who didn't work at all scored 484.[43] Two conclusions follow from these data; American students work more than do students elsewhere, and the relationships between hours worked and academic performance are complex.

Citizens want students to be well-rounded. In the 1996 *Phi Delta Kappa/Gallup Poll*, respondents overwhelmingly said that if they had to chose, they would prefer their sons or daughters to receive C grades and to be active in extracurricular activities as opposed to making A grades and not be involved in extra curricular activities (60% to 28%). These are strong data that suggest that American children are under pressure to achieve in multiple areas and that parents view schools as more than simply institutions that help students sharpen their academic skills. Similarly, the 1997 *Phi Delta Kappan/Gallup Poll* indicated citizens' tolerance for less than stellar academic performance. "Regardless of whether you have children in public school, what would be the lowest grade a child of yours could bring home on a report card without upsetting or concerning you?"[44] Sixty-three percent of public school parents and 64% of non-public school parents indicated that the lowest grade would be a C.

Some educators and policymakers have been upset by the fact that citizens in general view their school favorably and that they condone C's from students. For example, a recent study conducted at the University of Michigan examined how American children (13 and under) used time and compared it to how students used their time in 1981. In contrast to media-generated images of the "couch potato generation," in 1997, American children, in contrast with those in 1981, spent more time in school, on homework, and doing household chores. In 1997, children, in contrast to those in 1981, spent less time eating, playing, watching television, and engaging in free play. Steven Holmes observed that some of the time pressures experienced by parents are being transferred to their children. As parents' lives become more frantic and fragmented, children's lives have become more structured. He wrote, "Increasingly rare are the days when children had the time and ability to organize their own games of marbles, stick ball or cops and robbers. In their place are more time doing homework, more time running around with parents doing errands and more time participating in organized sports like soccer."[45]

CONCLUSION: THE TRUE FACE OF EDUCATIONAL ACHIEVEMENT

The evidence makes it clear that American students of today are not academically inferior to those of yesterday. Like many myths of a glorious past—the belief that today's children underachieve their parents and grandparents is shattered when the light of evidence is placed on the topic. Despite the cry of failing schools, it is clear that in some areas American students are doing very well. In particular, students' performance on advanced placement tests is outstanding—more students of all ethnic groups are taking advanced placement exams; doing sufficiently well on them to earn college credit; and maybe even saving themselves, parents, and citizens money by reducing the number of college courses required for graduation. However, the data reveal many thorns as well as roses in the educational system. Some American schools are among the worst in the world; performance in some states is shocking, and it is instructive to know that, in many of those states, the funding level for education is comparatively low. We know that educational achievement is low when children from poor families attend schools that are inadequately funded.

Given our conclusion that there is no crisis in public education (e.g., a large deterioration in pupil achievement), it does not necessarily follow that vouchers or public charter schools are not needed. The absence of a crisis suggests that in many public schools, reform can be thoughtfully considered and that citizens and policymakers can take the time to build a convincing case for what needs to be changed. There is ample evidence that in some states and in some school districts, more urgency is required. Even in those situations, however, the history of reform in American education suggests that today's quick and easy answer often becomes tomorrow's problem; intended solutions are so singularly focused that they address one problem but create another.

The Case for Needed Reform

Although much of the crisis language has been associated with the alleged low performance of students and subject-matter assessments, it is both possible and reasonable to argue for needed school reform on other grounds. Even if, on average, American schools have students who are performing on subject-matter tests at least as well as their parents and grandparents, it still may be the case that school reform is needed and that, in some cases, this may represent a major problem. Even given the results of our analysis, it is useful to consider four reasons why one might support school reform. First, although many schools have students who are generally performing adequately on assessment measures, some schools have verifiable deficiencies that beg for reform. Second, some groups of students may not be served well by the "one size fits all" public schools system. Even in schools or school districts where considerable efforts are made to accommodate individual differences in students, there may be some specific needs and certain students who are better served by a different type of school. Simply put, a school may be at a B level in its general performance in helping students to learn, but at an F level in responding to certain students.

Third, it could be argued that by resequencing the current curriculum or making relatively minor adjustments the curriculum could be improved in important ways. For example, instead of having science for five, 45-minute periods a week it might be preferable to have science three days a week but to extend the period so that students meet for 2 hours. That is, even if one grants that schools are doing okay as rated by traditional measures of academic progress, these measures are based on school curriculum that is outdated and needs major reform. Obviously, it is hard to evaluate this general claim, but we are certainly open to the possibility that some outcomes of schools that were appropriate and valid in 1910 will not be appropriate in 2010. Fourth, many have claimed that public schools are too bureaucratic to change. Such critics have argued that the competition of voucher plans and charter schools will require public schools to innovate. Accordingly, it will be instructive to see what novel and exciting curriculum changes are argued by those who want to open charter and other forms of alternative schools.

Voucher Plans, Charter Schools, and Reform

When we discuss proposed forms of school reform it will be useful to see the extent to which the four reasons we advanced do, in part, motivate the particular efforts of voucher plans or charter schools. Is it the case, for example, that some voucher plans are an attempt to transform curriculum in new and important ways? Alternatively, it will be informative to see the number of charter schools that appear to be simply doing the business of schooling as it typically unfolds in public schools. In the next two chapters we look at voucher plan and charter school proposals and assess their potential value as an investment of citizens' funds.

It is instructive to note that part of the zeal for public charter schools is to restore more local, immediate decision making to parents about the nature of schooling. Interestingly, early in 20th century, the school reform movement was focused on deterring the structure of local control and its abuses to more centralized forms of schooling in order to reduce the problem of cronyism and nepotism.[46] Now, as we turn to the 21st century, there is movement away from centalized control in favor of local control. The next chapter discusses the history of school reform as well as less extensive reform efforts such as magnets schools and school vouchers. The chapter also demonstrates how local control varies from state to state.

Endnotes

1. Bracey, G. (1997). *The truth about America's schools: The Bracey reports, 1991–1997.* Bloomington, IN: Phi Delta Kappa Educational Foundation.
2. Berliner, D., & Biddle, B. (1995). *The manufactured crisis: Myths, fraud, and the attack on America's public schools* (p. 41). New York: Addison-Wesley.
3. Henig, J. R. (1994). *Rethinking school choice.* Princeton, NJ: Princeton University Press.
4. Rose, L. C., Gallup, A. M., & Elam, S. M. (1997). The 29th annual Phi Delta Kappa/Gallup poll: Public's attitudes toward the public schools. *Phi Delta Kappan, 79,* 41–56.
5. Rothstein, R. (1997). *What do we know about declining (or rising) student achievement?* Arlington, VA: Educational Research Service.
6. Biddle, B. (1997). Foolishness, dangerous nonsense, and real correlates of state differences in achievement. *Phi Delta Kappan, 79,* 8–13.
7. Hoff, D. J. (1999, May). Board won't revise state NAEP scores. *Education Week, 18*(36), 1, 13.
8. Jordan, W. J., Plank, S. B., Partland, J. M., & Legters, N. E. (in preparation). *Report card grades in disadvantaged urban middle schools: School, teacher, and student influences on course failures.*

9. Entwisle, D. R., & Hayduk, L. A. (1978). *Too great expectations: The academic outlook of young children*. Baltimore, MD: Johns Hopkins University Press.

10. Ibid, p. 136.

11. Enwisle, D. R., & Hayduk, L. A. (1978). *Too great expectations: The academic outlook of young children*. Baltimore, MD: Johns Hopkins University Press.

12. College Board. (1997). *SAT averages by state for 1987 and 1994–1997* [Online]. Available: http://www.collegeboard.org/index_this/press/senior97/table02.html

13. For more information on state variation in Advanced Placement test rates, please see College Board Online. (1998). *Table 1: Advanced placement growth in states, 1988–1998*. Available: http://www.collegeboard.org/press/senior98/html/aptable1.html

14. Bronner, E. (1999, June 12). For '99 college application stiffest competition ever. *The New York Times,* pp. A1, A11.

15. Ibid., p. A1.

16. Ibid., p. A11.

17. Ogle, L. T., & Dabbs, P. A. (1998). The media's mixed record in reporting test results. In G. Maeroff (Ed.), *Imaging education: The media and schools in America* (p. 92).

18. Ibid., p. 95.

19. Ibid., pp. 85–100.

20. President's State of the Union Address. (1999, January 21). The text of the President's state of the union address to Congress. *The New York Times,* p. A22.

21. Stevenson, H. W. (1988). *A TIMSS primer* [Online], p. 32. Available: http://www.edexcellence.net/library/timss.html

22. Ibid.

23. Ibid.

24. Ibid.

25. Forgione, P. (1998, June). Responses to frequently asked questions about 12th-grade TIMSS. *Phi Delta Kappa, 79.*

26. Bracey, G. W. (1998, September). Tinkering with TIMSS. *Phi Delta Kappa, 80,* 32–38.

27. Good, T. L., Grouws, D., & Beckerman, T. (1978). Curriculum pacing: Some empirical data in mathematics. *Journal of Curriculum Studies, 10,* 75–81.

28. Berliner, D., & Biddle, B. (1995). *The manufactured crisis: Myths, fraud, and the attack on America's public schools*. New York: Addison-Wesley.

29. Stevenson, H. W. (1988). *TIMSS primer* [Online]. Available: [http://www. edexcellence.net/library/timss.html]

30. Faison, S. (July 1, 1998). Clinton enjoys radio stint: No violence, drugs or sex. *The New York Times,* p. A10.

31. Bustamante, M., & Samuelson, M. (1998, July 1). Student test scores edging up. *Tucson Citizen,* pp. 1A, 3A.

32. Ministry of Education. (1998). *Learning to think thinking to learn: Towards thinking schools, learning nation*. Singapore: Ministry of Education.

33. Ibid., p. 58.

34. Rose, L. C., & Gallup, A. M. (1998, September). The 30th annual Phi Delta Kappa/Gallup poll of the public's attitudes toward the public schools. *Phi Delta Kappan*, 41–56.

35. Rose, L. C., Gallup, A. M., & Elam, S. M. (1997, September). The 29th annual Phi Delta Kappa/Gallup poll of the public's attitudes toward the public schools. *Phi Delta Kappan*, 47.

36. Cuban, L. (1998). The media and polls on education—over the years. In G. Maeroff (Ed.), *Imaging education: Media and schools in America* (p. 81). New York: Teachers College Press.

37. Education Week on the Web. (1999). Public agenda: Reality check. *Education week on the Web, 18*(17). [Online]. Available: http://www.edweek.org/sreports/qc99/pub-agn.htm

38. Shepard, L. A., & Smith, M. L. (1989). *Flunking grades: Research and policies on retention*. New York: Falmer Press.

39. Applebome, P. (1997, September 14). Scold war: Yelling at the little red menace. *New York Times*, D1, D5.

40. McCaslin, M., & Infanti, H. (1998). The generativity crisis and the "scold war:" What about those parents? *Teachers College Record, 100*, 275–296.

41. Ibid., pp. 289–290.

42. Berliner, D., & Biddle, B. (1995). *The manufactured crisis: Myths, fraud, and the attack on America's public schools* (pp. 52–53). New York: Addison-Wesley.

43. Bracey, G. W. (1998, September). Tinkering with TIMSS. *Phi Delta Kappan, 80*, 32–38.

44. Rose, L. C., Gallup, A. M., & Elam, S. M. (1997, September). The 29th annual Phi Delta Kappa/Gallup poll of the public's attitudes toward the public schools. *Phi Delta Kappan*, 51.

45. Holmes, S. (1998, November 11). Children study longer and play less, a report says. *The New York Times*, p. A18.

46. Ravitch, D. (1974). *The great school wars: New York City, 1805–1973. A history of the public schools as battlefield of social change*. New York: Basic Books.

Chapter 4

The Emergence of School Vouchers and Choice in American Schools

We saw in chapter 3 that the language of *crisis* is overblown. Yet, many Americans perceive that a crisis in education exists, and other Americans argue that, crisis or not, schools can be improved substantially. Here we discuss the case for improving schools generally and then examine issues related specifically to school vouchers. The next chapter looks at another form of choice—charter public schools—as a way of reforming American education.

A NATION STILL AT RISK

As noted in chapter 2, the report *A Nation at Risk* created a controversy about the quality of American schools. On April 30, 1998, a policy document entitled *A Nation Still at Risk* was released that contended the problems of education from the 1980s still had not been solved. The report was prepared by many advocates of choice, and hence, it is no surprise that the report enthusiastically endorsed choice, privatization, and charter schools.

The preface to the report assumed a decided stance of self-importance:

> On April 3, 1998—fifteen years after the release of a landmark education report, *A Nation at Risk*—a number of the nation's most prominent education reformers, business leaders and policy makers met at an

event sponsored by the Center for Education Reform, Empower America, the Heritage Foundation, and the Thomas B. Fordham Foundation. The purpose was to discuss the state of American education and to recommend far-reaching reforms. The following manifesto results from that meeting.[1]

As can be seen in Table 4.1 members of the Still at Risk Coalition asserted the need for ten "break-through" changes to enhance education in the 21st century. Prominent among these recommendations was the call for more parent choice and charter schools.

We agree with the premise expressed in two of these statements that teachers must be knowledgeable. On the whole, however, these recommendations were largely political and appeared more designed to lampoon extant schools than to provide serious policy recommendations. As one example, the recommendation to pay excellent teachers a high wage and incompetent teachers nothing was a needless

TABLE 4.1
Ten Recommendations From *A Nation Still at Risk*

(1) Solid national academic standards and voluntary assessments based on those standards.

(2) The present authoritarian system must go and students must have the right to attend a school of their choice.

(3) Every state needs a strong charter school law so that schools get adequate resources but are still accountable for results.

(4) More school choice—charter schools should not be the only choice—more private enterprise is needed as well.

(5) Schools should not harm pupils by using methods that have been proven not to work nor force children into programs that their parents do not want.

(6) Teachers must have good subject matter knowledge and the ability to express that knowledge.

(7) The monopoly that teacher education programs have on the certification process must be ended.

(8) High pay for great educators—no pay for incompetent educators (teachers should provide evidence that their students are learning).

(9) The classroom should be the focus of effort—all resources should be focused here—money, people, time.

(10) More involvement of parents and other caring adults so that schools can focus on what they do best—conveying academic knowledge.

Note. Empower America. (1998, April 30). *A nation still at risk* [Online]. Available: http://www.edexcellence.net/library/manifes.html

exercise in polemics. We agree strongly that incompetent teachers should be weeded out of schools, but beyond that the scholarly performance issue becomes complex. Consider that the 1998 Championship-winning Chicago Bulls were willing to pay Michael Jordan vastly more money than they paid Jud Buechler and Steve Kerr, two reserve players on the team. Would anyone think that Buechler or Kerr deserved to be paid nothing? We suspect that given the level of basketball skill they possess in comparison to the average American, most people would want and expect them to be paid a good salary. Indeed, the 1999 Detroit Pistons were willing to offer Buechler a contract with a level of compensation that the authors and many of our readers would love to have. Similarly, Kerr signed an even more lucrative contract in 1999 than did Buechler.

This, of course, is what market forces would encourage. Kerr was worth more money on the open market because, among other things, he scored more points than Buechler. However, it is important to note that these two individuals played different roles on the team. Kerr did not start but got ample playing time and often played in key situations when the game was on the line. Buechler received small amounts of playing time.

In 1999 the fortunes of the two basketball players turned. Buechler played more minutes and scored more points for the Detroit Pistons than did Kerr with the San Antonio Spurs. In 2000, should Kerr be paid less and Buechler more?

Obviously our point is not to evaluate the comparative worth of these two professional players. We use the comparison to illustrate how silly the argument is that good teachers should receive high pay and less competent teachers no pay. We, of course, also take this opportunity to remind readers of the too limited financial compensation that even our best teachers receive.

Defining the effectiveness of a teacher is difficult because the role of teacher is not homogenous and requires many different types of knowledge and skills. Further, a teacher's value is not measured only by the individual knowledge and skills the teacher possesses, but also by how he or she fits into the team.

We use another sports metaphor to further stress the need to understand that teachers, ball players, salesmen, computer scientists, doctors, managers, and others are dependent on the quality of the other employees they work with as well as the quality of the organization that provides resources, directions, and feedback to all employees. The need for teamwork and specialization is well known in the business and sports world. For example, the 1998 American League All-Star baseball team did not include a single New York Yankee on the first team even though this baseball team at the All-Star break had the best mid-season record ever achieved by any team in the history of base-ball! Despite the lack of individual stars, the Yankees, as a team, won a record 128 games and the 1998 world series!

We use this example of the "team success" of the New York Yankees to illustrate the shallowness of the recommendations from the *Nation Still at Risk*. A public school is as complex as a professional sports team.

Different skills are present in all professions. For example, some physicians do research, some operate, and yet others have a marvelous bedside manner for providing useful assistance for depressed patients. Teachers also have a range of skills—some design exciting classroom lessons, others help students develop skills for managing their own be-havior, some work well with parents, and others work especially well with disturbed teenagers. Moreover, teachers are not just the sum of their individual strengths. They also have to function as a team mem-ber—to work with the school counselor, to share information with teachers in adjoining grades to assure continuity and planning. It is one thing to argue that we should pay good teachers more. However, the real task is to go beyond this empty rhetoric and define what con-stitutes good teaching and how it can be measured. The authors of *A Nation Still at Risk* are silent on this important issue.

Thus, the report failed to recognize many aspects of team work and organizational skills that are required if an individual teacher is to be effective. For some time it has been well known that the effectiveness of individual teachers can be greatly enhanced by the quality and pro-fessionalism of other teachers and the administration of a school.[2]

Yet, it is hard to realize the organizational complexity of schools given the assertions made in Table 4.1. If a school, team, or corporation is to be successful, several features must be in place, including strong leadership, capable employees, an organizational structure that sup-ports business and financial operations as well as effective public rela-tions. A view of teachers as isolated performers is but one manifestation of how many choice advocates underestimate the com-plexity of teaching. Increasing rewards for good teachers is a desirable goal, but it is important to recognize the other resources that must be in place for teachers to continue as or become good teachers, such as adequate libraries, computers, laboratories, principals, and staff devel-opment. As we see later, this focus on individual teachers and neglect of teachers as members of an organizational team virtually guaranteed that many charter schools would fail. Some assertions presented in Table 4.1 are equally specious and other claims, although plausible, are presented as established fact rather than as an idea to be tested. We deal with these claims in subsequent chapters.

Current discussions over the so-called crisis in education have led to dramatic changes in school finance and in some states to the opportunity for greater school choice. Although choice is presented by many as a new educational panacea, it is important to review the rationale for choice. Some Americans and many politicians advocate the use of public monies for vouchers to allow students to attend the school of their choice, even private and parochial schools. We now examine the issue of vouchers for private schools.

VOUCHERS AND CHOICE: A BRIEF HISTORY

Historically, vouchers have been seen in various forms. The highly successful GI Bill that Congress adopted at the end of World War II provided government payment (i.e., vouchers) to veterans to support college costs at the institution of their choice. Similarly, vouchers have taken the form of food stamps and payments to supplement rent in the private housing market and in programs like Medicaid and Medicare. However, these vouchers are for decisions mature adults make for themselves, not decisions they make for their children. And, of course, despite the general consensus that the GI Bill has worked, most conservatives report that food stamps and welfare are unacceptable.

Support for school choice has come from presidents, governors, professional educators, corporate executives, and citizens from all ethnic groups for many years.[3] Milton Friedman, the economist, first put the issue of school choice in front of the nation roughly 3 decades ago.[4] Although he successfully focused policymakers' and academics' attention on the possibility of vouchers, his idea fell flat because it lacked political support. However, recently the issue of choice has reasserted itself, and an idea that once seemed so extreme as to be unsupportable now has considerable public attention. Next we discuss both the rationale behind vouchers and their increased political efficacy.

Why Vouchers?

Vouchers are complex to discuss because they have numerous aspects. However, as a starting point, we offer the definition provided by Austin Swanson and Richard King: "an educational voucher is an entitlement extended to an individual by government permitting that individual to receive educational services up to the maximum dollar amount specified. The holder can normally redeem the voucher according to preference at any institution or enterprise approved by the granting agency."[5] Further, Henry Levin has noted that there is no singular voucher system and that voucher plans differ in terms of finance, regulation, and information. It is beyond our purpose to discuss all possible variations in voucher plans. However, it must be understood that these variations, sometimes subtle, have important consequences, especially in terms of which students receive vouchers and the actual amount of the voucher. Levin stated,

> Clearly a voucher plan with "compensatory" vouchers for the poor, no "add-ons," extensive provisions for transportation and information, and regulation of admissions to ensure participation of the poor will have vastly different consequence than one which provides a uniform voucher with parental "add-ons," poor information system, no transportation, and a laissez-faire approach to admissions.[6]

As one example, a voucher plan that takes a laissez-faire approach to admission decisions (first come, first admitted) will have a different student body than one that admits students on the basis of a lottery or requires admission of a certain number of minority, low-income, or special learners.

Ideas supporting the freedom (and desirability) of parents choosing schools for their children are typically associated with competitive economic theories of market behavior. Henig noted one common argument for vouchers is, "if parents are free to act as rationale education consumers—able to take their business elsewhere if unsatisfied with the product that their local school provides—schools will be forced to increase the quality of education and the efficiency with which they deliver it or else risk going out of business."[7]

Milton Friedman and Rose Friedman expressed a similar argument that a fundamental way to improve schooling is to allow parents to have more choice:

> to give all parents greater control over their children's schooling, similar to that which those in the upper-income classes now have. Parents generally have both greater interest in their children's schooling and more intimate knowledge of their capacities and needs then anyone else.

School reformers, and educational reformers in particular, often self-righteously take for granted that parents, especially those who are poor and have little education themselves, have little interest in their children's education and no competence to choose for them. This is a gratuitous insult.[8]

There is probably some truth to the argument that some "do gooders" have underestimated the capacity of poor parents to provide resources for their children.[9] In addition, there is literature to suggest that some reform efforts have tried to usurp parental power. Still, it is the case that some children—from all socioeconomic classes—are marginalized if not abused by their parents, and such parents do not have "intimate knowledge" of their children's needs and capabilities.

It is argued that because schools are legislated as a basic monopoly, they have no external incentives to be competitive. Hence, choice advocates suggest that schools will improve only if market forces are applied. Still, it is difficult to apply economic theory to schools in any direct sense. Education is not like a new hair style or a new winter coat. Conventional wisdom in applying market forces to consumer goods (e.g., keep quality high, prices low) does not necessarily apply to a conception of schooling designed to serve the public good. Many citizens in opposition to vouchers have argued that schooling is a public good that must be provided by government in the same way that national defense is a requirement of government. Friedman's conception was to move from schools as a government monopoly to schools as influenced heavily by market responses. Vouchers allow parents freedom to select a school of their choice and in turn provide schools with a payment for educational costs.

However, if public monies are allowed to move from school to school with a student, many contend that accountability for the social good must also be present. Levin noted the difficulty of market models reconciling and the need for common educational experiences. He indicated that there is no assurance that private choices will lead to desired social consequences. Importantly, he contended that choice in schools often involves parents selecting an educational settings for their children that reflects their own political, social, racial, and religious values.[10]

Levin argued that the situation in some inner-city settings is so bad that neither the goals of democratic education nor basic literacy are being well served. Levin wrote, "That is, inner-city youngsters may not be receiving either a 'common educational experience' or basic skills for economic and social participation, and there seems to be little optimism that present school governance can alter this pattern."[11]

The case for a strong need to reform many of our inner-city schools has been made by numerous educators. Can vouchers help to improve student achievement? If so, must it come at the expense of providing a common educational experience for a large and diverse student body?

Swanson and King noted that long ago the Center for the Study of Public Policy (CSPP) conducted a comprehensive study of the likely effects of seven different voucher plans. CSPP concluded that even if schools received more funds for taking a poor student or a special education student, there was the likely problem that some public schools would become a dumping ground for students that other public and private schools did not want.

Some voucher programs have been proposed in an attempt to balance the benefits of vouchers (more choice to parents) with societal concerns for equity and fair play. The CSPP proposed a plan in which most students could receive a voucher equivalent to the cost of education in area public schools. Further, to make all students as attractive as possible, they suggested that students who were poor or eligible for special education get supplemental money. Swanson and King argued that under such a plan if schools wanted more funds they could do so by enrolling more students who brought supplemental funding. However, even with such an economic incentive, CSPP concluded that to prevent discriminatory admission practices it would probably be necessary for popular schools to develop a lottery for at least half the students that it enrolled.

It has long been argued by critics of private schools that private schools do not have to deal with all types of students. If a student is reticent or aggressive, private schools have various strategies for persuading children to withdraw. In contrast, public schools do not have this power and must go through extensive bureaucratic procedures before removing a student from school. Thus, in the spirit of fair play, the CSPP recommended that if private schools take a student and his or her publicly funded voucher, they would have to assume the same responsibility that public schools have for such children. Their argument, in its simplest form, is that if you take public money you must assume public responsibility and accountability.

At present there is limited research evidence in America to support the value of vouchers for improving students' academic success in school. However, other countries have had more experience in supporting private schools through vouchers.[12] Extensive work in Canada and in the Netherlands has indicated that using public funds for private schools has done little to increase educational diversity. Further, some research has indicated that private schools tend to lose their individuality when they accept public support.[13]

A Recent Voucher Proposal.   Matthew Miller recently proposed a voucher plan for possibly combining support from both conservatives and liberals.[14] Miller contended that opposition to vouchers generally rests upon five "dubious" arguments. What he identified as voucher foes' central arguments were: (a) there is no evidence that vouchers work, (b) vouchers drain money from public schools, (c) the capacity is not there, (d) profit is bad, and (e) vouchers are unconstitutional. Let's examine this first argument. Miller claimed that research on vouchers has involved only small samples largely because teacher unions had been successful in limiting the size of students involved in voucher experiments. He asserted that "it is impossible to make sense of these dueling studies, whose sample sizes are so small that results seem to turn on whether, say, three children in Cleveland handed in their homework on time .... for now the 'no evidence' argument says more about union chutzpa then about voucher performance."[15]

It is important to stress that the "size" argument he advanced has more to say about Miller's chutzpa than about a solid research argument. The sample sizes in Milwaukee and Cleveland were sufficiently large to detect modest differences if they were present. Further, if anything, a small sample favors vouchers—the experimental group—because of inevitable selection factors. ("I was picked," novelty effects, a new start, a new location). The fact that the Cleveland Voucher Program included students who were not from low-income families[16] makes it even more likely to find effects in its favor, especially because the sample size was low. We review research evidence on the effects of voucher programs later in the chapter, and unlike Miller, we conclude that the contention that there is no research evidence to show that vouchers work is reality, not myth.

However, we agree with Miller that larger sample sizes would be useful and acknowledge that the study he described in which rich conservatives are providing vouchers to 14,000 children in a poor San Antonio district may yield meaningful and important data. Also, some of his ideas for vouchers in inner-city schools have merit.

Political and Intellectual Opposition. Voucher plans were frequently discussed in the 1960s, 1970s, and 1980s, but they never became an actual point of policy. Jeffrey Henig argued that the political liability of vouchers was seen early on in the opposition of teachers' and administrators' unions (e.g., National Association of Elementary School Principals). Citizens also were resistive to experimental voucher plans. In various polls taken in the 1970s, the majority (often an overwhelming majority) of citizens indicated they opposed voucher plans. This situation has reversed itself, as now a slight majority of citizens generally support the use of vouchers.[17]

However, as Henig noted, there were also intellectual challenges to the voucher concept, and its initial failure to gain momentum was not due to public indifference or the political activity of public school educators. He argued that intellectual objections to vouchers took four forms: concerns about separation of church and state, inequality, administrative feasibility, and impact on the public schools.

Gradual Erosion of Opposition to Vouchers. Despite these intellectual arguments against school choice, advocacy for choice moved to active policy consideration in the early 1980s. When Ronald Reagan assumed the presidency, those political and economic forces that focused on lessening government control of schools had a powerful ally. Reagan indicated his willingness to take on the educational establishment in various ways, including his proposal to eliminate the U.S. Department of Education. Indeed, the White House attempted in 1983, 1985, and 1986 to obtain congressional support for an education voucher plan. All these efforts failed, and even the modest 1986 proposal could not garner support. The 1986 voucher plan left it up to local school districts as to whether to allow vouchers to be used for private schools; hence, this proposal eliminated the church versus state argument as a constraint for members of Congress. Still, in 1986, the congressional reaction was sufficiently resistant to voucher plans that a Republican president could not obtain support from a majority of Republican congressional members to mandate a voucher plan.[18]

These early attempts to bring vouchers to public attention had an effect over time. By the late 1980s and early 1990s, it had become acceptable to talk about vouchers as a possible policy. One reason for the erosion of resistance to choice was Americans' confidence in government. In the 1980s, sharp criticism of government was expressed in various ways (e.g., dissatisfaction with high taxes and high inflation, and political scandals). Henig noted that an erosion of belief in government:

> helped set the stage for the broad privatization movement and the anti-government, anti-bureaucracy message that was the unifying dimension of Ronald Reagan's campaign. Studies comparing public versus private forms for delivering services traditionally provided by the government, such as sanitation and fire protection, built a case that contracting out to private firms could save money without reducing the quantity or quality of services.[19]

The arguments linking public school and market ideas, the growing attractiveness of privatization (as little government as possible), and the Reagan emphasis on shifting government power from federal to state and local communities nudged the political community to, at best, accept choice as an experiment.

Henig noted that by 1992 the argument for choice had come full circle. From Milton Friedman's arguments for market solutions in the mid-1950 to improve public education, which was largely unsupported by the public, to active political support and at least tacit support for market solutions. Henig contended that Friedman's historical ideas were relatively easy to reject because citizens had a high opinion of government and had consistently seen the wisdom of using government to solve problems (e.g., the New Deal, victory in World War II). But, in contrast, in the 1980s and 1990s, Americans' commitment to the public good had dissipated. Henig argued:

> Without a stronger vision of collective purpose to counter balance a deep commitment to personal freedom, Americans were left with little sense about why they wanted government at all. Although tradition and loyalty provided a residual constituency for public schools, the philosophical rationale for keeping educational decision making firmly anchored in public institutions was being forgotten.[20]

Hence, the political winds have shifted sufficiently so that the subjects of vouchers and choice are no longer taboo and can be discussed as possible policy.

PRIVATIZATION

Chapter 1 alluded to the fact that some, perhaps many, who participate in the education debate have little interest in the details of educational processes, that is, what teachers and students do in the classroom. Many of these individuals can be included under the label of advocates for privatization. Thus, some partisans who advocate for more competition in education are not interested in public education per se, but are simply advocates of the private sector (i.e., they want to reduce the role of government in all aspects of society). In the past 25 years, many politicians and economists have increasingly argued the case for the virtues of privatization—turning over government functions to private companies. The arguments are varied, but the basic assertions are that government workers have little incentive to work for improvement (products, services) and that private companies stimulated by competition and profits will make services better and at less cost. This general philosophical trend toward privatization, of course, also has helped fuel support for vouchers and charter schools.

Robert Kuttner, in his book entitled *Everything for Sale: The Virtues and Limits of Markets,* has presented a convincing case that human motivation (e.g., the willingness to vote) cannot be understood only in terms of price, cost, profit, and market forces.[21] Citizens sometimes vote and hence waste resources (i.e., their time) from the market perspective, when they know their candidate cannot win. People can and do often act for the common good, not just on the basis of narrow economic interests as advocates of market force would argue. Further, Kuttner argued that even when one keeps the argument only to issues of price, cost, and profit, privatization of public institutions has resulted in increased costs and inefficiencies, not in improved products at lower costs as market forces advocate. We return to a brief review of the literature on privatization and its implications for school reform in chapter 8.

RESEARCH ON SCHOOL CHOICE

There is a substantial literature about choice issues and program effects from the last 25 years. It is estimated that more than 4,000 magnet schools now allow students to select a school (within the public school system) that has a special teaching or curriculum theme.[22] It is beyond our purpose to comprehensively review the extensive literature on magnet schools and other forms of choice (e.g., districtwide procedures for school choice, state-initiated open-enrollment options). There is a substantial body of evidence that illustrates that these findings are mixed (sometimes they appear to work, other times they appear to fail) and complicated (when they do work, they appear to be more strongly associated with factors other than choice).[23] For example, Jeffrey Henig noted that of the recent experiments in school choice that arguably could be called successful, all had the following characteristics: "dependent on strong political leadership, authoritative government, and the will to insist that parochial interests sometimes be challenged in the name of broader societal goals."[24] Henig concluded, "individual choice is a value worth protecting; it can also be a useful tool in the collective arsenal. But its effectiveness in addressing social problems depends on its being used in the context of confident and legitimate government authority, not as an alternative to such authority."[25] In contrast, the purpose of many forms of school choice seems to be to skirt governmental authority.

The bulk of research to date on school choice has focused on magnet schools. Magnet schools were attempts by school districts to encourage voluntary school desegregation by creating schools with distinctive themes that would be widely popular to certain groups of students. It is very difficult to learn from this research for various reasons. One important issue is the likely possibility that magnet schools often are selected by different types of families for different reasons. However, evidence is mixed. In some studies magnet schools have drawn more high-income families, and in contrast, in others, magnet schools have been more popular with low-income families.

Recent research has shown increasingly that, at least in a relative sense, income is still a factor in choosing magnet schools. The Harvard project on school desegregation has provided recent data to show the growing segregation of students in school districts across the country. This report concluded that "the racial and ethnic segregation of African American and Latino students has produced a deepening isolation from middle class students and from successful schools."[26] Earlier, Orfield concluded that a concentration of poverty makes it very difficult for students to maintain a commitment to education. Poor students arrive at school with many disadvantages associated with low-income households, especially parents who are often consumed by the discouraging and disabling effects of poverty. Claire Smrekar and Ellen Goldring have provided a comprehensive 3-year study of magnet and non-magnet schools in St. Louis and Cincinnati. Smrekar and Goldring noted:

> In the context of St. Louis and Cincinnati, our study paints a different portrait than the ones sketched by the Harvard researchers, but is nonetheless a pernicious pattern; despite racially desegregated schools, the

systems reflect, to some degree, a "creaming" of more socioeconomically advantaged parents and their children from neighborhood schools to magnet schools. Our scrutiny falls on the disparities in the socioeconomic composition of magnet versus nonmagnet schools. We argue that the differences in family income, parents' education levels, and employment status are troubling and should trigger efforts designed to expand opportunities for lower income families to participate more broadly in the system of choice envisioned in the magnet program.[27]

Two conclusions from this literature are important. First, the results are highly inconsistent from study to study. In some instances, school choice is associated with enhanced achievement, but in other cases it is not. Second, even in those studies that showed a positive relationship between student achievement and school choice, the impact of school choice was minor, and other variables appeared to be more strongly associated with student achievement. As a case in point, Lee Shumow, Kyungseok Kang, and Deborah Lowe-Vandell, in their study of school choice, concluded that choice might not be the most powerful way to intervene. They found that school choice was associated with a very small but statistically significant difference in mathematics achievement (but not reading achievement) but that this relationship made less difference than parent involvement in schooling did. They concluded that:

> Parent's involvement in their children's schooling is found to have a more powerful effect than school choice on both mathematics achievement and school orientation. In light of these findings, future studies are needed to determine whether policy and practice may be best directed at engaging parents in direct and active involvement with their children's schooling rather than in instituting school choice.[28]

And, indeed, we suspect that yet other variables and combinations of variables have more influence on student achievement than do parent involvement and school choice.

Adding to the complexity of determining the desirability of school choice, Shumow and colleagues found that, contrary to their predictions, parents who had chosen schools were found to be less directly involved in their children's schooling. In contrast, parents in assigned schools that were most typically located in their neighborhoods were more directly involved in their children's schooling. Shumow and colleagues acknowledged that this finding bolsters the arguments made frequently by critics of school choice that low-income parents may be unable to become directly involved systematically in their children's education even if they do choose the school, because of limited transportation, time, and other factors.[29] Further, they found that parents and children taking advantage of choice were more likely to be African American, lower-income, and high-risk children. Although there have been some strong claims about the effects of allowing more choice for parents in selecting a public school (both positive and negative[30]) the literature is mixed, and choice has not proven to be a consistent or robust variable, at least not in terms of effects on student academic performance.

THE CASE OF VOUCHERS

Private schools have always been a constant in America education, and today some 11% of American youth attend private schools; 85% of private schools are associated with a religion.[31] Historically, public funds have not been allowed to support the cost of private education. Recent legislation and landmark court decisions have started to erode this historic barrier, and in some locations it appears, at least in the short run (pending other legislation or court action), that public monies in the form of vouchers will be spent in private schools, even in private religious schools. For instance, in April 1999, the Florida legislature passed the nation's first statewide voucher plan allowing children in the state's educationally poorest schools to attend private schools (sectarian or nonsectarian) using vouchers.

An Example: The Milwaukee Parental Choice Program

The Milwaukee Parental Choice Program (MPCP), developed in 1990, allowed some low-socioeconomic-status students to attend private, nonsectarian Milwaukee schools with the aid of public funds. According to the mandate of the program, students had to come from families with incomes not exceeding 1.75 times the national poverty rate, and students could not have been in private schools in the prior year or in public schools in any district other than the Milwaukee Public School District (MPSD). Students enrolled in the choice program in participating schools were provided public funds equal to the yearly MPSD per-student state aid. In the initial year of the program, the to-

tal number of choice students was limited to 1% of the MPSD enrollment, and private schools had to restrict choice students to 49% of the
total enrollment. In the original MPCP, private schools had to comply
with antidiscrimination provisions and all health and safety codes
that applied to Wisconsin Public Schools. In addition, any school participating in the program had to define performance criteria and submit to the state certain financial and performance audits on an annual
basis. Under the original MPCP, the state of Wisconsin gave public
funds directly to participating private schools.

The New Milwaukee Parental Choice Program

In June of 1995, several significant changes were made in the MPCP. In
this new program, 1.5% of students were eligible for vouchers, and a
given private school could have an enrollment of up to 65% choice students. Among other major changes were: religious schools could now
enter the program, students in Grades K–3 who were already attending private schools would be eligible for the program, and all funding
for data collection and evaluation was eliminated. Reaction to the passage of this controversial law was mixed; however, proponents of the
use of public funds for private education were excited when Wisconsin's Governor Tommy G. Thompson signed into law legislation allowing for public funds to be used in parochial schools. None were
more jubilant than the governor himself as he remarked:

> What a day! This morning I signed into law the most revolutionary
> budget in our state's history. And this afternoon we are here to celebrate
> one of the most revolutionary parts of that budget—the expansion of
> the Milwaukee Parental School Choice Plan. "Revolutionary" is not
> over-stating the case—the Milwaukee school choice program was "the
> shot heard round the world." We were the first. And now others are fol-
> lowing our lead. Ohio is starting school choice in Cleveland. Washing-
> ton D.C. is talking about a voucher program.

> What school choice is doing, ladies and gentlemen, is very simple: it is
> redefining public education. Public schools must no longer be govern-
> ment-run schools. They will be schools that serve the public. School
> choice is more than a program. It is a philosophy. It is a belief that par-
> ents know best when it comes to their children. And it is a belief that
> poor parents have the same right to choose that other parents do. That
> it's education that is serving the public.

So today, we are leveling the playing field. We are saying it doesn't matter if you live on Lake Drive or 35th and North, you are going to have the right to choose the best school for your own child. Together, you and I have turned Milwaukee into the Lexington and Concord of the education reform battlefront. Today we are taking the next step. Everyone is looking to us. Let's show them what we've got! Thank you.[32]

These changes in the MPCP have fueled an ongoing legal battle about the constitutionality of providing public monies to pay for education at private, nonsecular schools.

Court Ruling.   In June 1998, the Wisconsin Supreme Court ruled that the use of public funds to support private parochial schools was not unconstitutional. Importantly, the court indicated that their ruling did not bear on the merits of this type of school choice. The court made it clear that it was not dealing with the effectiveness or appropriateness of the program nor the political consideration that motivated its adoption. The court considerations attended only to the constitutional issues presented in the case:

> In the absence of a constitutional violation, the desirability and efficacy of school choice are matters to be resolved through the political process. This program may be wise or unwise, provident or improvident from an educational or public policy viewpoint. Our individual preferences, however, are not the constitutional standard.[33]

The Wisconsin court ruled that students did not receive money because they were a Baptist or an atheist but because the student was from a low-income family. Further, the court took the position that the voucher money went to parents, not schools, and thus its purpose, with regard to religion, was neutral.

Within the revised MPCP, students and parents were eligible for an equal share of per pupil public aid no matter which school they chose to attend. Accordingly, participating parents could send children to a neighborhood public school, another public school within the district, a specialized public school, a private sectarian school, or a private nonsectarian school. Given that parents choose how to use the voucher, it was claimed that the program in choice was religion neutral. The court concluded that:

> The amended MPCP, therefore, places on equal footing options of public and private school choice and vests power in the hands of parents to

choose where to direct the funds allocated for their children's benefit. We are satisfied that the implementation of the provisions of the amended MPCP will not have the primary effect of advancing religion. … the amended MPCP does not require a single student to attend a class at a sectarian, private school. The qualifying student only attends a sectarian, private school under the program if the student's parent so chooses. Nor does the amended MPCP force participation in religious activities.[34]

The Wisconsin Supreme Court approved the use of public funds in private schools by a very close vote. William A. Bablitch wrote a dissent that Chief Justice Shirley S. Abrahamson joined. The dissent contended that:

The amended Milwaukee Parental Choice Program violated the use of state funds for the benefit of religious societies or seminaries. The case involved several issues but one principal issue was the extent to which the amended MPCP violates Wisconsin's public purpose doctrine requiring that public funds be spent only for public purposes.[35]

Supreme Court Inaction. In the fall of 1998, the United States Supreme Court refused to hear the Wisconsin case, hence, allowing the ruling to stand. As expected, the Court's ruling drew praise from those who favor vouchers. In contrast, an editorial in *The New York Times* was unequivocal in its condemnation of the Supreme Court's inactivity:

A voucher plan, such as Milwaukee's, does not reform anything. It is a funding mechanism that forces taxpayers to underwrite religious and private education. Improving education for all students, not just the few who manage to get vouchers, requires sustained community commitment and leadership. Vouchers are a convenient political diversion from that task.[36]

Other recent developments have also made it likely that more states will find ways to shift public monies to private schools. The Arizona Supreme Court recently ruled that a state law allowing for a tax credit of $500 for contributions to private schools was constitutional. Hence, a substantial amount of state money will be spent in private schools. It is estimated that the program will cost $50 million in the first year, but it may escalate radically if more citizens take advantage of the tax break. This ruling is especially important because Arizona's state constitution explicitly forbids the use of state funds in private religious schools. The majority opinion in the Arizona Supreme Court was written by Chief Justice Thomas Zlaket, who concluded that a tax credit was not use of public monies because the funds provided by the tax credit were not monies already in the public coffer.[37] Specific plans for attempting to appeal this decision to the U.S. Supreme Court are underway.

In addition, in Florida, the governor, in concert with the Florida legislature, has approved a state voucher plan. The plan was developed in response to the large number of low-rated Florida state schools. Under the voucher plan, students attending the lowest rated Florida schools would be eligible to receive a $4,000 voucher to attend the school of their choice, including private religious schools. Although the plan limits the number of students receiving vouchers by only providing them to students in schools who receive a grade of F on a conglomeration of statewide assessments, in the 1999–2000 school year it is anticipated that four schools will meet this criteria. However, in the 2000–2001 school year it is anticipated that as many as 169 schools may meet this criteria, making 156,000 students eligible for vouchers.[38]

As in the case of Milwaukee, critics denounce the program as violating the separation of church and state. Further, critics worry that vouchers will cause a mass exodus of the top students from the poorest performing schools, leaving these schools and their remaining students in a more dire position than they had been in previously. Although any student in a poor performing school is eligible for a voucher, critics feel that only the better students and those students with involved parents will take the voucher option. State officials see this plan as demonstrating to school administrators that poor school performance has consequences. This plan is likely to encounter many legal obstacles before being implemented.[39]

As noted at the start of the chapter, it is no longer heretical to discuss vouchers, and the political climate in some communities has allowed them to become social policy. However, in these cities and elsewhere, the debate on vouchers is intense and often contentious. We now turn to available research. Is there evidence that vouchers enhance the academic performance of our students?

Findings From Two Voucher Studies

Choice in Milwaukee. The Milwaukee Parental Choice Program (MPCP) has been evaluated by two different research teams, and the two groups have presented contradictory conclusions about the impact of the MPCP on student achievement. The original research was conducted at the University of Wisconsin, Madison, by John Witte, Troy Sterr, and Christopher Thorn.[40] On the basis of a 5-year-study, Witte and colleagues concluded that the outcomes of the choice program in terms of achievement were complex and mixed. They noted that achievement-gain scores varied considerably. For example, choice students' reading scores increased the first year, but fell substantially in the second year and essentially remained at that same level over the next 3 years. However, they reported that the sample size used in year 1 was very small, and accordingly, the improved reading scores were not statistically significant. In contrast, in the second year the sample size was larger, and the documented decline was significant. In terms of mathematics achievement, choice students were essentially the same during the first 2 years, made a significant increase in the third year, and significantly declined in the fourth year.

Students in Milwaukee Public Schools (MPS) gained in reading in the first 2 years, with a small but significant gain. In the next 2 years, there were small but not significant declines. Math scores for MPS students were varied as well. In the first year, significant gains occurred for the total MPS group and the low-income subgroup. In the second year the scores were essentially the same, but there were major declines in the third year. In the fourth year, there was basically no change for either of the MPS groups of students.

Witte and his colleagues concluded that the choice program had no notable impact on student school performance: "Statistical analyses generally indicated that choice and public school students were not that much different. If there was a difference, MPS students did somewhat better in reading."[41]

In sharp contrast, Jay Green from the University of Houston and Paul Peterson at Harvard University and their colleagues reached noticeably different conclusions about the effects of school choice in Milwaukee.[42] They reanalyzed the data from the program's original evaluation and not only quarreled with the data analysis strategy used by Witte and his colleagues, but also criticized the legislative restrictions that made it difficult for the choice program to succeed. In particular, their criticisms took three forms: (a) only a few hundred children from low-income households were eligible for the choice program, (b) the voucher children received was worth only one-half the cost of educating the student in the Milwaukee Public Schools, and (c) parochial schools were excluded, preventing parents from choosing from more than 90% of Milwaukee private schools. Greene, Peterson, and their colleagues contended:

> But despite these restrictions and limitations, data derived from a natural experiment that allocated students randomly to test and control groups suggest that students in choice schools in their third and fourth years, scored, on average from three to five percentile points higher in reading and five to twelve points higher in mathematics than a randomly selected control group. These are not trivial differences in educational achievement."[43]

However, inferences and conclusions can be drawn only if the data used are a reliable representation of program participants. Unfortunately, even these advocates of choice indicated that there were sufficient numbers of missing cases that "one can not draw conclusions with complete certainty."[44] There is no dependable research evidence available in the Milwaukee data to conclude that choice has had favorable impact on student achievement.

Still, the Milwaukee program has been a political victory, if not educationally successful. Tamara Lewin concluded:

> Nine years into the nation's first school-voucher program here, there is no question that the concept has taken hold. More than 6,000 poor children, 6% of the cities students receive publicly financed vouchers of merely $5,000 a year to attend private or parochial schools (however, there is still no compelling data that students who attend voucher schools do better than children who attend regular schools).[45]

Some, like Mary Zapala, the principal of Riverside High School in Milwaukee, have claimed that the public schools in Milwaukee lost millions of dollars for students who were already in parochial schools. Ms. Zapala was quoted as saying, "I like competition if it is fair. What seems to be wrong with this is that the playing field is not level. We have unionized teachers, licensing rules, required assessments they don't. We have to take everyone. They can take a kid, get the money, and if there is any misbehavior, they can send him back to us mid-year."[46] (We return to this financial issue later: Do vouchers and charters have undue financial costs?)

Choice in Cleveland. The Cleveland Voucher Program began in 1996 with an enrollment of roughly 2,000 students in grades K–3. In May 1999, the Ohio Supreme Court determined that the way the voucher program was passed in the legislature was unconstitutional; however, they also ruled that the voucher program was not problematic in terms of its link between government and religion.[47] So, at the end of the 1998–1999 school year, the voucher program will end in Ohio unless legislative changes are developed to address "procedural issues," and such legislation is expected to pass. However, voucher advocates are pleased with this decision; they feel that it strengthens their position in getting future voucher legislation passed because "the court rejected broader challenges to the voucher program based on the First Amendment's prohibition against government establishment of religion, as well as on a similar provision of the state constitution."[48]

Kim Metcalfe and his colleagues at the Indiana Center for Evaluation at the Indiana University School of Education performed the first analysis of the Cleveland voucher program. Their study examined the academic achievement of 125 third-grade voucher students and the achievement of approximately 450 Cleveland Public School third graders. They found, after slightly less than 1 year in the program, no significant differences in academic achievement between voucher students and Cleveland Public School children. Given such a short time period, Metcalfe and colleagues urged those on both sides of the school choice issue to wait until more comprehensive data are available before judging the Cleveland choice program a success or failure.

Despite this caveat, J. Greene (now at the University of Texas at Austin), Paul Peterson (at Harvard), and William Howell (from Stanford University) conducted a reanalysis of the Cleveland data and concluded that students in one school in Grades K–3 gained an average of 5.5 percentile points on reading tests and 15 percentile points in math.[49] Metcalfe noted that:

Unfortunately, though perhaps not surprisingly, a small though vocal group of voucher advocates has attempted to cloud the issue by manipulating the data in a reanalysis of their own. Though all of this may

seem to be nothing more than an abstract, academic "cat fight," the outcomes of this debate are likely to impact thousands of children and their
families. It is absolutely critical that families and policy makers are provided with legitimate, timely, factual information on which to make
their decisions about school choice."[50]

The Cleveland choice program has since grown to include about
3,700 students, or 5% of the student population. The program is popular, as 5,000 students applied who were not granted admission. Further, Warren Cohen noted that it is not surprising that people might be
interested in vouchers, since only 16% of ninth graders in Cleveland
pass the Ohio proficiency test and only a third of the city's students
graduate on time. He noted that the draw for voucher schools is because they are smaller and believed to be safer, and over 60% of
voucher students attend Catholic schools, which have highly regarded
academic programs. Despite the possibilities of a small school size for
innovation and other curriculum reforms, he suggested that the gains
in performance have not been demonstrated:

> Yet in other ways, the pilot program, advanced as a market-based rem-
> edy for public school ills, falls short of its promises. In theory, vouchers
> encourage public schools to improve by giving their students the option
> to leave. But in Cleveland, the program seems more a form of educa-
> tional triage than a catalyst for reform. With only 3 percent of Cleve-
> land's public school students participating, the voucher program
> hasn't, to date, had a reforming effect on the whole system."[51]

Although the program has grown, research evidence to support the
argument that vouchers will improve student achievement is still not
available. Ironically, two high profile voucher schools stand out because of students' poor performance. Students who scored especially
low were enrolled in Cleveland's two Hope Academies. "The test
scores of these students, who are the poster children for vouchers in
Cleveland, were not just lower, according to the study, but 'significantly and substantially lower' than those of public school students
and of voucher students in other private schools."[52] The private school
enrolling the biggest number of voucher students, Hope Central Academy, provides absolutely no services for leaning disabled students. Furthermore, a majority of the city's voucher schools have been found to
include religion during the school day, which has triggered a number of
lawsuits challenging the programs constitutionality.[53]

Public schools have been instrumental in teaching a common heritage. Some see this key role of schooling in a democracy (uniting with common shared experiences) to be challenged by Cleveland voucher schools.

> But Cleveland's voucher program threatens to replace the single-heritage credo of public schools with a system that teaches one faith in one school and a competing faith in another. That's because the hard truth of the city's voucher program is that the choice it offers parents is mainly a choice of religious schools."[54]

Critics of the voucher programs have also complained that the movement takes away the "publicness" of American schools, since in many communities the school has served to bring students together from different social classes and races.

Across both the Milwaukee and Cleveland choice programs we see that inadequate research design and incomplete data sets have rendered comparisons of student performance in choice and nonchoice schools difficult to interpret. Later in the book, we return to a discussion of how to improve future field studies of student school performance in order to yield useful data for both policy and program improvement purposes. However, it is useful to remind readers at this point that the voucher movement, like other reform movements (open classrooms, new math, etc.) is a large and vague concept under whose umbrella many variations operate. It is time to stop comparing only voucher and nonvoucher schools and to examine high and low-performing schools within each group.

CONCLUSION

Arguments for choice have been stimulated largely by economic and marketplace conceptions. The arguments presented were simple and direct. Public schools essentially constitute a monopoly; hence, if we want to improve them, we need to provide competition and economic incentives that encourage risk taking and growth. Although initially such arguments for choice and vouchers met with substantial political opposition in both parties, over time political support for vouchers grew across the board.

In part, political currency for choice occurred because of the general public decline in satisfaction with government control. When Milton Friedman first introduced vouchers, citizens largely believed in government as a source for public solutions. The great depression in the 1920s, the victorious war in the 1940s, the New Deal, and the economic boom following World War II all enhanced a sense of public trust and public good will toward government. In the ensuing years various events occurred (Watergate, high taxes, inflation) such that many citizens grew progressively more dissatisfied with central government.[55] Indeed, President Reagan was extremely successful in encouraging citizens to think about the need for reducing government power per se but especially in shifting federal responsibilities to the state and local level.

Eventually, voucher programs were given an opportunity to become actual policy in some settings. The Milwaukee voucher program has grown over time from a program that accepted only low-income youth for instruction in nonreligious school settings to one in which students are now allowed to attend private religious as well as private secular schools. The constitutionality of voucher plans has been tested in Wisconsin. There, the State Supreme Court upheld the constitutionality of using public funds for private schools.

Unfortunately, most of the arguments and conclusions about vouchers have been based on political arguments. This is the case in part because the amount of data available is extremely limited. A review of such data shows that there is no real evidence that vouchers are used in ways that encourage innovative forms of instruction or function in ways that pressure public schools to reform their curriculum or to work harder to align programs with parent and student interest. In particular, the data in student achievement from two high-profile voucher programs have shown mixed results. Further, many members of the research community have concluded that the programs have provided data that are difficult to interpret, because the research designs and incomplete data sets are not sufficient to allow for reliable or meaningful evaluation.[56]

Vouchers have scored a political victory. They have gained a foothold in American schools and, given events underway in many places, including Florida, it is likely the number of voucher plans will increase in the near future. However, there has been no educational victory. The impact of vouchers to date cannot be related to any improvement in student achievement or related issues (e.g., public schools working harder because of competition). Again, it is important to note that there can be countless manifestations of a voucher. Hence, in a very real sense the relationship between vouchers and achievement has only been expressed in the case of particular types of vouchers.

In the next two chapters we turn to a discussion of school reform as demonstrated by charter schools. We discuss the charter school movement and begin to analyze the logic and potential value that this reform represents in light of the current state of education in the United States. Since charter schools have spread quickly and enjoy wide political support, they merit careful consideration. We address questions such as: What are charter schools? Is a charter school in Arkansas the same as one in California or Arizona? Are charter schools more segregated or integrated than noncharter schools? How do the instructional programs differ in charter and noncharter public schools? Is there any evidence to suggest that students learn better or different things in charter versus noncharter public schools?

Endnotes

1. Empower America. (1998, April 30). *A nation still at risk* [Online]. Available: http://www.edexcellence.net/library/manifes.html.
2. Rosenholtz, S. (1989). *Teachers' workplace: The social organization of schools.* White Plains, NY: Longman.
3. Henig, J. R. (1994). *Rethinking school choice.* Princeton, NJ: Princeton University Press.
4. Ibid.
5. Swanson, A., & King, R. (1997). *School finance: Its economics and politics* (2nd ed.). New York: Longman, p. 414.
6. Levin, H. M. (1991). The economics of educational choice. *Economics of Education Review, 10,* 137–158.
7. Ibid., p. 57.
8. Friedman, M., & Friedman, R. (1980). *Free to choose: A personal statement.* New York: Avon, p. 150.
9. Moll, L. (1992). Bilingual classroom studies and community analysis. *Educational Researcher, 21,* 20–24.
10. Levin, H. M. (1983). Educational choice and the pains of democracy. In T. James & H. M. Levin (Eds.), *Public dollars for private schools* (pp. 17–38). Philadelphia, PA: Temple University Press.
11. Ibid., p. 36.
12. Erickson, D. (1986). Choice and private schools. In D. C. Levy (Ed.), *Private education: Studies in choice and public policy.* New York: Oxford University Press.
13. James, E. (1986). Public subsidies for public and private education: The Dutch case. In D.C. Levy (Ed.), *Private education: Studies in choice and public policy* (pp.113–137). New York: Oxford University Press.
14. Miller, M. (1999, July). A bold experiment to fix city schools. *Atlantic Monthly,* 15–16, 18, 26–28, 30–31.

15. Ibid., p. 26.
16. Archer, J. (1999, June). Obstacle course. *Education Week, 18*(39), 22–27.
17. Rose, L. C., & Gallup, A. M. (1998, September). The 30th annual Phi Delta Kappa/Gallup poll of the public's attitudes toward the public schools. *Phi Delta Kappan*, 41–56.
18. Henig, J. R. (1994). *Rethinking school choice.* Princeton, NJ: Princeton University Press.
19. Ibid., p. 75.
20. Ibid., p. 96.
21. Kuttner, R. (1997). *Everything for sale: The virtues and limits of markets.* New York: Knopf.
22. Smrekar, C., & Goldring, E. (1999). *School choice in urban America: Magnet schools and the pursuit of equity.* New York: Teachers College Press.
23. Henig, J. R. (1994). *Rethinking school choice.* Princeton, NJ: Princeton University Press.
24. Henig, J. R. (1994). *Rethinking school choice.* Princeton, NJ: Princeton University Press.
25. Ibid., p. 23–24.
26. Orfield, G., Bachmeier, M., James, D., & Eitle, T. (1997). *Deepening segregation in American public schools.* Cambridge, MA: Harvard Project on School Desegregation.
27. Smrekar, C., & Goldring, E. (1999). *School choice in urban America: Magnet schools and the pursuit of equity.* New York: Teachers College Press, p. 115.
28. Shumow, L., Kang, K., & Lowe-Vandell, D. (1996). School choice, family characteristics and home-school relations: Contributors to school achievement? *Journal of Educational Psychology, 88,* 459.
29. Ibid., pp. 451–460.
30. Henig, J. R. (1994). *Rethinking school choice.* Princeton, NJ: Princeton University Press.
31. Newman, J. (1988). *America's teachers: An introduction to education.* New York: Addison-Wesley, Longman.
32. Thompson, T. G. (1995). *School choice rally Messmer High School Milwaukee, Wisconsin.* [Online]. Available: http://www.pff.org/townhall/spotlights/9-11-95/thompsee.html
33. Wisconsin Supreme Court. (1998). Warner Jackson et al. vs. John T. Benson, Superintendent of Public Instruction, Department of Public Instruction and James E. Doyle. Case #97–0270, pp. 11–12.
34. Ibid., p. 33.
35. Ibid.
36. Editorial (1998, November 11). *The New York Times*, p. A30.
37. Fischer, H. (1999, January 27). Court oks school-aid tax credits. *The Arizona Daily Star*, p. A1, A10.
38. Sandham, J. L. (1999, May 5). Florida oks 1st statewide voucher plan. *Education Week 18*, 1, 21.
39. Bragg, R. (1999, April 28). Florida to allow student vouchers. *The New York Times*, pp. A1, A21.

40. Witte, J. F., Sterr, T. D., & Thorn, C. A. (1995). *Fifth-year report Milwaukee parental choice program* [Online]. Available: http://www.lafollette.wisc.edu/outreach/pubs/fifthyear/index.htm
41. Ibid.
42. Greene, J. P., Peterson, P. E., Du, J., Boeger, L., & Frazier, C. L. (1996, August). *The effectiveness of school choice in Milwaukee: A secondary analysis of data from the program's evaluation.* Paper presented before the Panel on the Political Analysis of Urban School Systems, San Francisco, CA.
43. Ibid., p. 27.
44. Ibid., p. 27.
45. Lewin, T. (1999, March 27). Few clear lessons from nation's first school choice program. *The New York Times*, p. A10.
46. Ibid.
47. See ftp://ftp.sconet.state.oh.us/opinions/1999/971117.html
48. Walsh, M. (1999, June 2). Ohio court issues mixed verdict on voucher program. *Education Week, 18*(38), 16.
49. Associated Press. (1998, August 13). Study shows voucher pupils thriving in private schools. *The New York Times,* p. A6.
50. Metcalf, K. K., Boone, W. J., Stage, F. K., Chilton, T. L., Muller, P., & Tait, P. (1998, March 16). *A comparative evaluation of the Cleveland scholarship and tutoring grant program: Year one: 1996–97.* Bloomington: The Smith Research Center, Indiana University.
    Metcalf, K. K., Muller, P. A., Boone, W. J., Tait, P. A., Stage, F. K., & Stacey, N. M. (1998, November 18). *Evaluation of the Cleveland scholarship program: Second-year report (1997–98).* Bloomington: Indiana Center for Evaluation.
51. Cohen, W. (1998, April 27). Vouchers for good and ill. *U.S. News and World Report*, 46.
52. Cohen, A. (1999, April 26). A first report card on vouchers. *Time Magazine*, 37.
53. Cohen, W. (1998, April 27). Vouchers for good and ill. *U.S. News and World Report*, 46.
54. Ibid., p. 38.
55. Henig, J. R. (1994). *Rethinking school choice*. Princeton, NJ: Princeton University Press.
56. Smrekar, C., & Goldring, E. (1999). *School choice in urban America: Magnet schools and the pursuit of equity.* New York: Teachers College Press.

Chapter 5

In the 1990s, Government Created Charter Schools

The number of charter schools has grown dramatically since they were first introduced in Minnesota in 1991. As of May 1999, approximately 1,400 charter schools were operating in 27 states, and 35 states had passed charter school legislation. President Bill Clinton, among others, has frequently asserted his commitment to a belief in charter public schools' capacity to innovate and experiment. At present, charter schools are being discussed in all forms of the media and in most state legislatures in the country.

In this chapter we systematically examine charter schools—what are they, what are their various forms, and why do their proponents feel they will be successful? Do charter schools provide new, effective solutions for old problems and identify new possibilities, or do they represent only the latest form of faddism in education? First, we consider the case for charter schools as described by some of the leading advocates of choice and school reform, such as Chester Finn and Diane Ravitch. We then return to arguments made by those specifically within the charter school movement, such as Joe Nathan and Louann Bierlein.

GENERAL ARGUMENTS FOR SCHOOL CHOICE AND CHARTER SCHOOLS

Charter schools are, of course, the newest form of choice. Thus, they have benefited from the general arguments that provide a rationale for

114

choice. We first review recent, general arguments for choice and then turn specifically to the issue of charter schools. Some of those who have spoken for charter schools have presented rationales that support choice generally, including vouchers as well as charter schools. Diane Ravitch stated that, in general, American public schools are likely to continue to be popular both to current American citizens and new immigrants "because they are free, convenient, and satisfactory to the overwhelming majority of parents."[1] However, Ravitch argued, "For many children, especially children who are poor and belong to racial minorities, both equality and excellence in education remain out of reach."[2] Interestingly, this conclusion about the quality of American schools, is highly similar to the conclusions discussed in chapter 3.[3] Ravitch also made a case that public funds be spent in new ways (e.g., schools sponsored by a religious group).[4] Based on her arguments, it is hard to understand what the problem is and what new forms of schools and sources of funding will do about it. What are the specific deficiencies in inner-city schools? If the problem is inner-city schools, it would seem useful to focus arguments on charter schools in those settings—what are the unique contributions that they can make in those contexts?

Other advocates of choice have also argued that school choice will especially help low-income Americans. For example, John Chubb and Terry Moe in their book *Politics, Markets, and America's Schools* asserted that over time the public school bureaucracy has developed to such an extent that low-income and minority students are poorly served in part because they have little political clout to use against school bureaucracy.[5] Hence, Chubb and Moe argued that charter schools offer parents more leverage and voice in dealing with curriculum and other issues that the large school bureaucracy in public schools presently denies them.

Chester Finn presented a somewhat confusing analysis with regard to his conception of the problem with current schooling.[6] In the same paragraph in which he asserted that public education had not improved the knowledge base or work habits of the average high school graduate, he acknowledged that changes in school persistence have improved (i.e., the dropout rate is lower). Obviously, work habits can be defined in numerous ways, but one aspect of work habits that seems to have increased is goal-related and successful persistence (e.g., staying in school). Similar confusions arose when Finn, after noting that Black and Hispanic Americans' achievement has been increasing on certain measures (although, he noted, still lagging notably behind the achievement of White and Asian students), reached the following conclusion: "But achievement is not rising, nor are employers and University professors any better pleased with the preparation of their entrants than they were a decade ago."[7] It is clear that Finn was dissatisfied with the high and increasing educational costs, but his notions of improved education were difficult to perceive. Table 5.1 summarizes his beliefs about public school problems that prevent reform.

In our attempt to learn about the problem of American education from two leading advocates of charter schools, we have not been able to understand how they have defined the problem. Even if we momentarily grant that Finn has correctly identified barriers to reform, after responding to this issue we still do not know what to do to im-

TABLE 5.1
Finn's List of Structural Barriers That Inhibit
School Improvement

1. The school system was designed to provide increasing services to an increasing pupil population—it does not have aspects necessary for boosting quality and productivity.

2. The educational policy and governance system is largely free from conventional politics and policy leadership.

3. Real educational decision making occurs behind closed doors and competing interests among stake holders are brokered with little regard to the public interest or the distinctive needs of clients.

4. Stakeholders make it difficult and dangerous for others to disrupt the intricate balance of power that the special interests have worked out—educational interest groups are both ubiquitous and powerless.

5. The educational establishments' interests are well-organized and generously financed—in contrast consumers have no effective organization.

6. Consumers and reformers alike are crippled by the absence of standards, goals, and meaningful accountability.

7. Teachers have a near-impregnability of their own classroom.

8. The education establishment successfully manipulates Americans' strong affection for the concept of public education.

9. Public education has formed a budget that directs most of its monies into salaries and treats every change as an additional cost.

10. The education profession does not attract risk takers and those motivated for change.

Note. From Finn, C. (1997). The politics of change. In D. Ravitch & J. P. Viteritti (Eds.), *New schools for a new century* (pp. 226–250). New Haven, CT: Yale University Press.

prove education. Do we want citizens who are clear, independent thinkers or docile students who do well on passive tests of knowledge? Would we prefer that our students move from the 70th to the 80th percentile on subject-matter tests if it means an extra 15% of students drop out? We hope that those who actually open charter schools are more focused on specific goals and outcomes than their philosophical advocates have been (we examine this issue more in chapters 6 and 7).

Although a couple of the barriers Finn identified merit consideration, we find much he has identified as barriers problematic, if not flatly wrong. For example, in response to items 4 and 5, the dramatic shifts in provisions of special education services to students with handicapping conditions largely occurred because parents were able to organize and affect legislation and practice despite the opposition of public school educators.

Finn asserted that the fundamental issue is that the present structural and decision-making arrangements associated with schooling are flawed. He wrote:

> The principal impediments to successful reform are elements of the system itself, structural and political problems that block us from making the kinds of changes we most need and from installing on a large scale the bold reforms with the greatest likelihood of yielding markedly better results.[8]

On initial reading, Finn's sentence sounds appealing, but on inspection its meaning is elusive. What are the bold reforms? What are examples of what would constitute markedly better results? (Students graduating from school who read at the seventh-grade level? Students who are fluent in two languages?) Although it is reasonable to provide some latitude for charter schools so that they can develop innovative reforms that may take new and unexpected directions and to call for innovative proposals that leave much of the decision making up to proposal writers, it seems irresponsible not to provide program developers with outcome goals. What is he proposing that charter schools should accomplish? How is he defining innovation?

Table 5.2 presents some possible reasons for creating charter schools. Clearly they are arbitrary, as numerous goals could be listed. Given Finn's most recent writing, we can't guess how he, Ravitch, or other charter school supporters would rank order the possible out-

TABLE 5.2

Possible Reasons for Creating Charter Schools

1. To keep the cost of teacher and administrative salaries as low as possible.

2. To encourage noncharter public schools to work harder and be more experimental.

3. To provide students with environments that allow them to develop new skills and dispositions.

4. To compensate successful teachers and schools at high levels so as to attract exceedingly talented people to educational careers.

5. To have even more students do well on college board tests and on advanced placement tests in particular subject matters.

6. To be sure that more students read at an eighth-grade level.

7. To enable more students to live as productive and satisfied citizens.

8. To enhance opportunities for students to learn with other students who represent a range of parent income levels, ethnicities, and religions.

9. To allow government officials (e.g., governors, mayors) to have more influence over what happens in public education.

10. To make it possible for students to work together with students who have similar goals and backgrounds.

11. To recruit and retain the best teachers no matter what the financial cost.

12. To give educators creative license or a forum to experiment with their personal educational philosophies.

13. To be sure that every student who graduates from high school can write an acceptable expository essay and deliver an acceptable public presentation.

comes presented in Table 5.2. Similarly, we suspect that legislators who have helped to pass charter laws in various states would disagree markedly in rating the reasons listed in the table. It is one thing to argue for reform and yet another to agree on its direction.

To have an experiment, we need to know what change(s) is wanted and what controls are in place. For example, given that Finn reported that mayors lament the fact that they have little leverage or influence over public schools, we suspect that at some level he would support item 9 in Table 5.2. But would he continue to support item 9 if it were found that in instances in which mayors were given more control teacher salaries increased dramatically (e.g., item 1)? It is important to consider Ravitch's historical work documenting the fact that school districts moved from local control to more centralized control because of patronage and cronyism.[9] We don't disagree that if mayors or governors were given more power over education, performance, in many cases, would improve, but we suspect the impact of enhancing mayors' power would show a wide range of effects. Clearly, in some cases, mayors do not do a good job in the policy areas they already control. The quality of police, transportation, and various departments varies from city to city. The basic line of argument that Finn presented is specious.

CHARTER SCHOOLS BEGIN

The early literature associated with the creation of charter schools and other forms of school choice often criticized traditional public schools on the basis of poor student achievement. Perhaps because of the effects of a counterattack (see chapter 3), more recently charter school enthusiasts have become somewhat less strident on the issue of achievement. As we shall see, rationales for creating charter schools are vaguely presented, especially descriptions of goals and curriculum. First, we attempt to answer the frequently asked question, What are charter schools?

Defining Charter Schools

Bruno Manno, a charter school advocate, defined a charter school as:

> An independent public school of choice, given a charter or contract for a specified period of time (typically five years) to educate children according to the school's own design, with a minimum of bureaucratic oversight. It may be a new school, started from scratch, or an existing one that secedes from its school district. It is held accountable to the terms of its charter and continues to exist only if it fulfills those terms. As a public school of choice, it is attended by students whose families select it and staffed by educators who choose to teach in it.[10]

In theory, as demonstrated here, the task of defining the term *charter school* is relatively simple. Charter schools are public schools that operate based on a contract or charter with a state-approved charter granting agency. Charter schools are held accountable for student outcomes and in return are virtually freed from state laws governing schooling (with the exception of federal special education laws and health and safety standards). States fund charter schools based on their student enrollment by allocating to them a similar per-pupil expenditure that is earmarked for noncharter public schools. As long as charter schools fulfill their contract, they continue to exist. One source labeled charter schools "hybrid public schools" because they seem to combine the open enrollment of public schools with the educational programming more common to private schools.[11]

Although, on the surface, this definition seems relatively clear, in practice charter schools vary considerably in a number of dimensions. Charter schools operate differently in some way based on each of the laws currently in effect. They vary based on simple criteria, such as how many schools are allowed and the length of the charter, and on more complex criteria, such as employees' relationship with the school district and the process through which the charter is established (e.g., is parent, teacher, or community support needed in order to file an application for a charter¿). Indeed, the Center for Education Reform described state charter school laws in terms of over 30 categories that fall under six headings: general characteristics, application/approval processes, operations, funding, teachers, students.[12]

There are different forms of charter schools. Charter schools may be newly created schools, transformed public schools, transformed private schools (secular or nonsecular), or home schools. The type of charter school depends on the specific state legislation; that is, in some states, charter schools may only be transformed public schools, whereas in other states, they may be transformed public schools or newly created schools. Charter schools also vary considerably in terms of financial arrangements. In some states, charter schools may be allowed to earn a profit but in others they may not, and although in some states charters may not be granted to for-profit organizations, these organizations can run a charter school under contract with the charter school founder. Further, the path through which the funding reaches the charter school varies from state to state. In some states, 100% of the funding goes directly to the charter school; in others only a percentage of the funding goes to the charter school either directly from the state or from the state through a related school district (e.g., the district in which charter school is located or the sponsoring district). Also of note is the length for which a charter is granted. In Arizona, a charter is granted for 15 years, but in Georgia a charter is granted for up to 5 years. These highly variable contract lengths may lead to very different school environments. For example, when charters are granted for longer periods of time, there is more time for school personnel to implement and document the success of their particular educational vision. In contrast, the downside of a liberal charter length is that if a charter school is a poor educational environment, its charter status could allow it to function for 15 years. We return to a discussion of other differences in charter state laws later in the chapter.

We now turn to a discussion of the rationale behind charter schools by examining the arguments presented by their advocates. Who will benefit from charter school enrollment and why will they benefit? What new innovations are being proposed?

Why Charter Schools: A Rationale

Joe Nathan, a charter school advocate, in his book *Charter Schools: Creating Hope and Opportunity for American Education*, described the charter school movement as bringing together four powerful ideas:[13]

- Choice among public schools for families and their children.
- Entrepreneurial opportunities for educators and parents to create the kinds of schools they believe make the most sense.
- Explicit responsibility for improved achievement, as measure by standardized tests and other measures.
- Carefully designed competition in public education.

These principles can be described more succinctly as choice, autonomy, accountability, and competition. Choice, as defined by Nathan is primarily choice for parents and students; others imply choice can be conceptualized on multiple levels, including choice for teachers, administrators, and anyone else who has a particular educational vision they want to actuate. For example, whether students should have a chance to be exposed to some content early on (e.g., algebra) in order to receive more advanced content in high school (e.g., calculus) is a choice that is a debatable issue. However, at some point, choice may be an illogical absurdity. Although parents and students may want to open a school that specializes in basketball, it does not follow that other citizens will recognize this choice as schooling or be willing to use public funds to pay for it. Choice is widely touted to be one of the underlying rationales for charter schools, but as demonstrated by Arkansas' charter school legislation described later in this chapter, charter schools are not always about choice.

Autonomy, the second rationale provided for charter schools, indicates that charter schools are free of the bureaucratic control of traditional public schools. This emancipation is intended to provide educators with the freedom to innovate in many areas, including curricular focus, financial arrangements, and in some states teacher qualifications. As with choice, however, the idea of autonomy is not universally associated with charter schools, because many states do not categorically release charter schools from state regulations. Moreover, when naive people (lack of educational experience, or lack of administrative, financial, and legal knowledge) open charter schools, any potential autonomy is consumed by the immediate pressures of running a school.

Accountability for student outcomes, widely touted as one of the main tenants of charter schools, is one of the more problematic aspects of the charter school movement. Although advocates broadly hail charter schools as having greater accountability for demonstrating increased student achievement, few charter schools have concrete plans for demonstrating this goal. One advocate noted, "today's charter accountability systems remain underdeveloped, often clumsy and ill fitting, and ... beset by dilemmas ... Truth be told, they [charter school authorizers and operators] are often content to leave charter accountability agreements nebulous and undefined."[14]

Finally, competition posed by charter schools is intended to spur traditional public schools to work harder in order to keep student enrollments up. In theory, through competition, traditional public schools are pressured to provide comparable or superior services.[15] However, without accountability measures, what is the scale for measuring the success of the services provided by charter schools? How are noncharter public schools supposed to learn about charter schools? And, if competition leads to better outcomes, then why is there not competition for charters?

The Center for Education Reform described one case of misguided competition:

> 5,000 students attend 20 charter schools within the boundaries of the Mesa School District, AZ (one of the better districts in Arizona). In response, the district purchased an ad in the local paper touting their services and academic accomplishments. It may purchase advertisements and billboards next year in an effort to keep pace with charter school innovation.[16]

Innovation in advertising? Competition for students based on attractiveness of billboards? This seems more like carefully designed competition for noneducation-related spending. And, if the district is one of the better districts in Arizona, why do they need competition pressure from charter schools? It seems that this kind of competition could lead to decreased education-related spending and result in decreased achievement and innovation.

Competition for Whom?

To reiterate, one premise behind charter schools is that public schools will improve only with increased competition. However, to take the premise full circle, it would seem equally important to use competition to produce charter schools that challenge public schools in important ways. It appears logical that competition will lead to increased charter and noncharter public school quality to the benefit of American education in general and student achievement specifically.

To further develop our hypothetical example, it is useful to draw on Finn's 10 structural barriers to meaningful public school reform (see Table 5.1). At least two of his stated problems with current schooling seem inconsistent with the need and advocacy for allowing virtually any charter school to open. Finn's first argument is that the current school system is geared toward quantity not quality. Thus, why not pressure applicants to design charter schools that are not just more of the same? What better way to develop new proposals than competition to encourage charter school applicants to conceptualize and operationalize new, innovative approaches? Similarly, Finn's 10th stated reason why public schools don't improve is because public schools do not attract risk takers. Perhaps one way to encourage risk takers to enter the educational field is not only to create risky, competitive conditions (i.e., only a few charters will be approved) but also conditions that yield attractive rewards (i.e., a larger market share for successful applicants).

Others are also confused about the benefits of competition. Nathan argued:

> People with innovative educational ideas should have several places they can go to get supervision and sponsorship for a charter school. Imagine people who want to open a new restaurant, gas station, hardware store, or restaurant having to get permission to open the new business from their competitors. It would be tough, right? That is why it is vital for people who want to establish a charter school to have the option of gaining permission and sponsorship from an organization other than the local school board.[18]

At first glance, this argument seems to pose a healthy attitude that could bring vigorous competition to designing new, innovative programs to enhance students' learning. However, it appears that Nathan's commitment to competition seems half-hearted, or at least one sided. At one level, he abstractly views and recommends competition and risk taking as good; however, when actually structuring concrete proposals, vigorous competition in obtaining charters is ignored. Perhaps the champions of charter schools differentially value competition—public schools will benefit from the competition with charter schools, but competition among applicants for obtaining a charter school is counterproductive.

Nathan also argued that teachers who decide to teach in charter schools should have their status guaranteed in their former school district: "The state should explicitly permit teachers to take leave from their public school systems and retain their seniority when they wish to try teaching at a charter school."[19] This argument is equivalent to providing assistant managers at McDonald's the right to work for a competing restaurant chain while maintaining their seniority and pension benefits at McDonald's! Although it might be reasonable to vest employees in public schools who participate in charter public schools under certain conditions—we are not opposed to a system that recognizes tenure in multiple settings—we quarrel with the numerous internal inconsistencies in the logic of advocates for choice.

Confusion of Form and Effect of Laws

Louann Bierlein argued that there are seven critical aspects that must be in place if effective charter schools are to outperform noncharter public schools, as Table 5.3 shows.[20] These conditions were presented as the seven principles that characterize enabling state legislation for charter schools as "stronger" or "weaker." Bierlein asserted that stronger laws will yield stronger charter schools and lead to increased student performance.

Unlike Bierlein, we believe that the language chosen to characterize state charter school laws as weak or strong is arbitrary and depends, in the absence of data, on one's perspective. For example, her characterization of "strong law states" would be interpreted by some as permissive, soft, "anything goes" laws. Indeed, these seven principles do not necessarily call for the higher levels of student performance that many politicians and business people urge. Some citizens who hold high

TABLE 5.3

Bierlein: Critical Charter School Law Components

1. A charter school must be allowed to be sponsored by some public entity other than a local school board—or be allowed to appeal a school board decision.

2. Any individual or group should be allowed to make charter school proposals.

3. Charter schools should be exempt from most state and local regulations (with the exception of health, safety, civil rights, and physical and pupil accountability).

4. Charter schools should have fiscal autonomy.

5. Charter schools should have legal autonomy.

6. There should not be limits on the number of charter schools that can be established in a given state.

7. Charter schools must be permitted to employ noncertified teachers.

Note. From Bierlein, L. (1997). The charter school movement. In D. Ravitch & J. Viteritti (Eds.), *New schools for a new century: The redesign of urban education* (pp. 37–60). New Haven: Yale University Press.

standards for public schools undoubtedly want procedures in place to verify at some minimal level that the proposed charter school has sound instructional plans with verifiable goals and that the state visit and carefully examine the charter school for purposes of monitoring and accountability. Indeed, some citizens prefer tough requirements and clear plans before charter schools are allowed to operate. For example, some want assurances that if schools are using public funds, they be forbidden from teaching racial or religious hatred or that teachers possess minimal levels of academic and social skills if they are to guide youth.

Our rejection of Bierlein's stated criteria for strong laws is not an argument for public schools or the status quo or against public charter schools and change. We argue that in the absence of empirical data, or adequate theory, it is impossible to use labels such as "stronger" or "weaker" particularly if the goal is to predict student achievement. For example, there is considerable distance between requiring certification from a teacher education institution and allowing anyone to teach. Do choices have to be so dichotomously simple? The removal of certification requirements does not guarantee that talented teachers will flock to charter schools and students will learn (an implied premise of Bierlein's position). Indeed, the removal of certification requirements coupled with some charter school directors' interest in cutting costs make it likely that many unqualified individuals will teach. In some cases, "reckless experimentation" may be more harmful than the status quo of no experimentation. It is possible that a homeless person with a BA in English might be a very good teacher, or a retired navy captain, or someone working at McDonald's. It seems that the critical question for citizens and their legislative representatives to address is, How much risk we are willing to take with the lives of youth (especially given that there are data to illustrate that teacher certification often has positive effects on student performance, at least under some conditions[21])?

Striking down laws so that anyone can teach is not necessarily strong, adaptive behavior. In contrast, an active interest in protecting students from poorly designed educational experiences may be seen by many as a strong, appropriate stance. However, it is equally possible to argue that in some instances more permissive state laws—those that make it easier to create charter schools—are capable of immediately saving students from certain inadequate public schools where students are failing. If one thinks that American schools are generally adequate, it might make sense to make charter schools demonstrate more fully their ability to serve students. If one is convinced that current schools are failing students miserably, then it is possible to assert the need for quick action and even radical experimentation. However, advocacy for strong or weak laws is premature and perhaps irresponsible. At best, advocating for a form of strong laws in the absence of data is another example of faddism in American education.

Similarly, we argue that Bierlein's logic concerning another strong criterion on her list is equally flawed. She argued that states should not limit the number of charter schools allowed to operate within the state. She defends this position in part by noting, "potential charter organizers are discouraged when the legal limit is small and may conclude, 'why bother?'"[22] In contrast, one could argue that if only a few charters are awarded, it would lead to more competition, resulting in more attractive and thoughtfully prepared charter provisions for stimulating students' learning. Further, if numerous charters are granted quickly it would seem to negate the state's ability to even routinely monitor charter schools (unless additional funds are spent for supervision).

To improve public education, it seems imperative that we define problems and intended solutions better. Those who are more satisfied with the extant performance of American schools might argue for a list of criteria for charter school laws that is strikingly different from the list Bierlein proposed. For example, Table 5.4 presents a different conception of how to design charter laws. Specifically, what are the guarantees that charter schools provide for students and their parents? In Table 5.4, we raise a few parent and student "warranties" that merit consideration.

Current Charter School Legislation

In reviewing the advocacy writing of those who favor charter schools, we have been somewhat polemical in making contrasting points to illustrate that many assertions (good, strong) are arbitrary and driven more by ideology than logic, theory, or data. There is ample room to improve public schools, but we believe the best way to improve public schools is through clear systematic arguments that lead to a specific delineation of what will be changed and what evidence will indicate the success or failure of innovation.

Although we have quarreled with the vague logic associated with the call for charter schools, it should be understood that others, including legislators, have found the logic sufficiently attractive to pass enabling legislation for charter schools in many states. How then have states responded to the call for strong charter laws?

TABLE 5.4

Charter Schools' Warranty:
Recognizing Students' and Parents' Rights

1. The charter will assure parents and students that a charter school will not close in midyear for financial reasons.

2. Teachers will be hired because of their knowledge of subject and students; not because they are relatives of the director.

3. Students will be able to transfer from one charter school to another with minimal administrative difficulty.

4. Parents who work during school hours will not be prohibited from enrolling their children in a charter school on those grounds alone.

5. Charter schools should be limited to the number that the state can review and hold accountable for students' academic and social growth.

6. Each charter school will have an explicit, understandable plan for evaluating student progress in the school and that data will be verifiable for public accountability.

7. That individual charter schools will be reasonably representative of the ethnic population of the state.

TABLE 5.5
Criteria for Addressing Charter School Laws

1. Number of schools (the more charter schools allowed and the more autonomously the schools function the better).

2. Multiple chartering authorities and binding appeals process (entities other than the local school board should be allowed to charter schools).

3. Variety of applicants (the more individuals or businesses that can be allowed to charter schools, the better … eligibility limited to applicants from public schools or public school personnel are seen as more restrictive).

4. New starts (new schools are preferred to those that permit only public school conversions—for-profit companies and home-based schools are encouraged).

5. Formal evidence of local support (charter schools should be formed without having to prove specified levels of local support—teachers and parents signing petitions, etc.).

6. Automatic waiver from laws and regulations (other than waiving civil rights laws or health–safety codes, the more autonomy from state laws the better).

7. Legal and operational autonomy (i.e., the more independent the unit the better—they can own property, control budgets, contract for services, etc.).

8. Guaranteed full funding (strong laws guarantee 100% of per pupil funding based on state or district per pupil cost and federal categorical funding).

9. Fiscal autonomy (charter schools have full control of their own budget).

10. Exemption from collective bargaining agreements and district rules (stronger laws give charter schools the right to fire and hire, etc.).

Note. From Center for Education Reform. (1998). *Charter school legislation: State rankings* [Online]. Available: http://edreform.com/laws/lawrank.htm

The Center for Educational Reform (CER) has divided the states into those that have stronger charter laws and those that have weaker charter laws and has noted that strong laws (also sometimes referred to as effective or progressive laws) are ones that stimulate the development of many autonomous independent charter schools. In contrast, weak laws (also referred to as a dead or ineffective laws) provide very little opportunity or incentive for charter school development. Table 5.5 presents the 10 criteria they offered to assess whether a charter school law is strong or weak.

Table 5.6 shows both the CER ranking of the strength of enabling legislation and the number of charter schools in each state as of December 1998.

TABLE 5.6
Number of Charter Schools by State and Ranking of Strength of State Law: From Strongest to Weakest

State	Opened	Rank
Arizona	271	1
Michigan	139	2
District of Columbia	19	3
Delaware	4	4
Massachusetts	34	5
Minnesota	35	6
New York	n/a	7
North Carolina	59	8
Texas	60	9
California	156	10
South Carolina	5	11
Colorado	61	12
Florida	75	13
Louisiana	10	14
Missouri	n/a	15
Pennsylvania	31	16
New Jersey	30	17
Wisconsin	24	18
New Hampshire	0	19
Illinois	14	20
Georgia	27	21
Connecticut	16	22
Ohio	15	23
Idaho	n/a	24
Utah	n/a	25
Alaska	17	26
Nevada	1	27
Rhode Island	2	28
Wyoming	0	29

(Continues)

TABLE 5.6 (Continued)

State	Opened	Rank
Virginia	n/a	30
Kansas	15	31
Hawaii	2	32
New Mexico	5	33
Arkansas	0	34
Mississippi	1	35
Total	1,128	

Note. Center for Education Reform. (1998). *Charter school legislation: State rankings* [Online]. Available: http://edreform.com/laws/lawrank.htm

CASE STUDIES OF SELECTED STATES' CHARTER LAWS

To further describe the breadth and variation of charter schools, we focus on some of the nuances of the charter school legislation in five states, Arizona, Michigan, California, Mississippi, and Arkansas.[23] Arizona, California, and Michigan have led the way in the charter school movement with less restrictive charter school legislation, whereas Mississippi and Arkansas, represent the other end of the spectrum, with more restrictive charter school laws.

Arizona. Arizona's charter school law, passed in 1994, is considered by charter school advocates to be the strongest in the nation. Moreover, it is also the most popular charter school state with more charter schools than any other state. Twenty-five charters may be granted yearly by the state board of education, 25 by the newly established state board for charter schools, and an unlimited number by local school boards. A charter may be established by an individual or a group of individuals, a public entity, or a private organization for a new school, or may be a converted public or private school. Initial charters are granted for a term of 15 years, with reviews every 5 years. Arizona charter schools are automatically granted a waiver from state and local education laws and regulations with the exception of laws governing health, safety, and special education. Teachers in charter schools are not required to hold teacher certification (i.e., individuals with only high school degrees and no teaching experience may be hired as teachers in charter schools). Teachers who currently work for a state school district may take a leave of absence of up to 3 years to work for a charter school. All students in the state are eligible to attend Arizona charter schools. Preference is given to students who are residents of the district in which the charter school is located (if sponsored by a school district) and to siblings of students already attending the charter school. Charter schools are not allowed to implement enrollment requirements, such as parent involvement, although several charter schools in the state have put conditions on student enrollment. Students in Arizona charter schools must participate in statewide achievement testing.

Michigan.   Michigan's charter school law was passed in 1993 and is one of the nation's least restrictive charter school laws. Unlimited charters may be granted by a number of state-approved entities, including local school boards, intermediate school boards, and community colleges. State universities may sponsor up to 150 charter schools through 1999. Charters may be granted to an individual, a group of individuals, or a legal entity. Charter schools may be new schools or converted public or private schools but may not be home-based schools. The term of the charter can be up to 10 years, with a mandatory review every 7 years, but most charter schools to date have been granted for 5 years, with a review after 5 years. Waivers for state and local laws, regulations, and policies are granted on a case-by-case basis. Existing public schools are also eligible for waivers. Teachers in charter schools sponsored by local school districts are covered by the district bargaining agreement. Teacher certification is required for all teachers in charter schools except if the school is sponsored by a university, in which case university faculty may teach at the charter school without certification. All students in the state are eligible for admission into charter schools sponsored by universities, but only students in the district are eligible to attend charter schools sponsored by local education agencies. Enrollment preference may be given to students enrolled in the charter school in previous years and to siblings of students enrolled in the charter school. Enrollment requirements are not permitted in Michigan charter schools. Students in charter schools must participate in the Michigan Educational Assessment Program.

California. California's charter school legislation, passed in 1992 and amended in 1998, is considered moderate in terms of restrictiveness. A maximum of 250 charter schools were allowed in California in the 1998–1999 school year, and as many as 100 additional schools may be created each year thereafter. Charters may be sponsored by local school boards, the state board of education, or city boards of education. Any individual or group of individuals may open a charter school, which may be a converted public school, a home-based school, or a new school but not a converted private school. New schools and conversion schools must be supported by either 50% of teachers in the school or 50% of parents or guardians. Initial charters are granted for 5 years. Waivers for most state laws are automatically granted; however, waivers from local legislation must be negotiated with the sponsoring district. Teaching certification is required in California, and teachers may be on a leave of absence from their school district if specified in the charter. All students in the state are eligible to enroll in a charter school, although students living in the enrollment area of the school or siblings of students attending the school are given preference. Enrollment requirements are not permissible in California. Previous provisions for enrollment requirements (in the 1992 legislation) led to at least one lawsuit in California.[24] The charter must specify how the school will serve low-achieving students and how it will seek to reflect the racial and ethnic diversity of the surrounding area. Students in charter schools must participate in statewide achievement assessments.

Mississippi. In contrast to these three states, Mississippi has the most restrictive charter school legislation in the country. Established in 1997, Mississippi's legislation allows the state board of education to charter six schools contingent on approval by the local school board. Only existing public schools are eligible for charters, and a majority of faculty, staff, and parents must show support for and involvement in the petition for charter status. An initial charter is granted for 4 years. State and local regulations and laws are waived automatically as specified in the charter school legislation. All teachers in charter schools remain employees of the school district, and certification requirements are the same as for noncharter public schools: At least 90% of teachers must be certified. Students in the district in which the charter school is located are eligible for enrollment as are children of charter school staff. Enrollment preference is given to students who previously attended the school. Enrollment requirements are not permitted. Students must participate in statewide assessments, and the school must meet statewide education goals.

Arkansas.   Similar to Mississippi, Arkansas has one of the most restrictive charter school laws in the country. Established in 1995, Arkansas' charter school legislation allows for an unlimited number of charter schools, although none have been established to date. Charters are granted by the state board of education to public school personnel. As in Mississippi, only converted public schools are eligible for charter status. As a part of the chartering process, two-thirds of school staff and parents must show support for the school. The charter is granted to the superintendent of the school district in which the school is located. The initial charter is granted for 3 years. State regulations and laws are not automatically waived; any waivers must be specified in the charters. Teachers in charter schools are covered under the collective bargaining agreement of the district and are required to be certified. Only students who attended the school before its conversion to charter status are eligible for the charter school. Thus, school choice is not a factor in Arkansas charter schools. Students must participate in statewide assessments.

Summary.   As is demonstrated by these five state case studies, charter schools vary considerably from state to state. Even at the ends of the continuum of less to more restrictive legislation, there is not a standard answer to the question, What is a charter school? Although charter schools are frequently synonymous with school choice, as demonstrated here, school choice is not necessarily a component of charter schools. A cursory review of the charter school legislation in participating states quickly reveals that charter schools are highly variable educational experiments. Perhaps the only consistent feature of charter schools in all states with legislation is that incorporation of educational research or techniques that have been proven successful is not a required component.

CONCLUSION

This chapter examined the rationale for charter schools as advocated by their proponents. Although some of the arguments are interesting and potentially important, we contend that extant rationales often beg the question, are somewhat confusing, and are unconvincing, because equally compelling arguments can be made from a different perspective. As a case in point, we have noted that proponents of charter schools encourage competition when it involves competing with existing public schools. However, they are extremely recalcitrant in recommending competition for a rigorous review of charter school applications before the awarding of charter school status. Similarly, we have seen that it is premature to label charter schools "weak" or "strong." The extent to which laws that make it easier or more difficult for charter schools to open awaits empirical evidence to clarify whether more or less restrictive laws yield better schools. Also, the analysis provided of teaching and learning is simplistic and offers simple models to address complex teaching and learning issues.[25] Further, the intellectual leaders of the charter school movement promised so much so quickly that initial results are problematic. Some opponents are apt to point to the discrepancy between what was promised and what has been delivered to date and be extremely critical of charter schools, perhaps overly critical.

In fairness to charter school advocates, it should be noted that to be politically successful they had to appeal to a wide number of lawmakers in order to obtain legislation for sponsoring the charter movement. And, to obtain political support, there are advantages to being vague in order to keep the constituency support base as large as possible.[26] Fortunately, those who applied for charter schools have considerable latitude in articulating specific plans and programs.

Having examined legislation in several states to illustrate how definitions of public charter schools vary as a function of state law, we can see clearly that the term *charter school* means different things in different states. Chapter 6 turns to a review of recent research conducted in charter schools, and explores the degree of innovation in curriculum and instructional programs, that is, to what extent charter schools offer students a different educational experience than public schools. Further, we study parent involvement and satisfaction as well as student satisfaction and achievement in charter schools.

Endnotes

1. Ravitch, D. (1974). *The great school wars, New York City, 1805–1973: A history of the public schools as battlefield of social change*. New York: Basic Books, p. 271.
2. Ibid., p. 252.

3. Berliner, D., & Biddle, B. (1995). *The manufactured crisis: Myth, fraud and the attack on America's public schools.* New York: Addison-Wesley.

4. Ravitch, D. (1974). *The great school wars, New York City, 1805–1973: A history of the public schools as battlefield of social change.* New York: Basic Books.

5. Chubb, J., & Moe, T. (1990). *Politics, markets, and America's schools.* Washington, DC: Brookings Institute.

6. Finn, Jr., C. (1997). The politics of change. In D. Ravitch & J. Viteritti (Eds.), *New schools for a new century: The redesign of urban education* (pp. 226–250). New Haven: Yale University Press.

7. Ibid., p. 231.

8. Ibid., p. 232.

9. Ravitch, D. (1974). *The great school wars, New York City, 1805–1973: A history of the public schools as battlefield of social change.* New York: Basic Books.

10. Manno, B. (1999, March). *Accountability: The key to charter renewal. A guide to help charter schools create their accountability plans.* [Online], p. 1. Available: http://edreform.com/pubs/center_for_education_reform.htm

11. Toch, T. (1998, April 27). The new education bazaar. *U.S. News and World Report*, 35–46.

12. Center for Education Reform. (1998). *Charter school legislation: State by state analyses* [Online]. Available: http://edreform.com/laws/states.html

13. Nathan, J. (1996). *Charter schools: Creating hope and opportunity for American education.* San Francisco, CA: Jossey-Bass.

14. Manno, B. V. (1999, March). *Accountability: The key to charter renewal* [Online]. Available: http://edreform.com/pubs/center_for_education_reform.htm

15. Center for Education Reform.(1999). *Answers to frequently asked questions about charter schools* [Online]. Available: http://edreform.com/faq/faqcs.htm

16. Ibid., p. 4.

17. Finn, Jr., C. (1997). The politics of change. In D. Ravitch & J. Viteritti (Eds.), *New schools for a new century: The redesign of urban education* (pp. 226–250). New Haven: Yale University Press.

18. Nathan, J. (1996). *Charter schools: Creating hope and opportunity for American education.* San Francisco: Jossey-Bass Publishers, p. 3.

19. Ibid., p. 4.

20. Bierlein, L. (1997). The charter school movement. In D. Ravitch & J. Viteritti (Eds.), *New schools for a new century: The redesign of urban education* (pp. 37–60). New Haven: Yale University Press.

21. Ashton, P. (1996). Improving the preparation of teachers. *Educational Researcher, 25,* 21–22, 35.

22. Bierlein, L. (1997). The charter school movement. In D. Ravitch & J. Viteritti (Eds.), *New schools for a new century: The redesign of urban education* (pp. 37–60). New Haven: Yale University Press, p. 45.

23. Center for Education Reform. (1998). *Charter school legislation: State rankings* [Online]. Available: http://edreform.com/laws/lawrank.htm

24. SRI International. (1997, December 11). *Evaluation of charter school effectiveness: Part I*. [Online]. Available: http://www.lao.ca.gov/sri_charter_schools_1297-part1.html

25. Saranson, S. (1998). *Charter schools: Another flawed educational reform?* New York: Teachers College Press.

26. Good, T. L., Clark, S. N., & Clark, D. C. (1997). Reform efforts in American schools: Will faddism continue to impede meaningful change? In B. J. Biddle, T. L. Good, I. F. Goodson (Eds.), *International handbook of teachers and teaching* (pp. 1387–1427). Boston: Kluwer Academic Publishers.

Chapter 6

Charter Schools: Effective Investment or Wasteful Experiment?

Chapter 5 examined various claims about the potential of charter schools. Now we review research evidence on charter schools to see if these claims can be substantiated. As mentioned previously, many policy leaders have concluded that charter schools are a success. And in this sense, charter schools, like voucher plans, have achieved a political victory. In contrast, the educational evidence presented in this chapter leads to a different conclusion. Despite their growing popularity, charter schools have produced no convincing data to illustrate that, on the whole, they are prudent or productive investments. However, as we show in chapter 7, some individual programs (at an anecdotal level) represent potential contributions.

After reviewing available evidence, we provide evaluations for charter schools in several important areas, including demographic composition of students, student achievement, parent involvement, and innovation in curriculum, instruction, governance structure, and choice. Our evaluations for charter schools range from "Good" to "Unacceptable." Making judgments is always difficult and to some extent subjective. We have used our judgments in comparing charter schools in the aggregate to their own goals and those mandated by the legislature. We stress that we are not evaluating individual schools but charter schools as a group. Within categories, as is the case with public schools, the evaluations for individual schools range from "Superior" to "Unacceptable."

Before we review the literature, it is important to acknowledge the difficulty of this task. First, charter schools differ from state to state, and variation within a state can be tremendous. Second, defining the impact of charter schools is difficult, because only a few studies have been conducted, and generally, charter school research has not benefitted from the advantages of peer review.[1] For example, sometimes reviewers require researchers to reanalyze their data with new analyses or models, and often substantial differences in findings occur.

A third issue is that most of the existing research has primarily used survey techniques, and the few studies that have included observational techniques typically have involved only short amounts of time in classrooms or have studied only a handful of schools. In some studies, survey techniques have been limited further by use of volunteer samples and low response rates.

A fourth issue is that reports have been prepared or sponsored by agencies that have an interest in charter schools. For example, given President Clinton's advocacy for charter schools, the Office of Educational Research and Improvement (OERI) is placed in a difficult political position when it awards contracts and reviews research reports. Although researchers have attempted to be objective, it is important to recognize that much of the research on charter schools has been conducted by researchers who work under the auspices of state or federal agencies that believe in charter schools.

A fifth problem is that research studies have not examined the same constructs. Some focus only on parent involvement, whereas some do not study parent involvement at all. Similarly, other researchers have studied only school achievement; or on other single issues. Hence, conclusions about charter schools are more possible in some areas than in others.

Despite these difficulties, it is possible to provide a tentative overview of charter schools. Largely, this is because the research has focused on Arizona, California, and Michigan. These states have the most charter schools currently in operation (roughly 50% of all charter schools are in these three states[2]). Further, these states represent both moderately strong and strong standards for charter school legislation, which assures that schools representing a range of funding conditions and degrees of autonomy are studied.

Many policymakers have already announced the success of charter schools, and local papers have written editorials favoring or disfavoring charter schools based on limited data. President Clinton has claimed that charter schools are successful, and he has actively encouraged that more of them be opened as soon as possible:

> Today I am pleased to sign into law H.R. 2616, the "Charter School Expansion Act of 1998." This bill will help foster the development of high-quality charter schools, consistent with my goal of having 3,000 charter schools operating by early in the next century, and will help lead to improvements in public education more generally. I am particularly gratified by the bipartisan manner in which this bill passed the House and Senate.
>
> I have long championed charter schools—public schools started by parents, teachers, and communities, open to all students regardless of background or ability, and given great flexibility in exchange for high levels of accountability. When I was elected President there was only one charter school in the Nation, and now there are more than 1,000 serving more than 200,000 students. This bill will help strengthen our efforts to support charter schools, providing parents and students with better schools, more choice, and higher levels of accountability in public education.
>
> As the charter school movement spreads throughout the country, it is important that these schools have clear and measurable educational performance objectives and are held accountable to the same high standards expected of all public schools. These important quality-control measures will help charter schools fulfill their potential to become models of accountability for public education.
>
> I am also pleased that H.R. 2616 provides new authority for successful charter schools to serve as models, not just for other charter schools, but for public schools generally. At a relatively low cost, such model schools will provide in-depth advice, materials, and other information on various aspects of their programs—helping to start up new public schools and helping existing schools learn from their successes. By drawing on the experience of high-performing charter schools throughout our Nation, this legislation will help bring the benefits of innovation and creativity to hundreds of thousands of additional children.[3]

Whether we like it or not, policy decisions are being made on extant data. Hence, it seems critical to examine available data carefully to determine what conclusions can be supported. Here, we limit the review of evidence to include only research reports, journal articles, dissertations, and papers presented at professional conferences. A brief description of research reports on charter schools can be found in the appendix. Anecdotal evidence from newspapers, news magazines, and informal interviews are presented in chapter 7.

ISSUES INFORMED BY RESEARCH

Rationale for Charter Schools

Charter school advocates have advanced several rationales to explain why charter schools are needed to improve public education. These include to provide parents with choice, to grant parents and educators an opportunity to create and implement innovative ideas, to have a mechanism for holding schools responsible for achievement, and to provide competition for noncharter public schools with the idea that competition will make all schools better.[4] These rationales come from the belief that public schools are failing and alternate forms of schooling are needed. They assume that charter schools will be different from noncharter public schools in some important ways.

In what ways then, do charter school operators see their schools as differing from public schools? Good and his colleagues asked charter school directors to rate their level of agreement with 17 possible reasons why their charter school was distinct from noncharter public schools in their area.[5] The ideas charter school directors most frequently agreed on regarding noncharter public schools were (a) the pace of instruction does not match learner abilities, (b) there is overcrowding, (c) there is not enough room for teacher innovation, (d) there are too many students who are difficult to control in public school settings, (e) students are not challenged, and (f) teachers have no voice in testing requirements.

In contrast, charter school directors did not think that in public schools: (a) there is too much stress on parental involvement, (b) there is too much emphasis on gifted students, (c) there is too much emphasis on the "basics," (d) teachers don't have enough subject matter knowledge, (e) teachers don't really care about students as learners, and (f) teachers don't really care about students as social beings. Interestingly, charter school founders differentiated between teachers and the conditions of teaching. Namely, *those who have started public charter schools have not blamed teachers for lack of student performance. In contrast, they have criticized the conditions of schooling.* This is an important distinction to make, because many advocates who have championed the cause of charter schools—as opposed to those who do the hard work of creating them—have criticized the motivation, knowledge, and abilities of public school teachers and administrators.

In contrast to charter school directors, Good and Braden found that Arizona public school superintendents had differing opinions.[6] Superintendents rated their perception of the degree of importance of 11 possible reasons why individuals create and run charter schools. The superintendents indicated that the following were moderately to highly important reasons: (a) to avoid state regulations, (b) to create charter schools for administrators to make money, (c) to implement a particular educational philosophy, (d) because they feel public schools are inadequate, (e) to provide services to a niche of students, and (f) to avoid special education. Superintendents reported that the least important reasons for creating a charter school were (a) to provide special education students with inclusive education, (b) to provide students with individualized attention, and (c) to increase parent involvement in education.

However, in examining superintendents' ratings of agreement with possible criticisms of public schools, they agreed that (a) there are not enough resources for special education programs, (b) resources in schools are too limited, and (c) there is inadequate budget flexibility. Areas that superintendents disagreed with included (a) teachers do not really care about students as learners or as social beings and (b) there is too much emphasis on parent involvement, the basics, or gifted education.

Horn and Miron found that the rationales for creating charter schools in Michigan were mixed and included individuals concerned about deficient public school conditions as well as individuals motivated for intrinsic and extrinsic reasons.[7] Among the many reasons for establishing charter schools, the five most popular reasons were (a) dissatisfaction by a group of parents with the educational program being provided by the local district; (b) opportunity to obtain a more stable financial base for a private school; (c) personal mission of one or more individuals to develop a school with a particular emphasis (e.g., service learning component); (d) opportunity to create a school designed to be safer; and (e) opportunity to create a financial profit by one or more entities in the private sector.

Enabling legislation for charter schools in Michigan stressed that one rationale for charter schools was the development of new creative innovations.[8] Horn and Miron concluded that the charter schools were remarkably similiar to the regular public schools, with few notable exceptions (e.g., smaller student enrollments, governance, and span of contracted management services)."[9] In contrast, the OERI III report noted that about 7 of 10 newly created charter schools were established to realize an alternative vision of schooling. Further, 2 of 10 schools were established to serve a particular population of students, and 4 of 10 public schools that converted to charter schools were seeking greater autonomy from district and state requirements.

The Hudson Institute final report described charter schools as being created by three different groups.[10] First, educators who hold a particular educational vision that they feel can not be obtained in the bureaucracy of the traditional school system. Second, parents who are looking for a better or different educational alternative for their children. And, third, organizations (nonprofit and for-profit), who for a variety of reasons, want to be involved in the development of a new type of school.

Types of Charter Schools

Differing state laws and rationales for creating charter schools have led to a wide diversity of charter schools. As described in chapter 4, some types are dictated by state legislation that allows only existing public schools to become charter schools or only new starts to be charter schools. The Hudson Institute final report described charter schools in general as belonging to one of two types: (a) conversions, schools that were already in operation and switched to charter status—private or existing public schools, and (b) start-ups, new schools that did not exist prior to obtaining a charter.[11]

In Michigan, Horn and Miron found four types of charter schools: (a) converted private schools; (b) converted public schools (in this category, all in the study were former alternative high schools); (c) "mom and pop" schools (schools started by individuals or small groups of concerned adults); and (d) "cookie cutter" schools (largely identical but legally separate schools that are created by management companies).[12] The authors stressed the notable diversity between and within these types of charter schools.

In Arizona, Garn and Stout reported that each of the 46 charter schools they studied roughly fit into one of three categories.[13] First, schools with a focus on students who had not been academically successful in district public schools (17 schools were in this category and 14 were for high school students). These schools often described their students as at-risk, low achieving, in trouble with the law, or suffering emotional difficulty. Schools in the second category were schools that had a prior existence as proprietary enterprises. There were 9 schools in this category (5 had prior experience as independent high schools or independent elementary schools and 4 followed Montessori methods). Schools in the third category had some form of special curricular focus but were designed for regular students. Nineteen schools were included in this category. However, the authors found that the range of curriculum within this category was noticeably large including back-to-basics schools, progressive schools, and art schools to list a few. Finally, they noted that there were also several schools with students of primarily one ethnicity (one of these schools focused on Hispanic students and two on African American students).

The OERI III report noted that in the 1997–1998 school year 70% of charter schools were newly created whereas 19% were preexisting public schools and 11% were preexisting private schools. The report also noted that the percentage of newly created charter schools has increased over time. In 1997–1998, 84% of the schools that opened were newly created in contrast to the 53% of schools that opened in the 1994–1995 school year or earlier.

Innovation

Many public school critics claim that public schools have become stagnant and have not evolved in ways required to address the needs of 21st-century students. Thus, for advocates who support charter schools primarily because they believed charter schools yield new forms of curriculum or teaching, data indicating the occurrence of innovation is critical. However, many charter school advocates who believe in back-to-basic programs have also espoused the belief that charter schools will lead to innovation in these areas (by introducing new approaches to presenting the basics). Policymakers especially use the language of innovation, change, and new directions. Virtually all available research studies have included a review of charter school innovation. There is wide consensus that little if any innovation has taken place in charter schools. The authors of the SRI report noted that although a major premise behind the development of charter schools in California is innovation, innovation is difficult to define:

> For example, innovation can be thought of as a *unique* approach—implying that charter schools are expected to implement new and uncon-

ventional classroom practices. On the other hand, innovation can be viewed in relative terms—suggesting that a charter school's educational program is innovative if it is different from the norm within its local district or, in the case of a conversion school, if it represents a change from its precharter program and practices. Some charter school proponents argue that innovation can also be accomplished through changes in a school's locus of control …. Charter schools can also be seen as innovative in competitiveness. By providing alternatives within the public school system, charter schools might create competitive pressure on school districts to change their practices in ways that improve education throughout the public school system.[14]

Although these possibilities and distinctions are useful, we suspect that legislators were relatively clear in terms of what they meant by innovation (something new) even though the term can be interpreted from multiple perspectives. The SRI study reported little evidence of new innovation (e.g., they reported that 87% of charter schools reported traditional classroom-based approaches to instruction).

The Good study found that respondents most frequently described their innovative efforts in the areas of curriculum, content, and educational approach.[15] Some schools reported missions or unique focuses that appear quite distinct from public schools. For example, Good and his colleagues identified 16 schools with dropout recovery programs, 20 schools that were trying to teach knowledge and skills appropriate for gaining post-secondary education, 15 with an individual focus, 10 that focused on teaching responsibility and decision making, and 11 that emphasized parent involvement programs. Other responses ranged from culture-specific missions such as teaching Native American Culture or Greek Cardinal Virtues to the use of specific teaching strategies such as direct instruction to deaf students, cooperative learning and whole language, to specific career preparation goals like manufacturing and automotive repair. However, how much emphasis (amount of class time) was given to these themes and how objectives were to be met was seldom spelled out.

Similar findings were reported in the OERI II study.[16] However, responses included in the report as examples of "realizing an alternative vision for schooling" were uninformative because only general labels and not specific plans were provided. For example, the report included: (a) school-to-work program–outcome based education; (b) high-quality education for students interested in the arts; (c) innovative techniques and ways of learning; (d) the use of technology; and (e) reduced class sizes and more project-based learning.

It was also difficult to find innovation as conventionally understood (e.g., something new) in Michigan schools. Horn and Miron reported that charter schools' mission statements were similar to traditional public schools' with the exception that specific issues related to particular themes could be identified (e.g., an African American centered approach or a fine arts theme). They concluded that charter schools' mission statements largely failed to include certain key dimensions that had been articulated in the legislation that created charter schools "such as innovative teaching methods; more effective, efficient/equitable use of funds; greater accountability at the local school level; and/or the creation of new professional opportunities for teachers."[17]

Horn and Miron pointed out that there are various ways to define innovation (is it something new or is it something improved in a significant way?) and they attempted to consider broadly educational practices that were infrequently found in other public school settings. Still, the list of innovations generated was relatively pedestrian. Few educators would agree that much innovation had occurred in instruction or curriculum in these settings, but some reported functions of school management appeared innovative. The "innovative" practices reported are presented in Table 6.1.

Little curriculum innovation occurred in part because teachers were *excluded* from making curriculum decisions. Horn and Miron reported that curriculum decisions were generally determined by the principal, who allowed teachers, in some instances, to decide how to implement the decisions. Teachers had little opportunity to define the curriculum.

Some have argued that teachers and charter school managers will improve their performance in student learning because market competition will encourage them to do new things (e.g., develop new curriculum). In contrast, others have reasoned that freedom from bureaucratic constraints will allow teachers to do what they already know how to do. Pack made his argument this way:

Teachers, freed from burdensome regulations, would have freedoms in the classroom that they had not had before ... teachers would innovate and finally be able to do what they knew was best for students ... Teachers would be able to do what they always wanted to do in their classrooms but were unable to do because of the regulations and accom-

TABLE 6.1
Innovative Practices in Instruction, Management, and Operations

Innovations in Instruction and Teaching Methods
- Specific focus of a curriculum, i.e., Native American, African American, fine arts, agriculture, ecology, etc.
- Community activity experiences for students with a mentor (K–12 school).
- Set aside time (~ 30 minutes/day) for reading.
- Coenrollment of high school students in community college courses.
- Multilevel (grade/age) classrooms.
- Before- and after-school activities program.
- Individual Education Plans (IEPs) for all students.
- Small class size with additional adults (aides or volunteers) assisting the teacher.
- Greater individualization.
- Use of teaching assistants and volunteers in the classroom.
- Montessori methods.

Other Practices—Innovative, but Not New to Schools
- Cooperative learning.
- Chicago math and Saxon math.
- Small- and large-group instruction.
- Learning labs.
- Foreign language.
- Outcomes based.
- Direct approach/differential approach to instruction.

Innovations in School Management and Governance
- School founders self- or board-appointed as administrative heads/managers of schools.
- Use of for- and not-for-profit management companies for diverse services ranging from the provision of limited financial services to general management of a school.
- Contracting for instructional services with a private company as opposed to employing individuals as teachers.
- Renovation of a variety of structures/buildings for school use.
- Nepotism in employment of spouses and sons/daughters.

(Continues)

146

TABLE 6.1 (Continued)

- Acquisition of bank loans and acquisitions of property for the development of schools and campuses.
- Parents responsible for transportation of students to and from school.
- Absence of lunch program for students, especially the lack of free or reduced-price meals for students with demonstrated needs.
- Personal assumption of school indebtedness by founder and/or parents.
- Shared or sole decision making by teachers in selected areas.

Note. From Horn, J., & Miron, G. (1999). *Evaluation of the Michigan Public School Academy* [Online]. Available: http://www.wmich.edu/evalctr/

panied bureaucracy. These changes would eventually improve student achievement.[18]

Pack concluded that on the basis of his observational and interview studies of two California charter schools (a new start-up school and a conversion school) that charter school status had little impact on actual classroom teaching. He reported that teachers did not teach any differently than previously when they were not in charter schools. Further, the charter school milieus per se had no impact on how teachers described their motivation for classroom innovation.

The Horn and Miron study also concluded that a paucity of innovation had occurred in Michigan charter schools, suggesting that if one wanted to claim innovation, it would be "around a strong central theme—e.g., citizenship, leadership, character, entrepreneurship, locational preparation—and designing their entire program to support it."[19] Interestingly, some charter schools reported being innovative by their return to practices they suggested that public schools had largely abandoned—back to basics, strict discipline, phonics-based reading, and so forth. The report concluded, "the schools practice complete site-based management, and this allows them greater flexibility, which is their major innovation. They are able to create programs, change them, or discontinue unsuccessful, undesirable, or out-moded programs with much more ease than is possible in most traditional public schools."[20]

One goal of the Michigan legislature was to "create new professional opportunities for teachers in a new type of public school in which the school structure and education program may be designed with innovation and managed by teachers at the school–site level."[21]

However, it was found that teachers were not really managing schools and that administrators were turning to external management firms for guidance and help. A likely reason that innovation has not occurred is because teachers are locked out of the process.

Overall, innovation in curriculum and classroom instructional strategies was virtually nonexistent in charter schools. Innovation that has occurred has been the creation of management structures to address the financial and administrative functions of schools. Given the low levels of innovation in charter schools, they exert little if any reform pressure on the curriculum and teaching practices in traditional schools. The only study reporting that innovation was occurring was the Finn study.[22] However, the examples of innovation that they cite seemed problematic to us.

Special Education

Special education services have been a part of public education since the turn of the century. Educators have consistently acknowledged the need to provide certain students with services not available in the general curriculum. The provision of special education has taken many forms. At differing points in history, students with special needs have been institutionalized; placed in self-contained special education classrooms; mainstreamed into "typical" classrooms; been a part of "typical" classrooms leaving for brief periods to obtain special services (e.g., occupational therapy, speech therapy); fully included in regular classrooms; or some combination of these. In order to ensure that students receive necessary services to benefit from their education, federal legislation regulates special education.[23] Charter schools are generally notable for their failure to serve the needs of students with disabilities in an integrated setting.

Charter schools, in theory, should provide a natural niche for special education students with their purportedly smaller classes, more optimal student–teacher ratios, and consequent ability to provide services while limiting the use of special education labels.[24] However, provision of special education services seems to be the Achilles's heel of charter schools. Across the board, in studies that addressed the issue, special education was found to be problematic. Key issues in special education included whether it was offered at all in many charter schools, the amount of charter school funding spent on special education, the distribution of special education students in charter schools, and whether students previously labeled as needing special education services continue to be labeled as such and to receive special services on entering charter schools.

The Office of Educational Research and Improvement reported that in the 1997–1998 school year, 8% of students enrolled in charter schools nationally had received special education services before being enrolled in the charter school.[25] In contrast, the Hudson Institute 1997 final report noted that special education enrollment in charter schools was 12.6%.[26] Compared with 11% nationwide in noncharter public schools, these figures do not appear to be terribly deviant from the national norm. However, the figures are misleading. They do not indicate the percentage of students that continued to receive special services once they enrolled in charter schools or whether they chose or were forced to give up their special education status in order to gain charter school admission. Further, it is not clear whether these students were distributed among a variety of schools or whether there were only a few speciality schools that enrolled only special education students and others that did not enroll any special education students. For example, Good and his colleagues in their national study found that many charter schools did not have any special education students, whereas others had only special education students. Thus, the report that on aggregate special education students are represented in charter schools is highly misleading.[27]

Other studies have reached more critical judgments. For example, Garn and Stout reported data on the amount of money charter schools in Arizona spent on special education.[28] They found that most charter school budgets reflected a significant difference between the amount of money spent and the amount of money budgeted for special education. Almost half the charter schools they studied reported spending no money on special education students. Charter schools, on average, were reported to spend about 1.4% of their funds on special education in contrast to 10% in public schools. However, of the funds spent they found that one school accounted for almost half the total funds charter schools spent on special education in Arizona in the 1996–1997 school year. Consistent with this, in Michigan Horn and Miron found that some charter schools had no or very few students with special education needs, whereas others had more than schools in their host district.[29]

Mulholland reported that at the Arizona Center for Disability Law, approximately 20% of calls from parents regarded special education violations or concerns at charter schools.[30] Further, she reported that charter school directors were relatively unaware of their legal responsibilities for special education, unwilling to provide services required by federal law, or engaged in efforts to discourage parents from enrolling students in their program.

Although states do not have the authority to relieve schools of the responsibility for complying with federal special education laws, many charter schools practice as if they do not have to accommodate this responsibility. Charter schools in some cases exclude special education students altogether and in other cases seek to enroll a majority of special education students, effectively segregating them from less restrictive forms of education.

Student Demographics

As in traditional public schools, consideration of the ethnic and racial composition of teachers and students in charter schools is a contentious issue. There are both legislative and court rulings against segregated instruction yet we know that school populations in many locations (inner-city schools) often involve teaching students in primarily segregated groups. Even extensive attempts at busing have not altered the fact that much instruction in American schools is to segregated groups of students. Moreover, many minority parents have complained about the time their children spend in taking public transportation to other schools and their children's inability to attend a local neighborhood school.[31]

Despite these difficulties, we find it untenable for one to argue on legal (or moral) grounds for a policy that would further segregate American students along ethnic, racial, or income lines. The "law of the land" stresses that educational practices should move toward inclusiveness (e.g., including special education students and achieving a diversity of ethnic mixes) and should avoid more segregated instruction. However, it is also the case that attempts to desegregate schooling in some settings have appeared to be the only response to poor performance in some inner-city schools (no efforts have been made to bring in exemplary teachers, revise the curriculum, etc.). This is unfortunate, because all students need to be educated in schools that are equitably funded.[32] But it is our belief that these problems can be addressed in other ways (see chapter 8).

Making distinctions in this area is complex for various reasons. There are schools that are segregated due to community composition, which is reflected in the noncharter public schools. For example, if one opens a charter school on an Indian reservation, in many cases it follows that most students will be Native Americans. Similarly, if one opens a charter school in a rural Iowa or South Dakota farming community, most of the charter school students will be White, and if one opens a charter school in inner-city Detroit, most students will be Black.

The unit-of-analysis problem further complicates demographic comparisons. Data can be aggregated at different levels. First, one can take the population of all students in charter schools across the nation and compare that with enrollment patterns in all public schools. However, one can (and many reports have chosen to) combine data at the state level (e.g., looking at the demographics of teachers and students in charter and noncharter schools in California). Or, one can look at the composition of students in individual charter schools and compare the range of students in individual charter and regular public schools. One can even compare factors in some states with those in other states (e.g., demographic characteristics in states with strong vs. weak charter school laws).

There is wide variation in the research literature with regard to whether charter public schools have increased the segregation of students. It is possible to untangle most differences in research studies by understanding the unit-of-analysis issue. When data are aggregated at a national level, the conclusion is that charter and noncharter public schools enroll students with similar demographic characteristics. In sharp contrast, when one looks at individual schools or at schools clustered for neighborhood comparisons, the conclusion is that charter schools contribute to increasing segregation in American education.

The studies that reported data only at a national level (OERI I, II, III, and the Hudson Institute final report) reached the conclusion that public and charter public schools were serving similar demographic populations of students, with charter schools serving a higher population of minority students.[33] In contrast, the national survey conducted by Good and his colleagues reached a different conclusion because they examined individual profiles of data.[34] However, data from the Good study are only suggestive.

A better study for making statements about segregation using a smaller unit of analysis was conducted by Casey Cobb and Gene Glass in Arizona schools. In their January 1999 research report, they concluded that charter schools were more ethnically segregated than public schools. They contended that the unit of analysis—using the entire state or an entire city or school district—masks potential information about the degree of ethnic segregation. They argued:

To see the ethnic separation in Arizona charter schools, one must examine the geography of the situation. The crucial question is not what percents of ethnic groups either are or are not in charter schools; rather, the crucial question is how are ethnic groups distributed between propinquitous charter and traditional public schools. This question is addressed differently in small rural places and in large metropolitan areas. In the former, because attendance catchment areas are small, it is sufficient merely to list small towns that have charter schools and compare their ethnic composition to the traditional public school or schools in the same town. In the case of large metropolitan areas, it is necessary to plot actual maps of these areas and inspect the ethnic distributions of adjacent charter and traditional public schools.[35]

They studied matched pairs of 55 urban and 57 rural schools. Among their findings were:

1. Forty-six percent (21 urban, 18 rural) of the charter schools demonstrated substantial ethnic segregation. Several other school districts appeared to represent a degree of ethnic segregation—bringing the total number of charter schools contributing to ethnic separation to 61% (24 urban, 28 rural).
2. The rate of Hispanic students participating in charter schools was half that of traditional public schools.
3. Arizona charter schools were typically 20 percentage points higher in White enrollment than comparison public schools.
4. Those charter schools that were disproportionately White in general emphasized academic programs for students who were competitive for attending college.
5. Those Arizona charters that had a majority of minority students were most likely to be either vocational education secondary schools, (i.e., education, not leading to college) or schools for students who had been expelled from the public school system.

Cobb and Glass concluded that some students might be benefitting from charter schools but the majority were probably not:

The claim by choice advocates that charters equalize educational opportunity by offering minority students options previously available to more advantaged (White) students does not stand up very well to the evidence here. Although it is true that many ethnic minorities are well represented by several charter schools, most are in voc-ed schools and at-risk schools of last resort. This is not to say that all of the at-risk and voc-ed charter schools do children a disservice. It is probably the case that several of these schools serve students better than their former public schools. Similarly, this is not to say that all the non-voc-ed, non-at-risk ethnocentric charter schools are poorly serving students. It could be argued that minorities are using the charter vehicle for some interesting and worthwhile purposes. However, though some students undoubtedly benefit, the majority probably do not.[36]

The SRI International study of demographics in California charter schools also showed how data aggregation influenced obtained conclusions. Using data aggregated at the state level, they reported that charter schools were attended by student groups that were similar to statewide demographic averages. When using a different unit of analysis they reached different conclusions. "Within-district comparisons, however, showed that in about 40% of charter schools students were more likely to be White, and in about 60% of charter schools students were less likely to be low-income than other students in their sponsoring district."[37]

Although some readers may find our comments about the level of analysis needlessly academic, it is important to understand that the popular media often rely on general figures without realizing the important distinctions that are lost when reporting averages. For example, James Traub in a generally well-written and insightful essay on charter schools wrote "charter schools also attract the same percentage of Black and Hispanic students as public schools, according to a report commissioned by the United States Department of Education, though the percentage of students in poverty is slightly lower in charters."[38] It is clear that such a statement can be supported only in the context of national averages. What happens in individual charter schools is notably different than the national average. Thus the judgements issued in the OERI reports are careless statements that misrepresent what is occurring.

Student Achievement

Charter schools are supported in large measure because they are expected to increase student achievement. In fact, in some states (e.g., Arizona) the enabling legislation specifies that the primary reasons charter schools exist are for their purported ability to increase student achievement. Those who have studied student achievement in charter and noncharter public schools have suggested that it is either premature or virtually impossible to compare student performance between charter and noncharter schools because of inadequate research designs or sampling procedures. Further, many evaluators lament the fact that achievement comparisons are limited primarily to standardized tests. With this important caveat in mind, we turn to a discussion of available evidence.

Garn and Stout studied student achievement in charter and noncharter public schools but expressed concern about two issues. The Arizona Department of Education changed test mandates, and the sample size of schools in their study was too small to draw sound conclusions about student progress. In addition, they noted that given the quality of data from charter schools for at-risk students, they could not conclude that charter schools have made any significant inroads into improving test performance of at-risk students.

There were originally 9 schools studied that were formerly proprietary schools (the authors reported achievement from 7 elementary schools). Achievement in these schools was generally high, but as Garn and Stout noted, the schools serviced the same population of students that they had previously serviced. Originally, 19 schools were classified as special focus curriculum schools. The authors obtained data for 13 schools (10 elementary and 3 high school). Perhaps not surprisingly, these schools showed the most variability in achievement test scores. The authors concluded that "student achievement, as measured by the Stanford-9 test looks just about the way one would expect, and very much like that reported in district public schools."[39] Unfortunately, no data were presented in an attempt to explain the variability of student achievement in charter schools as a function of program features (e.g., do charter schools that have smaller classes have higher achievement than charter or noncharter schools that have larger classes?) Garn and Stout concluded that the charter schools they visited included some of the best and worst examples of public education.

Mulholland also studied student achievement in Arizona charter schools. One major conclusion presented in her report contended that charter school students were achieving similar academic gains to students attending regular public schools. The report later qualified this assertion by stating "however, an experimentally controlled research study over a longer period of time is needed to adequately understand achievement group differences and trends."[40] And later, the report made it clear that the achievement comparison was flawed: "clearly, the proportion of students used to describe charter high schools is markedly below what we had hoped for and caution needs to be used when making inferences about this group"[41] There is a major discrepancy between the initial bold claim that charter school students were achieving similar academic gains and the more qualified findings presented later in the report.

SRI International reported that the 1992 California Charter School Act mandated that charter schools were to improve achievement; however, the report indicated that data were not available to support that the mandate had been achieved. The SRI team noted, "In short, neither the state of California nor the Nation's larger educational community as a whole have been able to agree on specific definitions of academic achievement or how it should be measured."[42] Further, sponsoring agencies were found to focus more on and to hold districts more accountable for fiscal operations rather than educational outcomes.

Horn and Miron concluded that as a group, charter schools had lower scores on the Michigan Assessment of Educational Progress than host districts. Still, when schools were compared at an individual level, some charter school students had higher scores than students in the host district.

Public Sector found that Michigan charter schools under-performed the average of neighborhood traditional schools.[43] First-year charter schools scored more poorly although second- and third-year schools performed more closely to traditional public schools:

> In general, looking at the results of the Michigan study, we feel that charter schools in southeastern Michigan have not provided evidence to suggest that the legislative intent was successfully met. For example, there were simply no data to illustrate that the first two objectives were achieved (improving student achievement across the state and in stimulating innovative teaching methods).[44]

In comparing charter to comparison schools, these researchers concluded:

> Only four percent of study-area charter schools had a percentage of students achieving satisfactory scores that would place them in the top 25% (first quartile) of all schools in their comparison district. Fourteen percent of study-area charter schools were in the second quartile, 27% in the third, and 43% in the lowest, or fourth, quartile. An additional

12% had a composite MAEP score lower than any score in their comparison district.[45]

The Public Sector report, like the Horn and Miron Michigan report (and most reports, for that matter) was extremely sympathetic to the problems of measuring achievement in charter schools. For example, they reported the laments from charter school directors that pen-and-paper tests only measure a part of the curriculum, that such tests may be culturally biased, and that these tests fail to measure educational objectives that are central to the mission of their school and fail to consider the previous achievement level of charter school students. Similarly, many public school administrators have argued that pen-and-paper tests do not measure objectives central to their goals and that, unlike charter schools, virtually the entire special education population in their schools must be accounted for in testing programs. As some researchers have reported, charter schools are (a) drawing off a higher percent of parents who are involved in their children's education, and (b) using smaller classes—both conditions that are strongly associated with student achievement. It seems that both public schools and public charter schools have legitimate arguments about the use of standardized tests to assess student achievement.

Bruno Manno, an advocate of charter schools, has pointed out that there may be problems with standardized tests, but if charter school operators ignore them they do so at their own risk:

> It's vital for a charter operator to recognize that items like state-wide tests are part of the accountability deal with the state and the charter authorizer. It is naive to design a curriculum that doesn't prepare students to do well on them. Conversely, the chartering authority must realize both on the testing side and when designing other forms of accountability monitoring, that if it wants some school to be truly different—especially if it wants them to serve at risk youngsters—it has got to be imaginative and sensitive in monitoring their performance. There is no simple solution to this dilemma, but a charter accountability compact should be clear about what's expected by the charter authorizer.[46]

Manno also noted, "In simplest terms: what a charter school was founded to teach may not be exactly what the state (or district) measures. And the ways in which the charter school most desires to demonstrate its effectiveness may not yield the kinds of information that the larger world seeks from schools."[47] However, this again raises the issue of whether or not charter schools should be exempted from the "poor curriculum" and associated assessment measures of the state. To grant such an exemption would be illogical. After all, policymakers who have claimed that public schools are inadequate do so because public schools are believed to be doing poorly on the state curriculum and associated assessment measures.

Parent and Student Satisfaction

Because parents and students choose to attend a charter school, it is expected that they would report high levels of satisfaction. Consumer satisfaction data come from a variety of perspectives which include reasons that parents and students choose charter schools, areas of satisfaction and dissatisfaction in the charter school concept, satisfaction and dissatisfaction related to attendance at charter schools, and areas of dissatisfaction with their formerly attended public school.

Mulholland's 1999 report on Arizona charter schools examined areas of parent and student satisfaction and concern.[48] She found that the most popular reasons parents stated for moving their child to a charter school were that in their previous school, class sizes were too large (34%); their child was bored or under challenged (32%); their child experienced negative social environment interactions with classmates (29%); and teachers–staff of former school were not able or willing to help their child (29%).

Parent data were very supportive of charter schools, and parents scored the following items as: children were doing either a lot or a little better than in their previous school: how's your child doing academically at this school compared to the previous school (79%); how's your child's attitude toward school learning compared to the previous school (77%); how does your child feel about his or her teachers compared to the previous school (73%); and how does your child like classmates compared to previous school (63%).

However, parents reported that they had some continuing concerns about funding for building or campus improvements (38%); operational funding for the school (37%); lack of sports or extracurricular programs (37%); and transportation for students (24%). (Of note is that parents' concerns about funding and extracurricular activities more than doubled from initial concerns.) Parents also expressed significant concerns about their child's charter school experience. On the basis of parent focus groups, parents expressed concerns about the transferability of credits from a charter school to another public school or about the use of a charter school diploma for college admission. One parent was reported as saying:

> We lost a full scholarship at NAU [Northern Arizona University] because ... he couldn't get math classes, so I just don't know what we're going to do. We thought he was already qualified for the scholarship and now we find out he is lacking math and foreign language. The school is having a hard time getting the information from the colleges. It is just so different from the rest of the system and the schools just don't know how to handle it yet.[49]

Qualitative analyses of parent complaints indicated that the majority of complaints (24%) were regarding staff, administration, or governance issues. A close second were complaints about communications and expectations (21%), followed by policy (11%) and special education (10%).

Students' reasons for choosing a charter school were consistent with those expressed by their parents. A majority of students (58%) indicated that they wanted to attend the charter school because it had a special program that they liked. In general, students reported that they were not happy at their old school because: "teachers couldn't help me when I needed it" (38%); "I wasn't doing well in my classes" (36%); "I was bored" (32%); "my classes had too many students" (29%). Student data concerning perceptions of performance and attitudes at their present school compared to their earlier school were even more positive (combining statements indicating they felt a lot better and a little better): "how are you doing in your classes compared to your last school" (83%); "how do you feel about going to school compared to your last school" (73%); "how do you like teachers compared to your last school" (77%); and "how do you like the other students compared to your last school" (64%).

However, student reports about attending school for the next year were a bit more problematic. For example, in response to the question, "if you're going to another school next year, what type of school will you probably attend," 50% reported a regular public school and 17% another charter school. Why did students not indicate that they would be staying at their current charter school? In terms of "do you think you will go back to this charter school next year," 62% responded yes; 18% said no (either because the grade they would be attending was not taught there, or they were graduating or moving); 7% reported no for other reasons; and 13% reported not sure.

Similarly, students also raised some concerns about the charter school they attended. A few students shared the belief expressed by parents that their credits may not transfer, and many students were concerned about the lack of extracurricular activities. Mulholland reported that these two quotes illustrated some of the general concerns that students had:

> One good thing about public schools is the other activities. Some colleges look for that ... We need groups, clubs, like drama. Other high schools have classes like dance, band, music. Here we just have P.E. and computers.[50]

Increasing competition for college admissions, particularly at the top universities, is likely to be a significant problem for charter schools.

Parent satisfaction with charter schools was also noted in Michigan. In the Public Sector study, parents expressed overall satisfaction with charter schools. Ninety-one percent of parents reported that the school has a bright future, and 88% of parents reported that students feel safe at the school. However, not all areas of parent perception were so supportive, as only 55% of parents agreed that the school has good facilities, and only 51% of parents reported that they would be able to influence the direction or activities of the school and that adequate support services were provided (e.g., counseling, etc.).[51]

The Horn and Miron Michigan study reported similar results. Consumer satisfaction data in charter schools were positive, as 75% of parents indicated that they were satisfied with the school curriculum; however, of note is that 41% of teachers reported that they were unsure, dissatisfied, or very dissatisfied with the curriculum. Over 50% of students indicated that they agreed or strongly agreed with the statement, "I wish that there were more choices I could choose from."[52] More positively, 64% of students indicated that they were learning more in the charter school than at their previous school, slightly over 50% of students agreed that their assignments were regularly returned with corrections and suggestions for improvement, and 72% indicated that their teacher was available to talk about academic matters.

The Hudson Institute final report, also reported high levels of parent and student satisfaction.[53] Both parents and students reported that they favored the charter school to the previously attended school.

At the start of the chapter we noted that most surveys of parents and students had problematic samples; however, the reported response rate in the Hudson Institute study was very good.[54]

Parent's reasons for higher levels of satisfaction were opportunities for parent involvement (76%); smaller class (75%) and school sizes (74%); individual attention (71%); and better academic standards (68%). Student's reasons for higher levels of satisfaction were good teachers (59%) and teaching methods (51%). Similar to the Mulholland study in Arizona, students reported some dissatisfaction with sports programs (29%) and lack of "other" activities (29%).

Parent Involvement

Involving parents in their children's education, in the abstract, is a laudable goal. Some research exists to suggest that when parents are involved in their child's school learning, children have higher records of academic achievement.[55] But in practice, the term *parent involvement* can include such different tasks as fund raising, grading papers, providing active instruction, making photocopies, participating in school decision making, and providing a child with transportation to school. Parent involvement provisions may be related to creating collegial partnerships or, alternatively, may be an attempt to influence parents to conform to school goals and expectations. In some cases, parent participation may be a blatant attempt to conduct admission screening through the filter of parents' reported interest and support. Indeed, it has been suggested that although Catholic schools may not have been selective in terms of parent income levels, it can be argued that they have been notably selective in assuring that parents were actively interested in the academic success of their children.[56] Becker and colleagues contended:

> The literature on parent involvement thus supports its importance in building a school community. But in using parent participation to build community and increase achievement, an unintended consequence is that schools may sometimes alienate or penalize parents who are unable to meet the expectations for involvement. Such alienation may exacerbate social-class and ethnic differences in schooling by eliminating or excluding less-involved families from attending schools where expectations for involvement become codified, such as in charter schools.[57]

Overall, charter school research has documented increased levels of parent involvement. Some researchers have concluded that parent involvement is a defining feature of some charter schools.[58] Parents were reported to be a strong presence in charter schools including volunteering in the classrooms, participating in parent training programs, and assisting with large scale fund raising. In California, SRI International reported that 88% of parents were included on governing boards, and 88% of parents participated in parent-teacher conferences.[59] Similarly, a Michigan study reported parent involvement to be much higher at charter schools than at noncharter public school including parent attendance at school events, assistance in classrooms, and parent assistance with homework completion. Further, in an Arizona charter school evaluation, Mulholland reported that parents felt that in their child's charter school they had more communication with the school, more opportunities to be involved, more input into decisions made, and better treatment in general than they had experienced in the last school their child attended.[60]

Despite the seemingly positive review of parent involvement in charter schools, significant problems also can exist. Before a 1998 revision in legislation, California charter schools could make a child's enrollment contingent on parents agreeing to specific parent participation requirements. One study reported that 41% of charter schools studied required parents to participate in school governance or to attend parent meetings, and 40% required that parents volunteer for a minimum number of hours. Most schools did not articulate specific consequences if parent involvement contracts were violated, but 23% of schools reported that they had dismissed students because parents failed to comply with parent involvement contracts.[61]

Another California study reported that charter schools denied admission to students both because of parents' and students' lack of commitment to the school philosophy and because parents were not willing to accommodate parent involvement requirements as specified by the charter school.[62] Further, despite increased parent–school involvement contracts, in a Michigan study parent contracts were not associated with increased school-related activities or arrangements. Becker and colleagues reported that charter schools, in comparison to public schools, were (a) less likely to have a drop-in center for parents, (b) slightly less likely to have classes for parents, (c) less likely to have a family support professional making home visits, and (d) slightly less likely to assign a staff person to work on planning family involvement.

Parent involvement contracts were found to work against the involvement of low-income parents. Indeed, some speculated that the parents who send their children to charter schools were more likely to have the time and resources to be highly involved in their child's education. One study noted, "The act of removing their child from a traditional school and finding the right charter school tends to occur among parents who are engaged in their child's education. Moreover, few charter schools provide transportation, so most parents are at the school twice a day dropping off and picking up their child."[63] The researchers concluded that if *creaming* (a term advocates of public schools frequently use meaning that choice schools cream off only talented and motivated students) had taken place it was in the form of attracting and selecting the most involved and motivated parents. However, the effects of parent involvement are complex; as noted in chapter 4, research by Shumow and colleagues found that parents who chose magnet schools for their children were less likely to be involved.[64]

Thus, like many of the issues surrounding charter schools, the effects of parent participation are far from clear. A number of studies have reported higher levels of parent involvement in charter than in noncharter public schools. However, what manifests as parent involvement is highly variable. In some schools it is voluntary and in others required. In some schools children are asked to leave the school if parents don't fulfill involvement contracts, and in others they are not. In some schools parent involvement occurs during the school day, and in others it occurs exclusively outside the school day. And, in some schools something as basic as transporting a child to school is considered participation, whereas in others involvement constitutes a more substantial parental role in the school. Finally, parent involvement requirements may be veiled attempts to attract certain kinds of parents and students to a charter school and, alternatively, to keep others away.

Relationships Between Charter and Noncharter Public Schools

One core premise behind charter schools is that experimentation and educational innovations will be shared with noncharter public schools. However, mechanisms to facilitate this transfer have not been fully developed. Several researchers have studied this area and have noted that the relationships between charter schools and noncharter public schools are still developing (if they exist at all).

In Arizona, Garn and Stout reported varied types of relationships between charter schools and local school districts.[65] Some were positive; in one case, a charter school enabled a local public school to solve its crowded condition, and in another case a charter school was actually using the district curriculum and textbook and subcontracting for transportation and teachers. Administrators frequently mentioned that local districts were referring students to them (e.g., students who had dropped out of school or who had been expelled). Some administrators saw this as more beneficial than others. For example, one administrator reported hesitancy about wanting to become a dumping ground for students unwanted by the traditional system.

In contrast, other schools essentially had no relationship with local districts or had a distinctly negative relationship. In one case, a charter school was unable to negotiate a lease on an empty school that the district owned. There was a suggestion that conflicts between charter and noncharter public schools were being played out in the newspaper to everyone's detriment. Garn and Stout reported that relationships between charter schools were loose and typically not effective.

Good and Braden approached the issue from another point of view by asking noncharter public school superintendents to list ways they felt charter schools might inform public education.[66] Of the 40 respondents, 57% stated that charter schools cannot inform public education, and only 25% indicated that charter schools can inform public education. Those who noted that charter schools cannot inform public education felt that (a) the transfer of ideas from charter schools is impeded by the differences between the context and circumstances of charter schools and other public schools, (b) charter school practices are not innovative or even significantly different from public school practices, and (c) charter school practices are unacceptable and should not be replicated in public schools. In contrast, those who noted that charter schools can inform public education felt that charter schools (a) present a research opportunity to determine best practices in education, (b) can establish partnerships with public schools to improve all public education, and (c) provide a competitive market atmosphere that could improve education.

In California, Wells and her colleagues noted that the idea of collaboration seemed to contradict the notion of charter schools improving education by forcing noncharter public schools to compete for students. Further, they reported that there was no evidence to suggest that noncharter public schools were competing with charter schools or that they were learning from them. In fact, no mechanisms were in place for information transfer:

> One reason for this lack of sharing was a general lack of communication across the schools, especially in situations where the charter schools were more independent from the districts and where the charters were established to be in direct competition with the public schools ... we found little evidence that educators in public schools are learning about new innovative ideas from charter school educators.[67]

Charter school and regular public school communication is important. Even when state laws indicate that charter schools are to contribute generally to the improvement of education in the state, few collaborative efforts are apparent. In general, charter schools have had little impact on other public schools because there is very little experimentation and there appears to be no basis or reason to communicate. For whatever reasons, there is no systematic effort on the part of charter schools to provide information and ideas to public schools.

Teacher Efficacy and Empowerment

The Hudson Institute final report noted, "The teachers feel empowered. Charter school teachers are a diverse lot, but nearly all are finding personal fulfillment and professional reward."[68] In contrast, in a study completed in April 1999, Crawford concluded that contrary to popular belief, teachers in 9 charter public schools did not report feelings of higher efficacy and empowerment.[69] Crawford made use of the school participant empowerment scale[70] and based on responses from teachers completing the instrument, he concluded that teachers in noncharter public schools believe that they: (a) have more opportunities for decision making than charter school teachers do, (b) have more opportunities for professional growth than charter school teachers do, (c) enjoy a higher level of status than charter school teachers, (d) report a higher level of self-efficacy than charter school teachers have, (e) make more of an impact than charter school teachers make, and (f) overall, are more empowered than charter teachers. A seventh finding showed no significant difference between charter and noncharter teachers in terms of autonomy.

Charter school advocates have consistently argued that charter schools should be autonomous environments with decentralized management, which would allow teachers greater freedom and more opportunities for decision making. The argument follows that teacher efficacy and empowerment would therefore be increased. Teachers in the Crawford study completed a 38-item instrument designed to study empowerment. The instrument included six dimensions: decision making; professional growth, status, self-efficacy, autonomy, and impact. Crawford reported that teachers in noncharter schools are older, have more teaching experience, and have attained a higher level of education than charter school teachers. He noted teachers in charter schools had an average of 2 years teaching experience in their particular charter school, but in contrast, public school teachers in the sample had almost 7 years of experience in their particular school. Several other differences related to teacher empowerment were found between charter and noncharter public school teachers. Teachers in regular public schools perceived that they were more empowered than charter school teachers and that they had more opportunity for professional growth than charter school teachers. Furthermore, teachers in regular public schools in comparison to teachers in charter public schools reported the perception of having more status and a higher level of self-efficacy.

In Colorado, charter school teachers believed that they had more decision-making opportunities and more autonomy than noncharter school teachers. In Michigan, there were no differences on these two dimensions between charter and noncharter school teachers. Crawford noted that there was no significant difference between charter schools and regular public school teachers in terms of perceived autonomy. He also noted that overall, public school teachers perceived themselves as being more empowered and having more opportunity to participate in the decision-making process than charter school teachers. Crawford concluded that "even though charter schools have been granted certain levels of autonomy through state legislative acts, it appears that the autonomy has not reached teachers in charter schools themselves."[71]

Pack, in his study of two California charter schools, noted that in comparison to their earlier teaching in noncharter schools, most teachers reported little difference in the amount of classroom autonomy they perceived. Charter school teachers did believe that they had more autonomy in some school decisions such as in influencing the budget and other teachers who were hired. However, this autonomy came at a certain price. Pack noted that teacher-led decision making processes brought more micro-politics and responsibilities for teachers. Most teachers thought this time burden influenced their classroom performance.[72] At the start-up charter school, teachers were required to take on additional support services and noted that such extra duties meant less classroom planning time. Teachers in the start-up school were involved in workshops, scheduling, and other operational responsibilities that typically are covered by support personnel (principals, security personnel, librarians, and so forth). One teacher reported:

> There are so many jobs that need to be done because we don't have administration, and we don't have custodial services, that my job description changes daily from I am not only a teacher, I am also the counselor which I did [pause] ... I am also the custodian, I am also the principal, I am also the nurse. So I wear a lot more hats here than I did before.[73]

Horn and Miron noted that according to state law, the purpose of Michigan charter schools was to improve instruction for all people in the state and to provide empowerment opportunities for teachers.[74] In contrast to the legislative intent, it seemed that charter schools rarely fulfilled this purpose.

Charter School Funding

Many charter school advocates have asserted that charter schools are cost free experiments, because funds used to support a student's costs are simply transferred from the public to the charter school. Careful analysis suggests that in many situations this claim is problematic, because the creation of any new school virtually guarantees that some of that public money will be spent on administration. Charter schools that are sponsored by a public school may receive many services at a fair cost, but in many situations the administrative layer needed to support a new charter school is large and costly (director, associate director, budget officer, insurance costs, sanitation officers, etc.). Thus, even if public monies have not increased as charter schools are added, many public dollars are necessarily reallocated from instructional to administrative budgets. The "value" question then becomes, would citizens prefer higher administrative costs or lower student-to-teacher ratios?

Furthermore, many advocates for public schools have noted that costs for new facilities and various forms of duplication, such as for libraries and computer centers, drain large amounts from monies that otherwise could be used for instructional purposes.[75] Although existing schools that convert to charter status may not have additional facility expenses, funding a new facility can be costly.

Calculating financial cost per pupil also has to be done at the state level, because funding formulas vary as a function of state law. In some states, charter schools are funded at the same level as other public schools even though they do not provide all the services performed by public schools (e.g., transportation, cafeteria services). Hence, in this sense charter schools receive additional funds. Further, some states provide monies for physical facilities; others do not.

Some claim that charter schools are overfunded. In some instances, charter schools receive funding as if they had the same number of at-risk or special education students as do other public schools. Those charter schools that do not have any or have only a few special students are substantially overfunded in comparison to public schools that serve the majority of these students. In fact, Nelson has concluded that unless charter schools primarily serve at-risk students, it is likely they are overfunded.[76] Given these financial perks, it is not surprising that some schools have gained charter status primarily for financial reasons (more on this in chapter 7). Nelson examined various factors associated with charter school funding and concluded that on average charter schools were overfunded in each of the six states he examined.[77] The extra funding per pupil for charter schools was in Arizona, $1,000; in California, $500; in Massachusetts, $1,307; in Michigan, $600; and in Minnesota overfunding ranged from $200 in elementary schools to $1,000 in high schools.

Nelson also examined other issues related to charter school financing.[78] Oddly, given the literature showing that many small businesses often fail, how assets will be disposed of if charter schools fold is not addressed in all state laws. Some states have made it clear that assets revert to the school district or state (e.g., Colorado); however, in 10 states the situation about asset ownership is either unclear or left to the charter school to decide. Ironically, in the three largest charter school states (Arizona, California, and Michigan) there is no clear provision as to what happens to charter school resources if schools close.

States also differ regarding whether they provide funds for capital costs. For example, California and Michigan do not provide funds for facilities, whereas the state of Arizona provides generous funding. Moreover, in Arizona funds provided for capital funding can be spent on items that typically fall under general operating expenditures. This is unusual because school districts can almost never mix capital funds with monies intended for the general operating purposes. Further, "Arizona is the only state where charter schools get more capital funding than equivalent public schools, primarily because charter schools are funded like small districts, not like the school districts in which they are located.[79] An examination of the financial data provided by Nelson and his colleagues led to our conclusion that if one's primary motivation in opening a charter school is to make money, Arizona is the prime location.

As can be seen in Table 6.2 we have identified 10 aspects among the array of advantages for Arizona charter school operators. Why have Arizona legislators been so hospitable to charter school legislation? Obviously there is no way to answer the question of motivation, but among the possible reasons for this attractive climate for charter schools are (a) a deep belief in market principles and competition, (b) a deep distrust of the public schools system, (c) an active interest in al-

TABLE 6.2

**Ten Reasons Why Charter School Operators
Might Want to Be in Arizona**

1. In Arizona, provisions are in place for charter schools to receive "speeded up" payments (to get state aid sooner).*

2. Arizona charter schools are eligible for capital funds. Arizona schools are not only eligible for capital funds but Arizona is the only state in which charter schools are favored over other public schools. Further, capital funds can be used for general operating expenses.

3. Arizona charter schools can acquire debt.

4. Arizona charter schools can maintain a positive fund balance.

5. Arizona charter schools do not have to hire certified teachers.

6. Arizona charter schools do not have to participate in mandatory teacher retirement programs.

7. Arizona charter schools do not have to transport students (even though they receive transportation funds from the state).

8. Charter schools are exempt from state facility standards.

9. Arizona (and only Arizona) gives charter schools an advantage over other public schools for "geographic funding variations."

10. In Arizona, assets (computers, cars, buildings) can revert to charter school operators if the school closes.

Note. For further details, see F. Howard Nelson (in preparation). *National charter school finance study.*

lowing parents more control of education, (d) a belief that the problems are so acute in public education that radical experimentation is required even if it poses some risk for students, and (e) a commitment to privatization.

In comparison to host public schools, Arizona charter schools receive more funding if they enroll fewer special needs students but relatively lower support if they serve many special needs students.[80] The same effect is observed when enrolling low-income pupils. In comparison to host districts, charter schools that have enrolled few low-income pupils get more resources than those that enroll more low-income students. Many charter schools do not have this type of funding pattern. California and Michigan are similar to Arizona in that they are financially "penalizing" charter schools for enrolling many special needs students, but there is no economic disincentive to enrolling low-income pupils in these states. Given that problems of learning are more acute in schools serving low-income students, it seems that state dollars, if designed to improve learning, initially encourage charter schools to develop in those areas with the most need. It seems counterproductive to make funding for charter schools more attractive by discouraging them from enrolling special education students and students from low-income families.

David Arsen studied expenditures of public schools versus charter schools in Michigan.[81] Charter schools in Michigan received approximately the same funding as noncharter public schools. For example, in the 1995–1996 school year, charter schools' total average revenue was $6,345 versus $6,494 for traditional public schools. In contrast, the amount spent on instruction, instructional support, and business and administration differed in notable ways. Charter schools spent $1,035 less on instruction, $401 less on instructional support, and $721 more on business and administration. In terms of resource allocation, charter schools designated 54% of their current operating expenditures for instruction (vs. 63% for noncharter public schools) and 30% for business and administration (vs. 12% for noncharter public schools). Of note is that the variation in how resources were allocated in charter schools was notably higher ($\pm.18$) than in noncharter public schools ($\pm.03$).

Also of interest is that on average charter schools focused on the primary grades spent less on instruction (43%) than those serving secondary (55%) or mixed (66%) grades. Further, primary-level charter schools spent more on business and administration (41% vs. 26% and 22% respectively) and more on operations and maintenance (14% vs. 10% and 9%). Of note is that, on average, charter schools serving the elementary grades were able to bankroll approximately $1,600 in funds per student at the end of the year. So, although less was spent on instruction, it was not because funds were unavailable.

However, as we have stated before, average figures are often misleading. It appears that in some situations the extent of charter school funding is dependent on the knowledge and negotiation skills of those who manage charter schools. Julie Slayton noted that California charter schools are required by state law to be revenue neutral. That is, if a district sponsors charter schools the district should not receive extra revenue. However, she reported that one school district noted that charter schools present an economic drain because they tend to increase the number of teachers in a district but do not increase the amount of revenue that students generate.

> Students are pulled from all over the district, not just one location. As a result, a school may lose a few students increasing the financial burden of the school because they have lost the ADA [average daily attendance] but they cannot get rid of a teacher because they still have too many students to do that. So the school becomes more expensive to operate. As there are more charter schools in the district they present a financial risk to the district.[82]

Thus when choosing a charter school, parents must be aware of not only the educational program the school offers but also the ability of the director to obtain sufficient funds to implement the program.

There are arguments, however, to show that some charter schools, especially in some states, receive less money than intended by the legislature. This is particularly likely to be the case when charter schools are sponsored by a public school district. These arrangements require that charter school directors negotiate for various services and costs, (such as bookkeeping, legal and insurance fees), and also for access to certain types of funding.

Slayton, using data from the UCLA study, reached the same conclusions as did the 1997 SRI study: Many charter school directors know little about finances, and the charter school directors understanding of finances made a huge difference in how much money charter schools received.[83] Indeed, in some instances, charter school leaders were able to negotiate for more money than other charter schools in the same district.

The financial viability of some charter schools is further questioned because of their inability to raise the extra private funds needed to cover facility costs. School districts in California, unlike charter schools, can pay for facility costs in other ways (e.g., bonds). Charter school directors, of course, feel that this is an unfair advantage for public schools. Wells noted that this was especially the case for schools in low-income neighborhoods:

> We saw how difficult it was for charter schools in low-income communities to acquire these additional resources. As a result, charter schools in well-off neighborhoods were more likely to have adequate resources then schools in poor neighborhoods. The illusion of efficiency that this creates could lead to diminished political supports for public funding of education as a whole.[84]

It appears that in some instances charter school directors had to be more than sharp negotiators. Sometimes charter schools had to pay a premium to operate. In Arizona, some public schools were found to sponsor numerous charter schools (sometimes a couple of hundred miles away[85]) and charged them high administrative fees and provided few if any services. These public schools sold schools a charter for a "finder of sponsor fee." Such public schools not only charged high fees to charter schools but also failed to provide any supervisory control of charter schools as expected by public officials (more on this in chapter 7).

Charter schools claim, and rightly so in some cases, that they do not receive their fair level of funding. And, of course, public school advocates have claimed that they loose valuable resources to charter schools. We suspect that both arguments are valid. Some charter schools are unfairly funded and some public schools have their instructional budgets markedly reduced because of charter funding.

The real loser is the public. The funding of charter schools is not a revenue-neutral act. Charter schools are not a free experiment. If public dollars for education remain constant yet are spread over more schools, then it follows that more funds will be spent on administrative and other noninstructional expenses. If effective and informative experiments are wanted, citizens need to understand that they have real costs. An unintended effect of adding more schools and more choice while holding funding constant is to dilute the overall quality of American education.

DISCUSSION

Research on charter schools is relatively new, and many charter schools have been in operation for only a short period of time. We would be more sympathetic to supporters of charter schools and their need for more time to analyze effects on student performance if, in fact, they had set forth their agenda before they opened their schools. Unfortunately, advocates of charter schools often proclaimed quick and dramatic strategies for improvements in student learning that they boasted could be applied to public school settings.

There are several plausible reasons why charter schools initially may record high effects on student achievement that are unrelated to innovative educational practices. For example, in many charter schools there are motivated parents, teachers, and students eager to work in a new setting. If people work harder in the short run, there may be gains that occur simply because people work harder, not because an approach is of higher quality. Thus, when the motivational novelty wears off, students' work effort and results may drop notably (i.e., to a normal level). Indeed, there is a considerable literature to suggest that reform plans often appear to work initially but that the effect dissipates as the newness fades.[86] Many charter schools are as good as they will ever be after a couple of years of operation, and of course some will decline and others will improve in important ways the longer they operate. On average, the performance we describe here may be as high as it will ever be for charter schools unless new laws and practices are forthcoming.

Given these qualifications, it is our conclusion that charter schools as a group essentially have replicated the systemic aspects of American education. That is, some charter schools represent high-quality education, whereas many do not; some represent exciting learning opportunities, but many do not. At present, we estimate that the average performance of charter schools is lower than comparable public schools. In part, this is due to inadequate state supervision and the employment of administrators who simply were not prepared for the multiple tasks of providing instruction while also maintaining a business. Given time, with more adequate supervision and higher selection criteria, performance in charter schools may increase. (More on this in Chapter 7.) However, the present below-average mean performance is also a comment on the adequacy of ideas that charter schools have implemented.

What have citizens received from the charter school investment? We describe our reactions in the form of general judgments: Superior (S), Good (G), Meets Expectations (ME), Needs Improvement (NI), and Unacceptable (U). Again, we want to stress that there are charter schools that function at an "S" level on all of the dimensions we consider. We are not describing individual schools but charter schools as a group.

Innovation.   In terms of innovative experiences that stimulate students to learn in new and important ways, we assign charter schools a U. Their failure arises from the fact that in general there are no new educational methods being tried; most charter school curriculum and instructional ideas already have been implemented in public schools. Some readers might argue that our grading is too harsh in that charter school programs largely duplicate the public school curriculum. It is critical to note, however, that charter school legislation often mandates innovation—and virtually no exciting new approaches to teaching have occurred despite smaller class sizes (in some cases), freedom from many bureaucratic structures, and the use of management companies to run schools.

In terms of organizational innovations, the advent of private ownership and for-profit schools certainly is innovative. The experiment gets a G+ in this area. In time, evidence will indicate whether these are useful innovations, but at present, there is prima facie evidence that management structures are more varied in public school settings.

Special Education and Student Demographics

In terms of composition of student body and provision of services to a diversity of students including special education students, we would assign an U. Charter schools as a group have not decreased segregation; indeed, they have increased it. Students with similar racial backgrounds and income levels are increasingly being taught together in charter schools. Further, many special education students are being excluded systematically from many charter school settings. As we show in chapter 7, there is growing parent dissatisfaction with charter schools' provision for special education, and it is anticipated that lawsuits will be litigated in the near future.

Student Achievement.   Although advocates consistently agree that charter schools will improve student achievement, to date there is no available evidence to support this assertion, because extant data are flawed by small samples and inadequate research designs. It is important to understand as well that available data do not show charter schools to be categorically less effective than other public schools. On the basis of a limited set of data, the evidence shows a wide variation in charter schools, but the mean performance levels in charter schools are lower than in public schools. Charter schools, as with other public schools, show a range of achievement outcomes. Based on the evidence, we give charter schools an ME- on improving student achievement.

Parent and Student Satisfaction. Charter school consumers seem satisfied with their chosen schools; high satisfaction rates are reported by both students and parents. The experiment gets a G+. However, in one study it was found that parents' concerns about certain aspects of charter schools had risen considerably since they initially enrolled their children in the school. Students approved of what they received in the classroom; their primary concerns focused on what they gave up to attend the school (e.g., they now have fewer extracurricular activities). Consumer satisfaction is high in charter schools, as it is in many public schools.

Parent Involvement. In the area of parent involvement we would grade charter schools an ME+. Parents are involved in more aspects of charter schools than they are in public schools and are particularly more likely to serve on boards. (Hence, some individual schools rate an S.) Overall, parent involvement rates in charter schools are not much greater than in public schools, and key decisions still tend to be made by administrators in charter school settings. This is particularly true in for-profit charter schools. And, unfortunately, in some cases parent involvement is arguably a ruse for keeping certain types of students out of the school.

Relationships Between Charter and Noncharter Public Schools. The competitive impact of charter schools on other public schools (e.g., to enrich or expand their instructional options, or to recruit parents more vigorously) appears negligible. Some public schools (in Michigan, for example) have created their own charter schools. However, in general, charter schools have had less impact than they might have had, because there is very little experimentation and appears to be no systematic effort to provide information and ideas to public schools. Reciprocally, there appears to be very little active interest on the part of public school administrators to learn from charter school initiatives except on those occasions in which the public school sponsors the charter school. However, the mere presence of charter schools appears to have increased discussion of local schools in newspapers, and the heightened attention to schools (and the reactivity of measurement and accountability) may have some general but diffuse effect on public schools' improvement efforts. We give charter schools an ME+ in this area.

Teacher Efficacy and Empowerment.   Many have asserted that teachers would be more empowered by the more flexible arrangements in charter schools. However, at best we can give the experiment only an NI in this area. Two large studies in Michigan found that teachers generally were excluded from curriculum decision making. Further, the Crawford study indicated that because of the multiple constraints teachers face in these environments their beliefs that they can teach successfully are lower than teachers in regular public schools.

Charter School Finances.   The data reviewed have indicated that the charter school experiment is not cost free. Charter schools as a group have led to a significant percentage of state funds' transference from instruction cost to administrative costs. This may be a short-run problem while charters form collaborative arrangements; advocates have strongly asserted that charter schools will reduce administrative cost and make more dollars available for the classroom. Just the opposite has occurred to date. We assign an ME- in this area (leaving ourselves open to the charge of grade inflation).

Choice.   In terms of choice, we assign charter schools a G at this point in time. This is a difficult grade to assign because the variation among schools is enormous. It is the case that in most states with charter school legislation, charter schools offer a degree of choice to parents; whether these choices are good ones is a separate issue. However, it is clear that charter schools do offer an array of possibilities, even though the array, in some cases, is relatively minor. Interestingly, parental choice is mainly at the school level. That is, parents may choose a school that has a relative difference (i.e., an offering they cannot find in a public school); however, once within that school setting, parents are as limited in trying to change school practices as they are in public school settings. The choice, especially in for-profit schools, is largely take it or leave it.

CONCLUSION

This chapter reviewed extant data to see how charter schools vary in several important areas. The major conclusion is that charter schools, like regular public schools, are highly varied. Some schools appear top notch, and others are dreadful. On average, charter schools have not performed as well as public schools even with the advantage of highly motivated teachers, parents, and students. To be fair, charter schools have had to fight on many fronts, finding property, securing curriculum, and so forth.

Although most of our policy recommendations are made at the end of chapters 7 and 8, we draw attention to some major flaws that must be resolved if any useful data are to be gleaned from this movement. First, if policymakers want innovation, they must define the term and require that charter school directors demonstrate an intent and a plan before a charter is granted.[87] Second, more attention must be directed toward defining student achievement and how it will be measured; otherwise there is no experiment. Two major buzz words associated with charter schools are innovation and enhanced achievement; on these grounds charter schools are a dismal failure.

Third, more research talent and more educational practitioners need to be drawn into the evaluation process. If a governor and state legislature are largely in favor of charter schools, it seems to present a potential conflict of interest in asking state departments of education to evaluate charter schools. Fourth, if state departments of education are deemed politically able to conduct such evaluations, most need additional personnel since they are already fully engaged in other tasks. Fifth, state departments of education need to become more open in making public records accessible to citizens and researchers. For example, in our experience in trying to get information from the Arizona Department of Education about charter schools, we largely met with excuses, delays, or silence. Sixth, although state laws do not have the authority to relieve school districts of federal legal requirements, many schools appear to behave as though they have a mandate to violate federal law concerning the education of special students. States appear to be largely unconcerned about special education issues, and as a result we predict that massive litigation will occur in the next several years.

Seventh, the reporting of data only at a high level of aggregation (i.e., state level) must stop. Researchers and policymakers have long known that the use of aggregated data can and typically does mask data on important differences in their sample. For example, it was shown in this chapter that when data are disaggregated in California fewer students of color and fewer students from low-income schools are enrolled in charter schools. Thus, the charter experiment in California does not include all children. Data need to be reported for individual schools and for certain types of schools (i.e., where the needs of particular students are satisfactorily met). Eighth, researchers must be more willing to examine achievement data (as limited as they are) as a function of school type ("mom and pop" school, "cookie cutter" school, converted private school) and student type. General comparisons of charter and noncharter schools are virtually meaningless.

Despite their uneven, and in some cases dismal, performance records, charter schools may eventually make a positive contribution to American education. Although we argue at present that the charter school movement remains a disorganized and wasteful experience, not an effective investment, chapter 8 offers some strategies for gleaning useful information from this movement.

Endnotes

1. In time more peer review of the literature will be available, including Wells, A. S., Grutzik, C., Carnochan, S., Slayton, J., & Vasudeva, A. (1999). Underlying policy assumptions of charter school reform: The multiple meanings of a movement. *Teachers College Record, 100*, 513–535.
2. Schnailberg, L. (1999, June 23). Oklahoma, Oregon bump up charter law states to 36. *Education Week, 18*(41), 20, 23.
3. Clinton, W. J. (1998, October 22). Statement by the President [Online]. Available: http://www.ed gov/PressReleases/10-1998/wh-1022.html
4. Nathan, J. (1996). *Charter schools: Creating hope and opportunity for American education*. San Francisco: Jossey-Bass.
5. Good, T. L., Braden, J. S., & Nichols, S. L. (1997). *Charter schools: Promising alternatives for educational reform or an illusionary panacea*. [Online]. Available: http://www.apa.org/ed/charter.html
6. Good, T. L., & Braden, J. S. (1998). *Public school superintendents' perceptions of charter schools*. Unpublished manuscript.
7. Horn, J , & Miron, G. (1999). *Evaluation of the Michigan Public School Academy*. [Online]. Available: http://www.wmich.edu/evalctr/
8. Ibid.
9. Ibid., p. xviii.
10. Manno, B. V., Finn, C. E., Bierlein, L. A., & Vanourek, G. (1997). *Charter schools in action project: Final report, part VI* [Online]. Available: http://www.edexcellence. net/chart/chart6/htm
11. Ibid.
12. Horn, J., & Miron, G. (1999). *Evaluation of the Michigan Public School Academy* [Online]. Available: http://www.wmich.edu/evalctr/
13. Garn, G., & Stout, R. (1998). *Arizona charter schools*. Unpublished manuscript.
14. SRI International. (1997). *Evaluation of charter school effectiveness: part 1* [Online], p. 21. Available: http://www.lao.ca.gov/sri_charter_schools_1297-part1.html

15. Good, T. L., Braden, J. S., & Nichols, S. L. (1997). *Charter schools: Promising alternatives for educational reform or an illusionary panacea* [Online]. Available: http://www.apa.org/ed/charter.html

16. RPP International. (1998). *A national study of charter schools: Second-year report.* Washington, DC: U.S. Department of Education, Office of Educational Research and Improvement.

17. Horn, J., & Miron, G. (1999). *Evaluation of the Michigan Public School Academy* [Online]. Available: http://www.wmich.edu/evalctr/

18. Pack, R. H. (1999). *Charter schools: Innovation, autonomy, and decision-making.* Unpublished doctoral dissertation, The University of Arizona, pp. 127–128.

19. Public Sector Consultants, & MAXIMUS. (1999, February). *Michigan's charter school initiative: From theory to practice* [Online], p. 35. Available: http://www.mde.state.mi.us

20. Ibid., p. 46.

21. Ibid., p. 7.

22. Finn, C., Manno, B., Bierlein, L. (1996). *Charter schools in action: What have we learned?* Indianapolis, IN: Hudson Institute.

23. See http://www.ed.gov/offices/OSERS/IDEA

24. Horn, J., & Miron, G. (1999). *Evaluation of the Michigan Public School Academy* [Online]. Available: http://www.wmich.edu/evalctr/

25. RPP International, & The University of Minnesota. (1999). *The state of charter schools: Third-year report.* Washington, DC: U.S. Department of Education, Office of Educational Research and Improvement.

26. Vanourek, G., Manno, B. V., Finn, C. E., & Bierlein, L. A. (1997). *Charter schools in action project: Final report, part V* [Online]. Available: http://www.edexcellence.net/chart/chart5.htm

27. Good, T. L., Braden, J. S., & Nichols, S. L. (1997). *Charter schools: Promising alternatives for educational reform or an illusionary panacea* [Online]. Available: http://www.apa.org/ed/charter.html

28. Garn, G., & Stout, R. (1998). *Arizona charter schools.* Unpublished manuscript.

29. Horn, J., & Miron, G. (1999). *Evaluation of the Michigan Public School Academy.* [Online]. Available: http://www.wmich.edu/evalctr

30. Mulholland, L. (1999, March). *Arizona charter school progress evaluation.* Phoenix: Morrison Institute for Public Policy.

31. Henig, J. R. (1994). *Rethinking school choice.* Princeton: Princeton University Press.

32. Wells, A. S., Grutzik, C., Carnochan, S., Slayton, J., & Vasudeva, A. (1999). Underlying policy assumptions of charter school reform: The multiple meanings of a movement. *Teachers College Record, 100,* 513–535.

33. RPP International, & The University of Minnesota. (1997). *A national study of charter schools: First-year report.* Washington, DC: U.S. Department of Education, Office of Educational Research and Improvement.
RPP International. (1998). *A national study of charter schools: Second-year report.* Washington, DC: U.S. Department of Education, Office of Educational Research and Improvement.

Vanourek, G., Manno, B. V., Finn, C. E., & Bierlein, L. A. (1997). *Charter schools in action project: Final report, part 1* [Online]. Available: http://www.edexcellence. net/chart/chart1.htm

34. Good, T. L., Braden, J. S., & Nichols, S. L. (1997). *Charter schools: Promising alternatives for educational reform or an illusionary panacea* [Online]. Available: http://www.apa.org/ed/charter.html

35. Cobb, C., & Glass, G. (1999). Ethnic segregation in Arizona charter schools. *Education Policy Analysis Archives, 7*(1), 8. [Online]. Available: http://olam.ed.asu.edu/ epaa/v7n1

36. Ibid., p. 31.

37. SRI International. (1997). *Evaluation of charter school effectiveness: part 1* [Online], p. 16. Available: http://www.lao.ca.gov/sri_charter_schools_1297-part1.html

38. Traub, J. (1999, April 4). A school of your own. *The New York Times*, pp. A30, A31, A42, A43.

39. Garn, G., & Stout, R. (1998). *Arizona charter schools* Unpublished manuscript, p. 26.

40. Mulholland, L. (1999, March). *Arizona charter school progress evaluation.* Phoenix: Morrison Institute for Public Policy, p. 1.

41. Ibid., p. 6.

42. SRI International. (1997). *Evaluation of charter school effectiveness: Part 2* [Online], pp. 31–32. Available: http://www.lao.ca.gov/sri_charer_schools_1297-part2.html

43. Public Sector Consultants, & MAXIMUS. (1999, February). *Michigan's charter school initiative: From theory to practice* [Online]. Available: http://www.mde.state.mi.us

44. Ibid., p. 65.

45. Ibid., p. 65.

46. Manno, B. (1999, March). *Accountability: The key to charter renewal. A guide to help charter schools create their accountability plans* [Online], p. 20. Available: http://edreform.com/pubs/center_for_education_reform.htm

47. Ibid.

48. Mulholland, L. (1999, March). *Arizona charter school progress evaluation.* Phoenix: Morrison Institute for Public Policy.

49. Ibid., p. 14.

50. Ibid., p. 18.

51. Public Sector Consultants, & MAXIMUS. (1999, February). *Michigan's charter school initiative: From theory to practice* [Online]. Available: http://www.mde. state.mi.us

52. Horn, J., & Miron, G. (1999). *Evaluation of the Michigan Public School Academy* [Online]. Available: http://www.wmich.edu/evalctr/

53. Vanourek, G., Manno, B. V., Finn, C. E., Bierlein, L. A. (1997). *Charter schools in action project: Final report, part 1* [Online]. Available: http://www.edexcellence. net/chart/chart1.htm

54. Minimum response rates for the Hudson Institute final report were 70% for students, 40% for parents, and 80% for teachers.

55. Bryn, A., Lee, B., Smith, J. (1990). High school organization and its effects on teachers and students. In W. Cline & J. White (Eds.), *Choice and control in American education* (Vol. 1, pp. 135–226). London: Falmer Press.

56. Cobb, C. (1992). *Responsive schools, renewed communities*. San Francisco: IS Press.
57. Becker, H., Nakagawa, K., Corwin, R. (1997). Parent involvement contracts in California's charter schools: Strategy for educational improvement or method of exclusion. *Teacher's College Record, 98*, 513.
58. SRI International. (1997). *Evaluation of charter school effectiveness: Part 1* [Online]. Available: http://www.lao.ca.gov/sri_charter_schools_1297-part1.html
59. Ibid., p. 21.
60. Mulholland, L. (1999). *Arizona Charter School Progress Evaluation*. Phoenix: Morrison Institute for Public Policy.
61. SRI International. (1997). *Evaluation of charter school effectiveness: Part 1* [Online], p. 21. Available: http://www.lao.ca.gov/sri_charter_schools_1297-part1.html
62. Wells, A. S. (1998). *UCLA charter school study. Beyond the rhetoric of charter school reform: A study of ten California school districts*. Los Angeles: Author.
63. Public Sector Consultants, & MAXIMUS. (1999, February). *Michigan's charter school initiative: From theory to practice* [Online]. p. 51. Available: http://www.mde.state.mi.us
64. Shumow, L., Vandell, D. L., & Kang, K. (1996). School choice, family characteristics, and home-school relations: Contributors to school achievement? *Journal of Educational Psychology, 88*, 451–460.
65. Garn, G., & Stout, R. (1998). *Arizona charter schools*. Unpublished manuscript.
66. Good, T. L., & Braden, J. S. (1998). *Public school superintendents' perceptions of charter schools*. Unpublished manuscript.
67. Wells, A. S. (1998). *UCLA charter school study. Beyond the rhetoric of charter school reform: A study of ten California school districts*. Los Angeles: Author, p. 62.
68. Vanourek, G., Manno, B. V., Finn, C. E., & Bierlein, L. A. (1997). *Charter schools in action project: Final report, part 1*. [Online]. p. 2. Available: http://www.edexcellence.net/chart/chart1.htm
69. Crawford, J. (1998, May). *A comparison of teacher empowerment between charter schools and non-charter schools*. Unpublished dissertation, University of Missouri-Columbia.
70. Short, P. M., & Rinehart, J. S. (1992). School participant empowerment scale: Assessment of levels of empowerment within the school environment. *Educational and Psychological Measurement, 52*, 951–960.
71. Crawford, J. (1998, May). *A comparison of teacher empowerment between charter schools and non-charter schools*. Unpublished dissertation, University of Missouri-Columbia, p. 103.
72. Pack, R. H. (1999). *Charter schools: Innovation, autonomy, and decision-making*. Unpublished dissertation, University of Arizona.
73. Ibid., p. 305.
74. Horn, J., & Miron, G. (1999). *Evaluation of the Michigan Public School Academy* [Online]. Available: http://www.wmich.edu/evalctr/
75. Nelson, F. H. (1997). How much thirty thousand charter schools cost. Paper presented at the 1997 Annual meeting of the American Education Finance Association, Jacksonville, FL [Online]. Available: http://www.aft.org/research/reports/private/chartfin/index.htm

76. Nelson, F. H. (1997). *How much thirty thousand charter schools cost* [Online]. Paper presented at the 1997 Annual Meeting of the American Education Finance Association, Jacksonville, FL. Available: http://www.aft.org/research/reports/private/chartfin/index.htm
77. Ibid.
78. Nelson, F. H. (in preparation). *National charter school finance study.*
79. Ibid.
80. Ibid.
81. Arsen, D. (1999, April). *Charter school spending: autonomous and accountable?* Paper presented at the 1999 Annual Meeting of the American Educational Research Association, Montreal, Canada.
82. Slayton, J. (1998). *School funding in the context of California charter school reform: Legislation versus implementation.* Paper presented at the 1998 Annual Meeting of the American Education Research Association, San Diego, CA, p. 21.
83. Ibid.
    SRI International. (1997). *Evaluation of charter school effectiveness: Part 1* [Online]. Available: http://www.lao.ca.gov/sri_charter_schools_1297-part1.html
84. Wells, A. (1999, Spring). California's charter schools: Promises vs. performance. *American Educator,* 24.
85. Toch, T. (1998, April 27). The new education bazaar. *U.S. News and World Report,* 36.
86. Sarason, S. B. (1998). Charter schools: Another flawed educational reform? New York: Teachers College Press.
    Good, T. L., Clark, S. N., & Clark, D. C. (1997). Reform efforts in American schools: Will faddism continue to impede meaningful change? In B. J. Biddle, T. L. Good, and I. F. Goodson (Eds.), *International handbook of teachers and teaching* (Vol. 2, pp. 1387–1427). Boston: Kluwer.
87. For similar conclusions about requiring competition see F. Howard Nelson. (Spring, 1999). Learning from California. *American Educator,* 22–23.

APPENDIX:
CHARTER SCHOOL RESEARCH

This review of the literature on charter schools is based on several recent studies. Each major study is described briefly.

One of the largest studies of charter schools to date was sponsored by the Department of Education's Office of Educational Research and Improvement (OERI).[1] Research Policy Practice (RPP) International and the University of Minnesota have completed this large-scale study of charter schools over the course of 4 years, from September 1995 to September 1999. We refer to this collaborative contract work as *OERI*. Their purpose was to document and analyze the charter school movement. The first-year report was completed in

May 1997 and was based on a study of charter schools in 10 states: Arizona, 38 schools; California, 83 schools; Colorado, 22 schools; Georgia, 3 schools; Hawaii, 2 schools; Massachusetts, 13 schools; Michigan, 38 schools; Minnesota, 17 schools; New Mexico, 4 schools; and Wisconsin, 5 schools.

In 1998, OERI published its second-year report.[2] This report updated the first-year report and included information from 89% of the 428 charter schools in operation in the 1996–1997 school year. The second-year report also summarized information collected during site visits to 91 charter schools. Some of the issues explored are why charter schools were started, educational programs, financial arrangements, and organizational structures.

OERI published their third-year report in 1999.[3] This reports detailed findings from "three waves of telephone surveys to all cooperating charter schools that were open to children during the 1997–1998 school year, visits to 91 field sites across the country, and extensive analysis of state charter laws."[4] Data are mostly reported from the 1998 surveys; however, when necessary, information was drawn from earlier surveys. Issues explored in this report include trends in the charter school movement in general, characteristics of charter schools (particularly those opening in 1997–1998) and students, and autonomy and accountability in charter schools.

Concomitant with the first OERI study, Tom Good, Jennifer Braden, and Sharon Nichols completed a National Charter School Survey supported by a small grant from the Spencer Foundation.[5] The purpose of this national study was to survey charter school administrators ($n = 86$ schools) in order to obtain (a) unique and important goals that charter school founders advocated, (b) demographic information, (c) descriptions of core program components, and (d) information on their beliefs regarding noncharter public schools. Good and his colleagues attempted to capture the intent of the charter school movement as reported by charter school directors.

Chester Finn, Bruno Manno, and Louann Bierlein reported in 1996 on their field work conducted in 1995–1996.[6] They interviewed over 700 people including charter school operators and people employed in the state departments of education. The research team visited 43 charter schools in seven states. Detailed information was collected on roughly 35 schools. They noted that site visits took place in approximately a day and a half.

In the second year, site visits were made to 45 charter schools across 13 states. Seventeen of these schools had been visited in the previous years and an additional 18 schools that had been visited in 1995–1996 participated in a follow-up telephone interview. In the second year, surveys were administered to parents, students, and teachers in charter schools. The analysis used 4,954 students (fifth grade and older) drawn from 39 schools, 2,978 parents of students attending 30 different schools, and a sample of 521 teachers drawn from 36 schools. The results from the follow-up report were presented in six "final" reports. We refer to this data source as the Hudson Institute final report.[7]

Casey Cobb and Gene Glass studied the extent to which charter schools in Arizona were contributing to the segregation of students using matched pairs of 55 urban schools and 57 rural schools.[8] They published their report in 1999 and concluded that Arizona charter schools were more ethnically segregated than traditional public schools.

Greg Garn and Robert Stout (with support from the Arizona School Board Association) analyzed the applications that schools submitted to obtain charter status in Arizona.[9] All 46 schools that were approved for the 1995–1996 school year were analyzed. They conducted site visits at over half of these schools and conducted interviews with the director or head administrator of each school. The authors also had informal conversations with parents, faculty, and staff and examined records and status reports filed with the state superintendent for public instruction.

Lori Mulholland in 1999 completed a report (sponsored by the Arizona Department of Education) evaluating the progress of Arizona charter schools.[10] Eighty-two charter schools were studied, including 303 parents, 171 students, 123 teachers, and 54 directors. Participants completed surveys concerning charter schools, interviews were held with several people who held policy-making positions, and 14 focus groups were held with parents, students, teachers, and directors of charter schools.

Tom Good and Jennifer Braden completed a study in 1998 examining whether public school superintendents in Arizona felt that they were receiving usable information from charter schools and public school superintendents' perceptions about what charter schools offered to public education. Each of the 244 public school superintendents in Arizona received surveys and 28% responded.[11]

SRI International, under contract with the Legislative Analyst's Office of the State of California released a charter school report in 1997.[12] This report presented preliminary findings on the effectiveness of California charter schools. The SRI study included an examination of (a) educational performance of students in charter schools versus noncharter public schools; (b) characteristics of charter schools including student body, educational programs, and finance; and (c) the association of certain practices or characteristics of charter schools with student outcomes. In addition, 11 charter schools were randomly selected as case studies from a population of 50 charter schools that had been in operation for 2½ years to ensure that schools had been given an opportunity to implement their educational program.

Another study of California charter schools was conducted by Amy Stuart Wells and her colleagues at UCLA.[13] The 2½ year study released in 1998 contrasted the claims of charter school advocates with the day-to-day occurrences in charter schools as reported by educators, parents, students, and noncharter public schools. Topics studied included accountability, choice, competition, and models of innovation. Seventeen charter schools from 10 school districts in California were used as case studies. Also, extensive interviews were conducted with policymakers to assess various beliefs about charter schools.

Also in California, Henry Becker, Kathryn Nakagawa, and Ronald Corwin studied parent involvement contracts.[14] They considered both the possible positive effects of parent involvement and the possibility that parent contracts in charter schools were used to restrict enrollment for certain types of children (e.g., of parents who cannot or are unwilling to perform required duties). The 45 charter schools opened by the fall of 1994 that served elementary or middle school students were surveyed. Thirty-four charter schools and 23 parent contracts were used in analysis.

Christy Dykgraaf and Shirley Lewis studied charter schools in the Grand Rapids metropolitan area.[15] The area contained 15 charter schools, and 11 of these were run by for-profit corporations. Research focused on the 11 for-profit schools and addressed three questions: How do cost cutting strategies impact areas such as transportation, special education, and the socioeconomic mix of students? Is there adequate communication between school managers and the stakeholders they serve? Does for-profit management shift ownership of public schools from the public domain to the private?

In 1996, the Michigan legislature required that two independent evaluations be completed on charter schools in the state. As a part of this initiative, Jerry Horn and Gary Miron released a 1999 study entitled "Evaluation of the Michigan Public School Academy Initiative."[16] These investigators studied about half the charter schools in Michigan (excluding those in southeastern Michigan).[17] Authors evaluated charter schools with regard to goal fulfillment and processes used in charter schools and also provided charter schools, parents, and students with information on the performance of their specific charter schools relative to other schools.

The companion report on Michigan's charter schools was prepared by Public Sector Consulting Incorporated and MAXIMUS, Inc.[18] The researchers addressed three general questions: Are charter schools meeting basic requirements including improving achievement, stimulating innovation, achieving school accountability, and providing parents and students with greater choice? Are the processes related to creating and monitoring charter schools effective? How can charter schools be informed of innovation and how can parents and students be informed about the effectiveness of charter schools? The report studied charter schools in 9 counties in the southeastern area of Michigan, and included many schools from the Detroit metropolitan center.

James Crawford studied charter and noncharter school teachers in Colorado and Michigan.[19] In particular, he sampled schools that had enrollments greater than 200, and in total, he collected information from 202 charter school teachers and 185 noncharter school teachers. He chose Michigan and Colorado teachers because of the strong legislation in those states that presumably leads to greater opportunity for autonomy, which he hypothesized might be related to teacher empowerment.

Robert Pack completed an observational study of two California charter schools.[20] He studied a new, or start-up, school and a conversion school that had been in operation for 70 years and had just been given charter status earlier in the school year. The schools had overlapping grades (7 to 9), and both schools emphasized the same curricular program (which many consider to be an innovative curriculum). These data focus on only two of the many charter schools that are operating and in no way could be considered representative. Still, 79 of 80 teachers in the two schools agreed voluntarily to participate in this study.[21]

Two other recent studies focused exclusively on charter school finances. We integrate the work of F. Howard Nelson[22] and David Arsen.[23] The National Financial Charter School Study directed by F. Howard Nelson provided a comprehensive, comparative study of public school and charter public school financing.[24] The report provided extensive information about various topics including the extent (a) to which states provide capital funds for charter schools, (b) that low-income students and special education students are funded on the same basis in charter and noncharter public schools, and (c) to which start-up funds are available and whether charter schools' teachers are required to participate in teacher state retirement systems. Readers are referred to that source for detailed analysis.

Appendix Endnotes

1. RPP International, & The University of Minnesota. (1997). *A national study of charter schools: First-year report*. Washington, DC: U.S. Department of Education, Office of Educational Research and Improvement.

2. RPP International. (1998). *A national study of charter schools: Second-year report*. Washington, DC: U.S. Department of Education, Office of Educational Research and Improvement.

3. RPP International, & The University of Minnesota. (1999). *The state of charter schools: Third-year report*. Washington, DC: U.S. Department of Education, Office of Educational Research and Improvement.

4. Ibid., p. 6.

5. Good, T. L., Braden, J. S., & Nichols, S. L. (1997). *Charter schools: Promising alternatives for educational reform or an illusionary panacea*. [Online]. Available: http://www.apa.org/ed/charter.html

6. Finn, C., Manno, B., & Bierlein, L. (1996). *Charter schools in action: What have we learned?* Indianapolis, IN: Hudson Institute.

7. Vanourek, G., Manno, B. V., Finn, C. E., & Bierlein, L. A. (1997). *Charter schools in action project: Final report, part 1* [Online]. Available: http://www.edexcellence.net/chart/chart1.htm
   Finn, C. E., Manno, B. V., Bierlein, L. A., & Vanourek, G. (1997). *Charter schools in action project: Final report, part II* [Online]. Available: http://www.edexcellence.net/chart/chart2.htm
   Finn, C. E., Manno, B. V., Bierlein, L. A., & Vanourek, G. (1997). *Charter schools in action project: Final report, part III* [Online]. Available: http://www.edexcellence.net/chart/chart3.htm
   Manno, B. V., Finn, C. E., Bierlein, L. A., & Vanourek, G. (1997). *Charter schools in action project: Final report, part IV* [Online]. Available: http://www.edexcellence.net/chart/chart4.htm
   Vanourek, G., Manno, B. V., Finn, C. E., & Bierlein, L. A. (1997). *Charter schools in action project: Final report, part V* [Online]. Available: http://www.edexcellence.net/chart/chart5.htm
   Manno, B. V., Finn, C. E., Bierlein, L. A., & Vanourek, G. (1997). *Charter schools in action project: Final report, part VI* [Online]. Available: http://www.edexcellence.net/chart/chart6.htm

8. Cobb, C., & Glass, G. (1999). Ethnic segregation in Arizona charter schools. *Education Policy Analysis Archives* 7(1), 8. [Online]. Available: http://olam.ed.asu.edu/epaa.v7n1

9. Garn, G., & Stout, R. (1998). *Arizona charter schools*. Unpublished manuscript

10. Mulholland, L. (1999, March). *Arizona charter school progress evaluation*. Phoenix: Morrison Institute for Public Policy.

11. Good, T. L., & Braden, J. S. (1998). *Public school superintendents' perceptions of charter schools*. Unpublished manuscript.

12. Powell, J., Blackorby, J., Marsh, J., Finnegan, K., & Anderson, L. (1997). *Evaluation of charter school effectiveness—Part I* [Online]. Available: http://www.lao.ca.gov/sri_ charter_schools_ 1297-part1.html
Powell, J., Blackorby, J., Marsh, J., Finnegan, K., & Anderson, L. (1997). *Evaluation of charter school effectiveness—Part II.* [Online]. Available: http://www.lao.ca.gov/sri_ charter_schools_1297-part2.html

13. Wells, A. S. (1998). *UCLA charter school study. Beyond the rhetoric of charter school reform: A study of ten California school districts.* Los Angeles: Author.
Written with Ligia Artiles, Sibyll Carnochan, Camille Wilson Cooper, Cynthia Grutzik, Jennifer Jellison Holme, Alejandra Lopez, Janelle Scott, Julie Slayton, and Ash Vasudeva.

14. Becker, H., Nakagawa, K., & Corwin, R. (1997). Parent involvement contracts in California's charter schools: Strategy for educational improvement or method of exclusion. *Teacher's College Record, 98,* 511–536.

15. Dykgraaf, C. L., & Lewis, S. K. (1998, October). For-profit charter schools: What the public needs to know. *Educational Leadership,* 51–53.

16. Horn, J., & Miron, G. (1999). *Evaluation of the Michigan Public School Academy* [Online]. Available: http://www.wmich.edu/evalctr

17. In Michigan the term *charter school* is synonymous with public school academies (PSAs).

18. Public Sector Consultants & MAXIMUS. (1999, February). *Michigan's charter school initiative: From theory to practice* [Online]. Available: http://www. mde.state.mi.us

19. Crawford, J. (1998, May). *A comparison of teacher empowerment between charter schools and non-charter schools.* Unpublished dissertation, University of Missouri-Columbia.

20. Pack, R. H. (1999). Charter schools: Innovation, autonomy, and decision-making. Unpublished dissertation, University of Arizona.

21. Dissertations from James Crawford and Robert Pack arrived as we were finalizing manuscript copy. We were pleased by their willingness to share their materials with us and have integrated some of their work into the discussion here. Time constraints prevented a more extensive examination, and we encourage readers to seek out these primary sources.

22. Nelson, F. H. (1997). *How much thirty thousand charter schools cost.* Paper presented at the 1997 Annual Meeting of the American Education Finance Association, Jacksonville, FL [Online]. Available: http://www.aft.org/research/reports/private/chartfin/index.htm

23. Arsen, D. (1999, April). *Charter school spending: Autonomous and accountable?* Paper presented at the 1999 Annual Meeting of the American Educational Research Association, Montreal, Canada.

24. Nelson, F. H. (In progress). *National financial charter school study.*

Chapter 7

Charter Schools:
Some of the Best and Worst
in American Education

It is estimated that more than 1,300 charter schools now allow students in the 29 states with charter schools to select a public school of their choice. As of July 1999, 36 states and the District of Columbia had charter school enabling legislation. Charter schools continue to grow rapidly. For example, the first eight charter schools in New York state were recently approved,[1] in Arkansas, new legislation was recently passed to allow charter school development,[2] and most recently several states have made the chartering process even easier. For example, New Mexico raised its cap on charter schools from 5 to 100 over the next 5 years, and Minnesota made it easier for existing schools to convert to charter status.[3]

In chapters 5 and 6, we discussed charter schools and their effects on students as described by research reports. Here we present charter schools on a concrete level and, accordingly, move to both a discussion of some particular schools and an analysis of their general efficacy as reported by journalists and other informal sources.

Although we discuss specific schools, we are not attempting to identify the best charter schools. Instead, we are trying to identify schools, approaches, or practices that seem useful or creative. Success is difficult to validate. It may take several years before we see if any school is truly successful in maintaining a niche for particular students who want to achieve particular goals.

Similarly, we do not attempt to identify the worst charter schools but to discuss issues that have emerged as problematic. If a charter school closes in midyear, if someone hires a relative at a salary far above market, or if money is used for personal gain in unethical ways, it is easy to say that the school is not successful. Establishing prima facie evidence for failure is considerably easier than for success.

Earlier we noted that the media at large has helped to create a misperception of schools. It is a well-established finding that when citizens describe the schools they know, they rate them highly. But, when rating schools known only through media reports, they grade them markedly lower. Some have labeled this tendency to trust local schools more than schools elsewhere as "media induced."[4]

Why then do we include media reports if we feel they are often incomplete or biased? First, the media is an important part of the current debate on public education. It disseminates news that citizens use to form opinions. Thus, it is prudent to see the media's position on charter schools. In the current climate in which education is politicized, a generally consistent media presentation, unfortunately, may have as much impact as demonstrated fact.

Second, the media is not a monolithic block, and although some may have a bias for reporting problems and sensationalism, other journalists share thoughtful and insightful perspectives. Third, some of the media have become experts on education through their continual visits to and study of schools. Fourth, there is a paucity of systematic observational work in the literature. Still, we do not want to leave the reader with any impression other than that accounts of charter schools in this chapter are simply media reports with all the strengths and weaknesses involved in such reporting.

Media writers, like educational researchers, have recorded their perceptions that charter schools represent a wide range of quality. Thomas Toch wrote, "the best charter schools pursue innovation and educational excellence with an enthusiasm sorely lacking in many traditional schools. But these schools are the minority. Much more common are schools with problems as bad as—and in some cases worse than—those found in traditional public schools."[5]

Toch, studying charter schools in Arizona and Michigan (two states that passed charter school legislation early in the movement), reported that a few schools were interesting examples of reform. For example, in Michigan, a secondary school created by the Henry Ford Motor Company allowed students to study museums' technology exhibits as an important part of the curriculum. Toch contended that a few schools have become specialized "power houses" including "Sankofa Shule, an Afro-centric Elementary School in Lansing, Mich., that includes instruction in four languages, and the Arizona School for the Arts, a junior/senior high school in Phoenix that couples a half-day program in arts with college-prep curriculum."[6]

Toch reported that in the worst instances, charter schools show problems rarely encountered in traditional public schools. He concluded, "in scores of charters in Arizona and Michigan, curricula and teaching are weak, buildings are substandard, and financial abuses are surprisingly prevalent."[7] He noted that roughly half of Arizona charter schools are high schools, most of which are managed by chains. He further noted:

> These companies take advantage of the fact that Arizona requires high school students to attend only four hours of school a day. They target kids on the margins of traditional public schools—lower achievers, discipline problems, truants—with pledges of swift and simple routes to graduation. And many of the companies increase their revenues by running two or three 4-hour sessions a day and substituting self-paced computer instruction for regular teaching staff.[8]

It is especially unfortunate that students who have demonstrated limited skills for learning from others are essentially taught in social isolation.

After we explore positive and negative examples of charter schools from other media sources, we turn to a more complex task: What can we do to improve charter school legislation and functioning? Based on the formal and informal evidence presented here and in chapters 5 and 6, we discuss recommendations for parents to help them in the difficult task of choosing an appropriate school for their child. We make several recommendations to state legislators, policymakers, and state departments of education for improving charter school legislation and oversight in general.

We argue that existing charter legislation and especially recently reversed charter laws are increasingly making it easier for charter schools to open. We urge legislators to become more concerned about program quality and protecting children's rights and to de-emphasize the rush to increase the quantity of charter schools.

POSITIVE MEDIA EXAMPLES
OF CHARTER SCHOOLS

As we have stressed throughout this book, charter schools represent wide variability in terms of innovation, achievement, and overall quality, but some schools appear notable in designing innovative features or in working with children not served well by the current system. Again, it is not our intention to contend that these are success stories, but rather schools that at one point were attempting to implement a distinctive program.

Laurent Clerc Elementary School

In Tucson, Arizona, the Laurent Clerc Elementary School provides an example of an innovative charter school. The special focus of this school is the education of deaf students, although those attending the school include both deaf and hearing students. They use a curricular focus based on research in bilingualism; specifically, they are assisting students in becoming proficient in American Sign Language, transferring ASL into a hybrid language called *gloss*, and then writing in Standard English. Techniques used at Laurent Clerc are based on research and include teaching students an alphabet of 31 symbols to help children sound out words spatially and recognize them as words they know in ASL. The techniques and model provided by this school have been recognized nationally by educators of individuals who are deaf.

The school provides a social environment for deaf children that they are not often afforded. Historically, deaf children have been educated in an environment that isolates them from hearing students. At Laurent Clerc, deaf and hearing children are educated together. Additionally, the faculty at the Laurent Clerc school documents their techniques and progress so that other educators of deaf individuals can learn from their experiences.

Laurent Clerc is also a model in dissemination of innovative ideas; local Tucson schools are using methods developed at Laurent Clerc.[9] For example, in the past, public schools have not provided deaf students with direct instruction in American Sign Language. However, based on methods developed at Laurent Clerc, local noncharter public school teachers are teaching both American Sign Language and Standard English, avoiding the use of slang, and avoiding the practice of speaking and signing simultaneously. One result of past shoddy teaching methods for deaf individuals is that their SAT reading scores plateaued around the fourth-grade level. So by developing, documenting, and disseminating techniques developed at Laurent Clerc, educators are supporting a movement toward increased literacy and achievement for deaf children.

The Charter School of Wilmington

Another distinctive school is the Charter School of Wilmington, in Delaware. The school is small and self-described as a school for students who want to engage in serious scholarship.

> It gives out academic letters as well as athletic ones and holds an annual academic banquet for students who make the honor roll. Students must take 24 courses to graduate rather than the 19 or 20 normally required in the district and 10 math and science courses rather than the usual 6 or 8.[10]

Given the existing school culture in which athletes are given attention and status not afforded to other students, it is edifying to see a school that is trying to recognize and embrace academic achievement.

In line with the serious academic focus, students are expected to be respectful and attentive. Instruction takes place with students in rows and teachers standing in front of the room. This school, in contrast to following a new, innovative model, is actually considered old-fashioned by today's standards, and so focuses attention on the problems of defining *innovation*. Is a return to earlier models innovative?

One aspect of the school is clearly innovative, in that it is sponsored by six of Delaware's major employers including DuPont and Bell Atlantic. Through this link with local employers, the Charter School of Wilmington has been able to supplement their budget allocation from the state.[11]

O'Farrell Community School

The O'Farrell Community School, located in San Diego, California, also takes an innovative approach to schooling. At O'Farrell the goal is to prepare sixth, seventh, and eighth graders to take a college preparatory curriculum on entering high school. The school provides an enriched interdisciplinary curriculum without tracking students by ability. Each student is a part of an "educational family" for instruction. All students maintain portfolios and complete community service.

The administrative structure at O'Farrell is also unique. There is not a traditional principal, vice principal, or school counselor. Instead, there is "a 'chief educational officer' (CEO) who is also referred to as 'keeper of the dream'."[12] The school includes a "family support area" from which psychologists, social workers, and representatives from a variety of social agencies work. By raising additional funds, they have been able to employ a gardener and to purchase additional facilities.

Minnesota New Country Charter School

The Minnesota New Country Charter School is a year round school that is based on five principles: "Extensive parent involvement, teacher/student accountability, use of the community as a place to learn, enhanced technology, and the Essential Principles of the coalition of Essential Schools."[13] Students work through a competency-based curriculum using a curriculum guide and completing projects in 9 curricular areas (arts, math, earth systems, communications, citizenship, technology, personal management, problem solving, and lifelong learning). Teachers work as facilitators and advise groups of students on projects, consult with parents, and assess progress.

> Each student and her or his parent meets with an advisor in August to develop an individual learning plan for the coming year. This plan is a guide for the student's intellectual, social, and physical growth ... Each personal learning plan includes a series of objectives that must be achieved through a variety of learning activities that are self-directed and connected to real-world experiences.[14]

Technology is a central part of the education at the New Country School. There is one computer for every two students, and all computers are networked and have Internet access.

The school is run by a parent–teacher school board. In addition, several teachers and original founders have created a corporation, EdVisions Cooperative, that "contracts with the charter board to handle personnel, staff development, and other services."[15] The Le-Sueur-Henderson school board, the chartering agency, has reportedly learned from the innovations and experiences of the Minnesota New Country Charter School, and based on what they've learned, they have implemented changes in the traditional public schools in this area.[16] For example, teachers from the LeSueur-Henderson school district have attended in-service programs at the Minnesota New Country Charter School to learn more about using computers.

Nataki Talibah Schoolhouse

The Nataki Talibah School in Detroit, Michigan, with a focus on social studies, hands on science, and arts, serves only minority students. The approach to curriculum is "teach from the norm." In this way, the school integrates subjects like African American history into the curriculum without placing abnormal emphasis on it. Students at this school have performed well in terms of public, private, and charter schools in the state. The principal, Carmen N'Namdi, attributes this success to the school's long history. Although the school has been a charter school for only 4 years, it was a well-established private school before seeking charter status.

This school is notable for its high test scores in light of the general lagging performance of students in other schools in Michigan. For example, Hornbeck reported:

> Nataki Talibah scored 68.8 percent in the 1997–98 fifth-grade science test; public and private schools, by comparison, scored 40 percent on that test. The charter school average was 27 percent. Nataki Talibah students did even better when it came to writing. They scored a perfect 100 percent, while private schools scored 69 percent, public schools scored 64 percent and the charter schools averaged 57 percent.[17]

Reactions to Positive Reviews

These examples of seemingly unique or innovative programs show good schools working; the fact remains, however, that all of these programs either have been or could be realized within the traditional public school system. For example, Gary Orfield noted:

> Magnet schools ... have been in operation for more than 20 years and offer many of the same possibilities as charters but more equitably and on a larger scale. Most of these schools provide transportation for students who can't get there themselves. And magnet schools are usually committed to helping achieve successful voluntary desegregation.[18]

Further, charter schools are fodder for those seeking to spread a prejudiced or troubling educational approach:

> A charter, after all, is not an educational program. It is a school that uses public money to advance a privately defined vision of education. In one

school that vision may be a positive plan put into place by dedicated teachers. In another, a biased or sectarian group may have a disturbing agenda.[19]

We agree with Orfield that a charter is not a program but a school; however, he perhaps overestimates the practical difficulty of getting a consensus on a schoolwide theme. Structurally, the charter legislation allows like-minded individuals to easily get together. Moreover, it is possible to argue that perhaps in time charter schools will prove to be of value because of their ability to attract new and talented people to the field of education from other disciplines and occupations. However, we share Orfield's basic observation that charter schools to date have not been very innovative, and because of this and other considerations identified in chapter 6, we restate that overall the charter school investment stands closer to being a wasteful experiment than an informative one.

PROBLEMATIC CHARTER SCHOOLS AND PRACTICES

Some charter schools have received public admonishment. Criticism has taken many forms and has spanned such areas as finance, school closings, and the use of management companies to run charter schools. We now turn to a discussion of various charter school problems reported by journalists.

Management Companies

The Edison Project is a management company that runs for-profit schools.[20] Founded by Chris Whittle, Edison runs schools through contracts with local school boards. Started in 1995 with four schools that educated 3,000 students, there are currently 51 Edison schools that educate 24,000 students. Approximately one-third of these schools are charter schools. The other two-thirds operate on a contract between Edison and a local school board. Among other advantages, the Edison schools offer longer school days, longer school years, and enhanced access to technology. Two-thirds of students who attend Edison schools qualify for free or reduced-price lunch; thus, it appears that these schools attract students from lower income families.

Tamar Lewin, writing for *The New York Times,* reported that although Edison schools are growing in popularity, they really do not represent anything new in education. Moreover, although the Edison Project claims to improve student achievement, the data are far from clear: "these data are a hodgepodge, some following a group of students from fall to spring, or grade to grade while others compare one year's third graders with the next year's."[21] Despite this, the Edison Project continues to expand.

Charter schools managed by for-profit companies in Massachusetts represent some of the worst schools for providing special education. They actively denied enrollment and "counseled out" students with disabilities prior to enrollment.[22] Nancy Zollers and Arun Ramanathan reported that these for profit schools, in particular those schools run by the Edison company, served fewer students with severe and complicated disabilities. In addition, they noted that parents of disabled students reported that when trying to enroll their child in one of these schools, school officials convinced them that their child would be better served in noncharter public schools, effectively counseling them out of enrolling in the charter school. Parents who managed to enroll their children frequently had to transfer them back to traditional public schools because of pressure from the charter school. In fact, 61 students with disabilities who enrolled in the two Massachusetts Edison schools, have left to return to noncharter public schools. In contrast, in not-for-profit charter schools, only two students with disabilities have left.

Children with behavior problems are reported to get particularly shoddy treatment in Massachusetts, at times being isolated from other students for extended periods of time. The charter schools advertised inclusive education, but what they provided was far from the type of inclusive education special educators advocate. Students frequently were either placed in typical classrooms with little or no support or removed from the classroom to resource rooms until they caught up to other students. Although clearly in violation of state and federal special education legislation, the charter schools continued these practices unimpeded. Regardless, these schools benefited financially because of the state funding formula that is based on public schools, which receive funding to cover special education, bilingual, and at-risk students. So, based on the population served in these for-profit charter schools, they were overfunded by the state. Although many parents and students report increased levels of satisfaction with charter schools run by management companies, they undoubtedly are not parents of or students with disabilities.

Unfortunately, the mechanism for parents to complain about charter schools was also riddled with difficulties. In theory Massachusetts charter schools are expected to obtain a charter before shopping for a management company (charters cannot be granted directly to management companies). In practice, the management companies solicit individuals to develop charters that the company then administers once the charter is granted. As a result, the charter school board of directors is not made up of impartial individuals trying to provide the best education to students but of individuals chosen by management companies, who are highly unlikely to fire a management company for mismanagement. Zollers and Ramanathan concluded:

> Unfortunately, the basic interest of these schools in making a profit has often been incompatible with offering an appropriate education to students who require expensive supports and services. To parents of these students, for-profit charter schools do not represent a choice. If the politicians and the state officials who support the for-profit charter school concept are going to give parents this choice, they must protect parents' rights by enforcing federal and state laws.[23]

A reported case of the "tail wagging the dog" was documented in Michigan. Horn and Miron reported that Michigan charter schools (called PSAs in Michigan) often existed primarily for management companies to make a profit. The evaluators concluded:

> While the logical development of the relationship between a PSA and a management company develops when the PSA searches for a management company to provide for its particular needs, we are not so aware of the increasing phenomenon of management companies who go in search of a "community" to host its schools. In fact, at several schools, we were informed that the impetus behind the school was not a local group of parents or educators; rather, it was the *management company*.[24]

Finance

One of the most perplexing issues in the charter school movement is that often charter schools are granted charters even when those who seek the charter have no business plan or even a leased property. Few banks would make loans to a business or an individual that did not have careful plans, and it seems inconceivable that a bank would turn over capital to a business that did not have a contingent rental agreement. Yet, many states have turned over funds for educating students when the charter school did not even have a property lease agreement in hand and before the state ensured that the facilities were safe, appropriate, and handicap accessible. Other financial issues concerning how charter schools use public dollars are questionable as well. Some appear to be wrong, decidedly unethical; others are in the "gray" area. That is, in these cases, no one is embezzling money or engaging in acts of nepotism, but the use of public dollars is atypical.

We start with some gray issues. For instance, the small Higley Elementary Schools District in Arizona has chartered 24 schools across the state. Charter schools in Arizona pay the sponsor district a fee for granting the charter school. These figures can vary widely from district to district. In the Higley Elementary Schools District, the fee was on a sliding schedule, so that districts paid a shrinking percentage as the number of students enrolled increased. In this case, if the charter school received $150,000 in state aid, they paid the sponsoring agent 10% of their funding; if the charter school received $2 million in support, the sponsor received 4%. To obtain a charter contract from Higley ESD, charter schools paid from a minimum of $9,600 up to $100,000.[25]

Larry C. Likes, the superintendent of the school district, has indicated that his primary motivation for chartering other schools was because of the financial difficulties in his own district:

> But we've been terribly cash-strapped for years, and if this was a way to get us the technology we needed, I was willing to take a look. When parents here were getting into this whole charter thing, I told them it was to pay for our computers, and they were satisfied.[26]

Certainly Mr. Likes has laudable intentions, to get money for his school district. However, on the other side of the ledger, he now has charter schools that he has at least paper responsibility for monitoring, including the putative need to visit schools throughout the state of Arizona and the necessity of answering phone calls from charter school directors who must deal with various problems (e.g., a principal leaving in midyear, deciding whether to go to a full-day kindergarten program).

Many would contend that a school district should not be pushed to the point where in order to get technology it must monitor other schools that have diverse programs and are scattered across the state.

Others would hope that Mr. Likes attend primarily to developing and supporting educational programs within his own district; after all, he has a full time job. Some probably would say that if there is no other way to obtain the money, then this is an innovative strategy for funding his school district. Still others might question his qualifications for supervising other schools.

Elsewhere it has been reported that two schools decided to obtain charter status because they had more teachers at the lower end of the salary schedule—their charter status got them funded as if they had average teacher costs. In another city, a higher SES school with an average cost faculty and few at-risk or special education students went to charter status because the charter law paid the costs of special education and at-risk pupils for the entire system.[27]

Converting from regular public school status to charter public school status can be profitable, but converting from a private school can be even more profitable. For example, William and Mary Delaney owned and operated a private elementary school in Michigan, and when they converted it to a public charter school in 1996, they began to charge the school district $200,000 a year in rent. It was estimated that the per-foot rental rate was about three times greater than that paid by several public schools and another charter school in that same geographical area.[28] More generally, Toch found roughly 20% of Arizona charter schools and 50% of Michigan charter schools were former private schools that converted to charter status primarily as a way to raise revenue.

The literature provides many more clear examples of financial controversy and scandalous behavior associated with charter schools. In 1998, Howard Blume and Kevin Uhrich reported that the Cato School of Reason used its public charter status to obtain millions of dollars in state apportioned money.[29] The Cato organization claimed to enroll hundreds of students who were either being home schooled by parents or attending private schools. When working with parents it was alleged that the Cato school provided minimal services and pocketed the rest of the state subsidy. When dealing with private school directors, Cato arranged to split state proceeds with individual schools.

The Cato School was created by Thomas A. Cosgrove, who was in his 60s before he obtained a teaching credential (in the 1990s). At the time he started his charter school, his educational experience was limited to student teaching and limited work as a substitute teacher. The growth of Cato (and Cosgrove) has been phenomenal. Blume and Uhrich reported:

In the 1996–1997 school year, Cato took in 3.9 million in government educational funds based on payments of about $20 per day per student. Just 56% of that money went to programs and expenses, giving Cato a whopping 1.7 million surplus for the year, and year-end reserves totaling two million. The following year was better still, with the school obtaining the 7 million dollar mark in revenues nearly doubling its take of state education funds.[30]

Further, some of the school expenses for operation are payments for administrative costs (in 1996–1997 totaling more than $320,000, which went to Cato's corporate parent, the Education Foundation for Ethics and Principles, a nonprofit organization formed and controlled by Cosgrove).

Initially, Cato's clients were parents already teaching their own children. For joining Cato, they received free books (which were often outdated and from a free source also available to the parents), sometimes computers and Internet access. Thus, for parents who were already home schooling, the deal seemed extremely attractive in that they received free assistance for something they would have had to pay for otherwise. At the same time, Cosgrove received virtually full state funding for students, about $3,600 per year. Moreover, Cosgrove did not have to pay teacher salaries or employee benefits or physically maintain classrooms.

After his initial success with parents, Cosgrove began to affiliate with already established private schools in order to build the clientele base more quickly. Many of these private schools were receiving not only money from parents for services but also funds from Cato for affiliating with his school operation. Although obtaining financial records was difficult (Cosgrove claimed to be a private business), Blume and Uhrich were able to document some specific instances of possible abuse (e.g., a draft letter that Cosgrove sent to the Orange Crescent School in Garden Grove, proposing to split state funding down the middle with Orange Crescent).

Similarly, in August 1998, an Arizona newspaper ran a five-part series on Arizona's charter school experiment entitled "Guinea Kids."[31] The paper noted that the state allowed for charter schools (a) to be staffed by poorly educated teachers, (b) to be directed by people with little or no business experience, (c) to take ownership of land building and buses that were purchased with tax payer dollars, and (d) to operate with virtually no monitoring from the State Department of Education. Kirk Mitchell wrote:

The guineas would move on to Noah Webster Charter School in Mesa where, like Sequoia, they would lease land to the school and hire their family members. At Noah Webster, Glen Gaddie earned $64,200 as director, another sister, Lisa Davies makes $28,355 as a teacher. Delite Gaddie is office accountant for $15,000 a year, and Ernest Gaddie makes $36,667 as teacher/custodian. The school employs four of Glen Gaddie's children and his wife as book keepers, maintenance workers, and part-time office staff. The school also employees Glen Gaddie's third sister, Laura Jonas for $19, 921 and her husband, David Jonas, Jr. for $18,340. None of the Gaddie family members has a college degree save Glen Gaddie.[32]

Glen Gaddie eventually was bought out of ownership by other board members, and he moved on to greener pastures at Nora Webster Charter School in Mesa.

There were many other grand sweeps winners in the Arizona charter school giveaway. Mitchell noted that Sandra Houston was given $3 million from the state of Arizona to run two charter schools and to educate 300 students. Mitchell reported:

Had the state board for charter schools made even a cursory check of Houston's resume you would have learned that her liberal arts degree from Susan B. Anthony University is mere paper—the product of a noncertified Midwest school. Houston attended no classes at Susan B. Anthony. She took no tests. She never even stepped foot in Missouri where the schools is located. She acknowledged all.[33]

Still, in fairness to the state board, Arizona law does not require charter school teachers or directors to have teacher certification or a college degree. Hence, the absence of a degree would not have provided a basis for refusing to grant the charter.

In May 1999, the Arizona Department of Education requested $18.8 million in supplemental funds to help them make the June apportionment payment to Arizona schools.[34] Part of the reason for this shortage of funds was transportation costs for district-sponsored charter schools. Because of a loophole in Arizona state legislation, charter schools were able to bill the state for miles driven by private vehicles. Using the transportation funding formula, the state Department of Education was charged up to $1.95 for every route mile generated by district-sponsored charter schools or school districts. When these miles were driven by private vehicles, they multiplied quickly. This transportation problem has led to the state's owing $4 million more than anticipated.

Competition

As an example of the theory gone awry that charter schools will compete with noncharter public schools to the betterment of noncharter public schools, the Inkster, Michigan school district may be closed down because of financial difficulties stemming from the loss of students to charter schools. "The exodus of students—and dollars ... could eventually mean closure or state takeover of the entire district."[35] The Inkster district admittedly had problems, including poor test scores, fiscal and management difficulties, and declining enrollment, but the introduction of charter schools into the area quickly pushed them closer to collapse instead of helping the system (through competition) to improve.

It can be argued that the community is better off because the competitive charter school environment resulted in the closing of poor schools and the continuation of better schools. However, the charter schools in Inkster can not currently accommodate the entire population of Inkster students, so if the public schools close due to financial difficulties, many students will be left temporarily without a school. Moreover, if one of the Inkster charter schools fails and there are no public schools, there will be no place for students to go. In addition, some charter school advocates do not want charter schools to be seen as a replacement for public schools but rather as an alternative. Dan Quisneberry, president of the Michigan Association of Public School Academies noted, "Charter schools are the lifeboats, not the iceberg."[36]

Special Education

Special education has proven to be a problematic issue for charter schools. As one example, the Children's Academy of Arizona was designed to meet the needs of special education students. However, Sarah Tully Tapia reported:

> Children's Academy of Arizona's Tucson campus has been the target of more special-education complaints—seven—than apparently any other Pima County public school in the past two school years. The Arizona Department of Education has received complaints about the

2-year-old school ranging from failing to evaluate children to failing to give them services on time.[37]

The school directors attribute the problems to a variety of causes, including not receiving records from previous schools in a timely fashion to not being prepared to handle special education when the school first opened. Unfortunately, these difficulties had negative impacts on students attending the school. For example, "one boy's reading skills slipped back three months in almost two years at the school."[40]

Some of the complaints that have been lodged against the school include the following. One parent complained because the school refused to initiate her sons' individualized education plan. The complaint had to be taken to a due process hearing to force the school to serve the student.[39] Another parent withdrew her child and filed a complaint when the school dismissed her daughter's diagnosis of attention deficit disorder, motor skills problems, and counseling needs saying "doctors always want to find something wrong and that one test on one day by one psychologist didn't really mean anything."[40]

The Children's Academy Charter School in Phoenix had similar problems. One parent sued the school after they refused to enroll her son who has AIDS and uses a wheelchair. The director of the school, Reginald Barr, claimed that they could not accommodate this student because the school was not wheelchair accessible; however, the student's lawyer, Jerri Katzerman pointed out, "that's beside the point—all public schools must be accessible to the disabled."[41]

School Closings

The Window Rock Unified School District in Arizona entered the business of "selling" charters in order to bolster the districts' financial position. However, this practice resulted in the development of several charter schools that were run with little oversight from their sponsor. As a consequence, several of the charters closed midyear because of problems stemming from financial mismanagement. A chain of charter schools named the Alternative Learning Center closed, leaving 150 students without a place to go. Some students were particularly upset, because they were only several months away from graduating and were unable to graduate on time after switching to district schools.[42]

A second chain of charter schools in Arizona, the Success Charter Schools, also closed a little over 2 months after opening. The state closed these schools down because they were doing a poor job of keeping track of the at-risk population of students they served. Commenting on the situation, Lisa Graham Keegan observed, "all we've seen from Success is an inability to track kids. And there are too many places in Arizona for these children to go that would be beneficial for them."[43] The OERI third-year report noted that as of the 1997–1998 school year, 32 charter schools in the nation had closed.[44]

Facilities and Property Ownership

In Tucson, Arizona, one charter school attempted to set up shop in a local residential neighborhood. When residents heard of the plan they organized a protest, citing traffic and noise problems as the basis for their protest. This led the Tucson city council to rethink their zoning laws and eventually block the development of the school on the purchased property.[45] It was also determined that the decision to purchase the property was not made publicly, thus, the property was purchased illegally. A further issue embedded in this property dispute was that charter school operators in Arizona, who are considered to be doing a public good, keep all property, equipment, and so forth accrued by their charter school when the charter school shuts down. So, this property initially slated to be a school later could have served as the directors' new home. As another example, we might open a charter school in September and purchase 400 computers; if the school closes in November, the computers belong to the charter school operators.

SHOPPING ADVICE FOR PARENTS

Given the questionable practices at some charter schools and the reports of school closings, some have been motivated to warn parents of potential problems. In response to the varying quality of charter schools, Gene V Glass at Arizona State University put together 10 questions parents should ask a charter school, which are listed in Table 7.1.[46] In addition to these useful questions, we have developed some of our own questions that parents should consider asking their child's current or future teacher.[47]

Before or after visiting the teacher who instructs or may instruct your daughter or son, you should visit with a few parents whose children the teacher taught the year before and see what their perceptions of the teacher's strengths and weaknesses are. Further, we think it is

TABLE 7.1

Ten Questions Parents Should Ask
a Charter School
(and Maybe the School They Are Already in Too)

Parents approaching a charter school have probably already decided to seek an alternative to traditional public schools which they have experienced either first or second-hand. Arizona charter schools are public schools, funded by tax payers, just as are the schools of the traditional public school system. Arizona leads the nation in virtually any aspect of charter schools that one would wish to measure: number of them, number of students in them, opportunities they create, problems they present.

And some few Arizona charter schools have indeed presented parents with problems. These ten questions that parents contemplating enrolling their children in a charter school might ask of that school are intended to assure the safety of their children, that their children's needs might be met, their time not wasted and that the intellectual, emotional and moral growth of their children will be fostered to the fullest. Good luck in finding the best possible education for your child.

1. Who—what school district or board—issued your charter? When was it issued? Were you previously a private or private/profit-making school or are you affiliated with a corporation that is running other charter schools?

In Arizona, individual school districts as well as the State Board of Education and the State Charter School Board may issue charters. Failures of charter schools with the resulting inconvenience and trauma to families and students tend to occur in charter schools whose charter was issued by small or remote school districts. Recently (February 1998) Window Rock and Ganado ceased issuing charters because the failure of some charter schools in Phoenix to whom they had issued charters brought them bad publicity and administrative headaches. The State Boards appear to exercise more accountability over the charters they issue than some school districts. Currently about 25 charter schools hold charters from school districts, the remaining 250 or so having received their charter from one of the two State Boards.

Other things equal, a charter school with a couple of years under its belt is safer than a brand new one. No parents want their children to be guinea pigs in someone's magnificent adventure. No charter school in Arizona can be more than 3 years old as of Spring 1998.

(Continues)

TABLE 7.1 (Continued)

2. a) What is this school's enrollment?
   b) What "Average Daily Membership" did you report to the State Department of Education last October?
   c) Of 100 students who would start the school year here, how many will still be here in June?

Parents should divide the answer to b) by the answer to a) to obtain a measure of how good attendance is in this charter school. If the answer is below .75 (or 75% of students attend school on any given day), then parents may have reason to be concerned. If, in addition, the answer to c) is 50 or fewer (more than half the students turn over in any one year), parents may legitimately worry that a highly transient student body could be absorbing the energies and attention of teachers that might be more available to their children in a more stable school.

3. **If for some unknown and unfortunate reason this charter school were to close before the end of the school year, has some coordination been made with another charter or a traditional public school to which my children would be sent?**

Although a lesser concern at the elementary and middle school level, an abrupt closure of a charter high school can wreak havoc with students' graduation and college plans. A parent contemplating enrolling children in a charter school might also do well to ask a traditional public school into which the charter feeds whether they anticipate any problems in receiving children who "graduate" from the charter school.

4. **Tell me about your teachers:**
   a) How many are there?
   b) How many have Bachelors degrees?
   c) How many of them are in their first three years of teaching?
   d) How many of last year's teachers are still teaching for you this year?

Divide the number of students in the school from Question 2 (a) by the number of teachers in Question 4 (a). If this school's student teacher ratio is above 30, your child will be in a bigger class than most Arizona school children; if it is under 20, your child will be showered with attention indeed.

Having certified—by the State of Arizona—teachers ensures certain background in a beginning teacher's training. Note that some charter schools hire uncertified teachers. Be sure these teachers have some background information about teaching and students.

Learning to teach is part book knowledge, part supervised training and a large part practical experience. Just as lawyers and doctors "practice" their profession after they leave school, so do teachers. Teachers in their first year or two or three after college are still learning to teach. Be sure uncertified teachers have some experiences that allow you to believe that they can be successful teachers.

(Continues)

TABLE 7.1 (Continued)

5. What is this charter school's discipline policy/plan? Are rules for student conduct printed? May I please have a copy?

What some schools regard as a serious infraction, some parents do not. Get squared away before you and the school are at odds over your child's behavior. Some charter schools have been created in reaction to what they regard as too lax conduct codes in traditional public schools. They may have discipline policies that seem Draconian to parents accustomed to the policies of large, traditional public schools, who can not so precipitously expel wrong-doers.

6. How do you encourage parent involvement in the school? Must I sign a contract pledging a certain number of volunteer hours during the school year?

These contracts have become common in certain areas and may work a hardship on single parent families and dual career couples.

7. May I have a copy of the school budget that you file with the State Department of Education?

Divide the total $ for teachers' salaries by the total budgeted $; if the ratio is less that 60%, inquire further into the salaries paid to key administrators (principals and assistant principals). Though rare, some charter schools have paid a few key administrators far more than their counterparts in traditional public schools. Charter schools sometimes lump administrators' salaries into an "Administrative Costs," making it impossible to tell exactly how much the principal or director is paid.

8. What if my child has, or develops while here, some special need—for counseling or psychological services or some adaptation to a learning or physical disability? Do you have personnel and facilities to take care of my child's need? Will you be able to help me find such care if it is not available here?

9. How are students grouped for teaching? Are classes "ability grouped"? Are children "age grouped" into grade levels?

Ability grouping tends to be beneficial for above average children and not so for average or below average.

10. Have you ever applied for or received special funds from the State Department of Education that are available to charter schools as well as traditional public schools?

For example, funds for (Title I) compensatory education, special education, bilingual or English as a Second Language instruction?

A well run and savvy charter school will know what help is available and how to get it. Some new and poorly managed schools—of all types—have not availed themselves of the resources that students ought to receive.

Note. Reprinted with slight modification from material prepared by Gene V Glass for the College of Education, Arizona State University, Tempe, AZ.

important to visit any other potential teacher at the school who will spend a lot of time with your children. Among the many questions that could be asked, we suggest that the following are useful in a 30- to 60-minute visit to get an understanding of the school, the teacher's conception of teaching and learning, and her or his ability to deal with certain situations.

Some General Questions

1. Does the school adhere to all state and federal mandates? For example, have all the teachers and other school employees been finger-printed and undergone a background check?

2. Teachers, like anybody else, have good and bad days—what would a good day for you be like as a teacher? How does a typical day go? (If the teacher has difficulty in understanding the question—it is broad—you might ask follow-up questions such as) Will my child spend most of his or her time in similar learning formats? In a typical day, how much time will my child spend learning alone (on book or paper assignments)? Learning alone with a computer? Working in a small group with a teacher? Working in a small group without a teacher? Working in a large group in teacher- or student-led discussion?

3. If my daughter or son did something really wrong, how would you handle it? Are students ever automatically sent to the principal's office for certain behaviors? When and why?

4. Students learn many things other than subject matter in school. What three or four other things do you especially want them to learn?

5. If my child were far ahead of the rest of the class in a particular subject, how would you deal with this situation? If my child were far behind other pupils in a subject, how would you deal with the issue? What services does the school provide for children who need remedial help? Does the school have the staff to complete evaluations for special education placement if necessary?

6. Do students who usually do well in one subject (say, social studies) also tend to do well in other subjects (say, reading)? If my child were really doing well in (say, math) but not in (say, social studies), what would you do?

7. What do you like best and least about teaching? What pupil behaviors or attitudes bother you the most?

8. What would be a good day for my child?

9. Kids sometimes pick on others; how do you deal with these situations? What separates appropriate teasing from something that is inappropriate? Is this true for both boys and girls?

10. Some say that girls and boys behave essentially the same as learners; others say they differ. What is your perspective?

11. When you group students for instruction, how do you decide which three to five students to place together?

12. What are your primary reasons for allowing or not allowing students to work in small groups? What do they learn from one another?

13. How much choice do students have in their classroom assignments? When do students have a choice and why?

14. Who picks the curriculum? How much say do teachers have in this school ? How much do parents have?

15. How do students know if you like them? What type of students do you work with best? Worst?

16. (If your child is in high school) What kind of diploma will my child receive? Will the diploma be accepted widely by colleges and universities? Will my child be taking all the prerequisite courses necessary to gain college admission? Do you have counselors on hand to assist my child in planning for after high school graduation?

17. May I come to the school anytime I want to and observe?

18. Your school has a special theme (say, performing arts). Tell me what this means. How does this school differ from a school that does not have a special theme?

19. Given this theme, how much time will my child spend in basic subjects such as English and mathematics?

20. This state has required tests. To what extent is your curriculum aligned with these assessments? Do you think the state's tests impact your curriculum? Positively or negatively? Why?

21. Can I see the application you submitted to obtain your charter? I'm especially interested in seeing your curriculum plan.

22. As a parent, will I be asked to pay any special fees (uniform, laboratory fees, etc.), and will I, or my child, be required to participate in any fund-raising activities?

Comments on the Questions

Unlike the first question, in which there is a clear yes or no answer, some of these questions do not have simple, correct answers. Still, this set of questions can provide a basis for considering how teachers think about particular issues. For example, question 4 might indicate the extent to which teachers are interested in students' growth as social beings and their development in ways other than academics. This would be an especially important question to ask in schools that stress academics (and may become a "pressure-cooker" environment).

Similarly, questions about students being ahead or behind are useful in looking at the extent to which teachers recognize individual differences in students' learning. For example, a student may be experiencing no difficulties in one subject but may be having more problems in other subjects. Is the teacher aware of such possibilities, and is the teacher willing to adjust instruction accordingly, or does the teacher tend to think that students learn in similar ways at similar rates across different subject matters?

Some young students may have difficulty attending to the various demands of a physical setting, particularly if a teacher uses only one instructional format hour after hour. Some teachers are so enthused about a learning approach, for example, that they may have students in cooperative learning groups for several hours a day, not realizing how demanding and frustrating group work can be. Similarly, working alone for an entire day can be isolating and unstimulating. Teachers can overuse and underuse learning formats, and it is instructive for parents to inquire about what a teacher thinks constitutes a good day.

Some of the questions concern a particular grade level, especially those involving individual differences in students. Teachers who are experienced in working with fifth-grade students, for instance, know there are many similarities between girls' and boys' learning but some distinct preferences as well, which can be used profitably when students are allowed to make choices about research reports, and so forth. At higher grade levels, it is important that teachers not believe gender-related or ethnicity-related stereotypes (e.g., girls don't like science and math and do poorly, boys are unlikely to be good art students) so that female students are not discouraged from taking advanced courses or male students from taking humanities courses. Needless to say, we hope teachers would not use ethnicity or performance as the primary reason for assigning students to groups, because students who vary in important ways can learn together in many settings. Much damage can be done by teachers who insist on teaching students in homogenous groups.

Questions About Special Education

Schools are required by law to provide special education services in the least restrictive environment. Further, services must be individualized and accommodate a child's needs, including provision of related services such as speech and occupational therapy. Schools must follow current individualized education plans (IEPs). Charter schools in general have earned a reputation for skirting special education laws and requirements, so if your child has a disability you may want to ask questions such as the following to determine how much the teachers and directors of the charter school know about special education and if they currently have special education programs in place or have not yet initiated them:

1. Do you currently employ special education teachers? School psychologists? School counselors? Speech therapists?

2. What type of training do your special education teachers have? Do they have state certification?

3. Will you follow my child's IEP at this school? If not, why?

4. How will you make sure that my child's individual needs will be accommodated?

5. How many other special education students attend this school?

6. How many special education students have left the school? Why did they leave?

7. Are special education students grouped together in a self-contained classroom, or are they included in typical classrooms with other students?

8. Will my child be pulled out for special services or will services be delivered within his or her classroom?

9. How many due process hearings have parents brought against the school? How have these been resolved?

10. May I see the application you submitted to obtain your charter? I am especially interested to see what you said about special education.

Comments on the Questions

As mentioned, the answers to these questions should specify that special education services are available and that they are tailored to meet the needs of the individual child. If the school indicates that they do not provide special education or do not seem to understand the questions they are likely in violation of federal law. To report any violations or to find out more about what your rights are as a parent, contact your state department of education. If you are currently having difficulty with a school your special needs child is attending, you may request a due process hearing to address the problems. Contact your state department of education for more information.

The Parent Information Network for the Arizona Department of Education's Exceptional Student Services described parent's rights (see Table 7.2). Because these rights are based on federal law, they are applicable to charter schools in all states.

School Visits

If you are favorably disposed toward a particular school after visiting with the teacher, talking with parents of students previously taught by the teacher, and examining various written documents, you should visit the school. The questions presented earlier represent a way of talking with the teacher about children in general and your child in particular. It is important to understand how the teacher thinks about children both as academic learners and as social beings. Teachers' informal ways of presenting their ideas may provide clues as to how they think about educational issues and the philosophy they bring to

TABLE 7.2
Parental Rights

Parents have the right to
- Participate in decisions about a child's educational needs, including their IEPs.
- Have their child receive special education services for free.
- Know about changes in identification, evaluation, placement, or delivery of services.
- Receive notice of the explanation for a school's refusal to grant a parental request for identification, evaluation, placement, or delivery of services.
- Give or withhold consent for an evaluation.
- Get an outside evaluation, paid for by the school, if they disagree with the school evaluation. The school has a right to have a due process hearing to prove the evaluation is appropriate.
- Use free mediation services from the Arizona Department of Education.
- Request due process hearings to resolve disputes.

Note. Reprinted with permission. Parent Information network. (1999). *Parental rights.* Phoenix: Arizona Department of Education.

the classroom. However, you can only learn so much in an interview, and we recommend that you actually visit the classroom and observe on one or more occasions.

Most charter schools that have good programs want parents and potential clients to visit the school. For example, in a letter to parents the directors of the Tertulia: A Learning Community Charter School in Phoenix, Arizona, wrote:

> We often say, and truly believe, that the only real way to appreciate the uniqueness of *Tertulia* and of our students is by visiting the school. If you haven't been able to do so, we extend an open invitation. In this way, you too can see the spirit and energy our students possess. They exhibit a thirst for knowledge and an understanding that learning is the single most important key to their success. While we had many goals when we founded the school three years ago, this was the one behind them all: to restore confidence that school is the place where a successful future is built.[48]

This is exactly the type of attitude parents should be looking for. Schools that are excited about what they are doing and genuinely want you in the school. In fact, we were sufficiently impressed by the Tertulia newsletter that we have included it in an appendix at the end of the chapter (see the appendix).

Questions About School Closing

It is also important for parents to find out from school administrators what happens if the charter school closes midyear. Important questions to ask include the following:

1. What is your plan for placing students if the school closes?
2. Will my child go to another charter school or a noncharter public school?
3. How much choice will my child have?
4. How long will the change in schools take?
5. How will my child's records be transferred (grade reports, discipline records, immunization records, etc.)?
6. (If your child is in high school) How do I know that my child's credits will transfer to another school?[49]

ADVICE FOR LEGISLATORS
AND STATE DEPARTMENTS OF EDUCATION

As we noted in chapter 4 when we presented the logic of choice, certain imposed definitions such as *strong legislation* and *weak legislation* have gotten in the way of analytical analyses of extant laws. Clearly, legislators are not to blame for the labels strong and weak legislation that charter advocates have imposed. And, as we pointed out before and many legislators would agree, descriptors of weak and strong laws depend on data that show which provisions within these two categories lead to schools that serve students better.

Unfortunately, our analysis of legislation leads to the conclusion that laws in some states are too permissive, allowing charter schools to be created with few restrictions, little oversight, and the granting of charters to applicants who do not meet the provisions of state or federal law. In many states, charter legislation benefits those who open charter schools and slights the needs of parents and students who use them. We understand legislators' initial excitement in their attempts to improve schools for students. However, we think that some fine-tuning now will have powerful effects on states with active charter schools and will provide guidance to states currently initiating charter school legislation.

In order to fine tune state laws and increase the responsible reviews of charter schools by the state, we offer 20 recommendations:

1. Make people compete for charters. Only the best and most complete charter proposals should be funded by the state. If charter schools are to improve education generally, citizens have a right to know, before they fund, the ideas that are being tested. Further, proposals should describe clearly how they are going to implement their ideas in educational practice.

2. Make sure that charter directors have a financial plan and understand state financial requirements, including reporting, before they are granted a charter. If necessary, they can take a class on school finances or pass an exam.

3. Consider setting a baseline for the amount of state funds that can be spent for purposes other than instruction. Some studies have shown a large variation between different types of charter and noncharter public schools in terms of what percentage of revenue is spent on instruction.[50]

4. Clarify the division of assets if a charter school closes. In several states, the situation concerning disillusionment and property ownership is ambiguous and rulings in some states have made it possible for charter school operators to retain assets (computers, books, buildings) after they close. If legislators view such forms of potential compensation and flexibility as imperative, a school should be required to serve students capably for a minimum number of years before venture capital supplied by state funds becomes private property. It seems incumbent that legislators take away incentives that encourage charter operators to enter the school business with the intent of cashing in quickly on short-term possibilities without any long-term commitment to improving education for students.

5. Create a clearinghouse for information on charter schools. Included as a part of this, all applications should be easily accessible by the public (those accepted and rejected) as well as public complaints about charter schools.

6. Inform parents that charter schools may close (sometimes midyear), and give them tips on how to protect their children against this possibility.

7. Make sure the law specifies whether special costs to parents are allowable (e.g., a materials or uniform fee).

8. Inspect charter schools before they open to ensure that facilities are safe and are handicapped accessible, meeting requirements of the Americans with Disabilities Act. In addition, states should rescind any legislation allowing charter schools to by-pass physical facility requirements in the sponsoring state. There is growing evidence that school building repairs are often handled poorly (even with such restrictions in place and given pressures to build facilities for the short run at considerable long-term expense), and capital expenditures should be closely scrutinized.[51] Guaranteeing safe and enduring buildings does not seem to impede the development of innovative charter schools.

9. Keep management companies out of the chartering process. If management company–run schools are involved, they, like other schools, should be monitored to ensure that they follow state and federal laws and do not cut corners to increase their profit margin. As a case in point, in Michigan it was noted that charter schools on average spent 51% of their budget on instruction, compared with 54% in surrounding public school districts. But in sharp contrast, charter school chains used only 35% of funds for instruction. Also, administration

costs consumed 32% of chain schools' revenue, as compared with 11% in surrounding public schools.

10. Ensure that all charter operators understand and are able to negotiate special education laws and paperwork. For example, require that they take a class or pass an exam on special education before granting their charter. Further, ensure that all charters include a plan for accommodating a range of students with special needs.

11. Make sure that the state has a plan securely in place to monitor charter schools before any schools are sponsored. Do not allow more charter schools than the state has the capacity to monitor.

12. If school districts are allowed to serve as charter school sponsors, make the districts demonstrate that they are prepared for this complex task (e.g., see item 6). Make districts compete for the right to sponsor charters. If districts indicate that they will charter schools outside of their district, have them explain their logic and defend this action. If it is justifiable, make sure that they have the adequate resources to manage the schools they charter.

13. Make sure that the state department of education is as neutral and responsive as possible to citizens, parents, teachers, charter school directors, and others.

14. Take a Government Accounting Office approach to information collection and dissemination. Provide all information about charter schools in a clear and descriptive format. Include details such as how many charter applications were reviewed by each sponsoring body, how many were accepted, how many were rejected, what age groups the schools serve, and so forth.

15. Provide information on individual school budgets in an easily understandable format, including how much money was spent by each school; what were the sources of revenue; what were the major expenditures (curriculum and instruction, maintenance and operations, facilities, etc.).

16. Produce a short report for each school discussing demographic information, including special education, bilingual students, and gender and ethnic composition. Also, describe teacher composition; certification status of teachers; and teaching specialties (e.g., bilingual education, special education). If schools are attracting individuals from other fields to be teachers, what fields are they from and how successful are they as teachers? What is the level of student achievement at the school? How does that compare with students' scores from previous years (i.e., has the charter school improved individual

student's achievement compared with their achievement level at their previous school?).

17. Present the information in an easily accessible format (e.g., written reports available by mail, the Internet).

18. Share complaints with the public in a nonbiased manner. For example, the number of complaints per year, how many for each school, what categories the complaints fall under (e.g., special education, curriculum and instruction, parent involvement).

19. Within the state department of education, employ adequate personnel to ensure that the described tasks (e.g., monitoring, paperwork, reporting) are accomplished in a timely manner.

20. As noted in chapter 6, many charter schools are not responsive to special education students and their parents. Hence, state legislators should enact practices to monitor for segregation.

21. Support research and development. The best way to demonstrate and to understand whether the charter school movement is successful in your state is to provide monies for research and development. Each new charter school should include in their charter a plan for evaluating their own progress, to be implemented immediately on initiation of the school. And each charter school applicant should be required to illustrate how they will contribute to the knowledge base—to understanding if a particular program or technique worked and why (more on this in chapter 8). In addition, monies for research and development should be provided for a range of people who are likely to give as unbiased an assessment as possible.

The logic for most of our recommendations appears to be generally straightforward. However, in two cases discussion of the argument may be helpful. Advocates of charter schools are apt to see our recommendations presented in items 3 and 4 as more of the unwarranted bureaucracy that has stifled public schools in the past. However, reasonable legislation can balance both the need to support innovation in schools and to provide safeguards that public funds are spent appropriately. For example, it could be specified that a baseline minimum expenditure of funds is expected for instructional costs unless a waiver is sought. The waiver need not even require extra work. For example, if the charter application requires, as it should, a statement of innovation, then the applicant would need only to site that feature as the basis for a waiver. If provided such information, then a state board or another granting agency could examine the soundness of the plan and decide to grant the waiver or not on the basis of the idea and its possible instructional benefit.

Our reason for making public schools compete for the right to sponsor charter schools (and the funds of sponsoring, which in some cases can be substantial) simply is a call for procharter legislators to follow their own argument. That is, if legislators have concluded that public schools are not having desired effects of student performance (to such a degree that we need charter schools), why are they content to let any public school sponsor charter schools? After all, as we have seen in this chapter, some superintendents' primary interest in sponsoring charter schools is to obtain funds to help their own school districts. If legislators believe many public schools are inadequate, then there should be provisions in place to make public schools compete for the right to sponsor charter schools.

Similarly, we feel that choice and alternative approaches to education can be achieved only when there is public scrutiny and openness of information. Citizens should be able to find out where charter school funds are being spent without undue effort. If approved charter applications (especially those approved by individual schools) are available for public inspection, it allows the competition and award process to be verified by competitors who lost and citizens who are interested in improving the quality of education. When such access is denied, it is impossible to determine the extent to which charters are granted for political reasons, because of friendship, or because of a high-quality proposal.

CONCLUSION

There is no way to convey concrete stories that represent the diversity of charter schools; there are simply too many different forms of charter schools. For example, in describing charter schools in Arizona, Tamar Lewin noted:

> These schools are mushrooming all over, from the River of Life Church in Phoenix to a concrete dome on a Navajo reservation. There are charter schools for students at risk of problems, for pregnant students, for those who want back-to-basics curriculums, or performing arts. Some are run by parents, some by experienced educators; some have no certified teachers at all, and some are even run by companies operating schools for profit.[52]

This chapter considered a few individual profiles of schools using information presented by journalists and other informal sources. Interestingly, the range of descriptions provided by the media is fairly balanced, as there are numerous positive and negative examples. Newspaper accounts also report the diversity of existing charter schools. Hence, although the media has been described by some as being unduly negative toward public schools, they have certainly demonstrated the capacity to be critical of new, alternative forms of public education as well.

In addition to presenting profiles of individual charter schools, we have also integrated information presented in this chapter with the more formal evidence we presented in chapters 5 and 6 in order to provide some guidelines and recommendations for parents. We shared some questions suggested by our colleagues at Arizona State University and provided our own list of suggestions for parents to consider. An examination of media reports reinforces our earlier conclusion that the range in the quality of charter schools is enormous with some individual schools performing at an "S" level; whereas, others perform at notably lower levels.

Further, we presented specific suggestions for state legislators and members of state departments of education to consider as they grant, renew, and monitor charter schools. In particular, we believe that legislators throughout the country have tended to be too willing to grant charters and, hence, to put students at risk. A few charter schools have proved to be informative sources of innovation and learning. Unfortunately, most have not. Part of the reason for disappointing charter school performance can be laid at the feet of lax legislation that fails to sufficiently encourage and require innovation and the active supervision and monitoring of charter schools. It may be that charter schools will eventually become a major source of informative experimentation, as educators struggle to find new ways of educating students, particularly students who have specific needs. Thus, as noted earlier, charter schools have experienced political success and are apt to remain a component of public education. However, if they are to become an educational success (e.g., a source for developing innovative ideas), at least some of the recommendations we have advanced here will need to be enacted.

Charter schools will not, by themselves, reform or markedly improve education. If effective public policy is to be developed, it needs to cover many fronts. Charter schools may be one of the avenues to pursue; however, they need to be improved considerably from how they are currently operating.

In chapter 8, we expand on our thoughts about charter schools and their role in research and development. Also in chapter 8 we advance an agenda for obtaining a broader consensus of citizens focused on the quality of educational programs. At present, education has become so politicized that the result is for pork barrel funding that creates the illusion that many reforms are taking place. However, in general these "reforms" are taking place in ways that often are both uninformative and without procedures that allow us to understand if their programs are working or not. We also argue that extant knowledge of learning and teaching could be put to better use in some schools but that in the schools where a real educational crisis exists we also have an acute shortage in our knowledge base. Thus, we consider the specific example of inner-city schools and the country's failure to adequately help children achieve success.

Endnotes

1. Hartocollis, A. (1999, June 16). State's first independent schools are picked, and criticism is swift. *The New York Times*, p. A25.
2. Arkansas Department of Education. (1999, June 9). Personal communication.
3. Schnailberg, L. (1999, June 23). Oklahoma, Oregon bump up charter law states to 36. *Education Week, 18*(41), 20, 23.
4. Bracey, G. W. (1997). *The truth about America's schools: The Bracey reports, 1991–97.* Bloomington, IN: Phi Delta Kappa Educational Foundation, p. 153.
5. Toch, T. (1998, April 27). The new education bazaar. *U.S. News and World Report*, 36.
6. Ibid, p. 37.
7. Ibid, p. 37.
8. Ibid, p. 37.
9. Samuelson, M. (1999, March 12). School's goal to improve deaf students' literacy. *The Tucson Citizen*, p. 8A.
   Samuelson, M. (1999, March 12). Deaf students reap benefits of having adult role models. *The Tucson Citizen*, p. 8A.
10. Traub, J. (1999, April 4). A school of your own. *New York Times: Education Life*, p. 30.
11. Ibid., pp. 30, 31, 42.
12. Stein, B. (1996, September). O'Farrell Community School: Center for advanced academic studies. *Phi Delta Kappan*, 28–29.
13. Thomas, D., & Borwege, K. (1996, September). A choice to charter. *Phi Delta Kappan*, 29–31.
14. Ibid., p. 30.
15. Ibid., p. 31.

16. Ibid.
17. Hornbeck, M. (1999, June 6). Charter schools fall short of expectations. *The Detroit News* [Online]. Available: http://detnews.com/specialreports/1999/schools/990606main2/990606main2.htm
18. Orfield, G. (1998, January 4). Charter schools are not the fix for ailing education. *The Arizona Daily Star*, p. F3.
19. Ibid.
20. Lewin, T. (1999, April 7). Edison schools say students gain. *The New York Times*, p. C28.
21. Ibid.
22. Zollers, N. J., & Ramanathan, A. K. (1998, December). For-profit charter schools and students with disabilities: The sordid side of the business of schooling. *Phi Delta Kappan*, 297–304.
23. Ibid., p. 304.
24. Horn, J., & Miron, G. (1999). *Evaluation of the Michigan Public School Academy* [Online], p. 71. Available: http://www.wmich.edu/evalctr/
25. Lewin, T. (1999, June 13). Arizona district profits from charter schools. *The New York Times*, p. A25.
26. Ibid.
27. Nelson, F. H. (1997). *How much thirty thousand charter schools cost.* Paper presented at the 1997 annual meeting of the American Education Finance Association, Jacksonville, FL. Available online [http://www.aft.org/research/reports/private/chartfin/index.htm]
28. Toch, T. (1998, April 27). The new education bazaar. *U.S. News and World Report*, 35–36.
29. Blume, H., & Uhrich, K. (1998, August 14). Charter school for scandal. *LA Weekly* [Online]. Available: http://www.laweekly.com/ink/98/38/blume1.shtml
30. Ibid.
31. Todd, C. (1998, August 23–27). Guinea kids: Arizona's charter school experiment. *The Tribune*. Special section reprinted from earlier Tribune series.
32. Mitchell, K. (1998, August 23). $500 down, $90,000 profit: Windfall from system legal, auditors say. *The Tribune*, p. 4.
33. Mitchell, K. (1998, August 24). Start your own school, no questions asked. *The Tribune*, p. 7.
34. Schimpp, S. (1999, May 26). FY 1999 Supplemental Request, Department of Education. Arizona joint legislative budget committee (staff memorandum).
35. Wildavsky, B. (1999, June 28). Why charter schools make Inkster nervous. *U.S. News Online*. Available: http://www.usnews.com/usnews/issue/990628/charter.htm
36. Ibid.
37. Tapia, S. T. (1998, June 28). Parents say charter school wouldn't meet kid's needs. *The Arizona Daily Star*, pp. B1, B3.
38. Ibid.
39. For more information on due process hearings and IDEA 97 please see: http://www.ed.gov/offices/OSERS/IDEA/index.html

40. Tapia, S. T. (1998, June 28). Parents say charter school wouldn't meet kid's needs. *The Arizona Daily Star*, p. B3.

41. Tapia, S. T. (1998, June 28). Mom says school rejected ill son. *The Arizona Daily Star*, p. B2.

42. Tapia, S. T. (1998, February 10). Parents worried by shut down of Willcox charter school. *The Arizona Daily Star*, p. A1.
    Tapia, S. T. (1998, January 3). Charter school in Benson closes; 64 kids shut out. *The Arizona Daily Star*, pp. A1, A8.
    Tapia, S. T. (1998, January 6). Charter school closure could bring suit. *The Arizona Daily Star*, p. B2.
    Tapia, S. T. (1998, February 4). Charter bankruptcy filing could shut schools permanently. *The Arizona Daily Star*, pp. B1, B2.

43. Staff and wire reports. (1997, November 26). Board closes Tucson site, all Success charter schools. *The Arizona Daily Star*, p. B3.

44. RPP International. (1999). *The state of charter schools: Third-year report.* Office of Educational Research and Improvement, U.S. Department of Education.

45. Tapia, S. T. (1998, August 14). Charter school's home purchase is ruled illegal. *The Arizona Daily Star*, p. B1.
    Tapia, S. T. (1998, August 13). Toss out charter school suit, neighbors say. *The Arizona Daily Star*, p. B3.
    Tapia, S. T. (1998, May 3). Charter schools free to move in, upset residents. *The Arizona Daily Star*, pp. B1, B6.

46. Glass G. V. (1998, February). *Ten questions parents should ask a charter school (& maybe the school they are already in too)* [Online]. Available: http://www.ed.asu.edu/coe/csfaq.html

47. The authors acknowledge the help of Mary McCaslin in the Department of Educational Psychology at the University of Arizona in generating the list of questions.

48. Aguirre, J., & Aguirre, M. L. (1999, Summer). Personal communication.

49. Adapted from Barclay, B. (1998, December 12). *Nobody wants to talk about it, but what if ... a charter school has to close?* Unpublished document.

50. Nelson, F. H. (1997). *How much thirty thousand charter schools cost.* Paper presented at the 1997 annual meeting of the American Education Finance Association, Jacksonville, FL. Available online http://www.aft.org/research/reports/private/chartfin/index.htm
    Arsen, D. (1999, April). *Charter school spending: autonomous and accountable?* Paper presented at the 1999 annual meeting of the American Educational Research Association, Montreal, Canada.

51. Sullivan, J., Drew, C., & Steinberg, J. (1999, July 26). Careless risk in fixing New York City schools. *The New York Times*, pp. A1, A16.
    3/D International. (1999, March). *Problems of underfunded maintenance are being compounded by the lack of capital renewal plans.* White paper. Houston, TX.

52. Lewin, T. (1999, June 13). Arizona district profits from charter schools. *The New York Times*, p. A25.

APPENDIX

Tertulia: A LEARNING COMMUNITY
CHARTER SCHOOL

Summer Update
1999

Dear *Tertulia* Friend:

Summer vacation is already upon us and we'd like to share some thoughts on our successes this year and a few ideas for next year. This third year of *Tertulia*'s existence has proved unique and exciting in many ways, and we're hard at work making plans to continue our success in the years to come.

We often say, and truly believe, that the only real way to appreciate the uniqueness of *Tertulia* and of our students is by visiting the school. If you haven't been able to do so, we extend an open invitation. In this way, you too can see the spirit and energy our students possess. They exhibit a thirst for knowledge and an understanding that learning is the single most important key to their success. While we had many goals when we founded the school three years ago, this was the one behind them all: to restore confidence that school is the place where a successful future is built.

Had you visited this year, you might have taken a walk through one of the two student gardens planted and maintained as students learned about desert ecology. Or perhaps you would have heard from a sixth grader about the overnight field trip to Northern Arizona in which students — many of whom had never been in the forest before — had a chance to put their astronomy studies to use away from the glare of the big city lights of Phoenix. Or maybe you would have been lucky enough to see the pride of a third grader who had just completed a Hyperstudio presentation on the animal they had chosen to study. Whenever visitors arrived, there was always something exciting to see.

On a different note, the response from the community in our third year has been the strongest yet. Our parents have established a crucial presence at school, due in part to a new program called P.R.I.D.E. in which parents earn small-but-important incentives for volunteering at school, actively participating in the Parents Association, and attending school functions. Through this program, parent involvement has expanded significantly and parents have earned uniforms, backpacks, school supplies, and museum tickets. Two parents this year among the leaders in hours volunteered even won grand prizes of a refurbished PC-computer.

Additionally, the corporate and foundation world has again rallied behind *Tertulia*. Hopefully you saw the news May 12th, because all the networks — both English-language and Spanish-language — reported on the grand opening of the

Una comunidad de aprendizaje

new *Tertulia* playground, generously provided by the Dial Corporation. Other corporations including GenCorp, Target, China Mist Teas, Best Western, and Microsoft also furnished important assistance this year. And many foundations supporting public education reform have again bolstered the *Tertulia* program; these include the Rainwater Foundation, the Challenge Foundation, the Greenville Foundation, and the Wharton Foundation. Finally, let us not forget to mention the special assistance given to us by a remarkable non-profit organization called Make A Difference.

We offer our sincerest thank-you to all of these organizations, and to the individuals from the community who have extended their time and commitment. Your devotion has already made an important difference for our students as they strive toward their goals.

To briefly look ahead: Next year we will have our first eighth-grade graduating class! We will also launch a new program (supported by many of the above organizations) to greatly improve the achievement levels of our students in the crucial subjects of Math and Science. Furthermore, we will continue the implementation of our technology plan, which is helping our students achieve in all areas while developing important technology skills.

We are constantly grateful for the dedication and hard work of our staff and families, and for the important contributions that you, as a friend of *Tertulia*, have made. Please accept our invitation for a visit in the Fall.

Sincerely,

Jesús Aguirre
Co-Director

Mónica Liang Aguirre
Co-Director

_____

Note. Reprinted with permission. Aguirre, J., & Aguirre, M. L. (1999, Summer). *Tertulia: A Learning Community summer update.*

Chapter 8

Dealing With Complexity and Uncertainty: Moving Schooling Forward

We begin this chapter with a brief review of the arguments made in the book, which set the stage for our recommendations for improving public education, especially in inner-city schools. Our analysis begins by noting that current reform efforts and pressures in education are part of a broader movement toward privatization—an attempt to minimize governmental action and size. In examining the privatization movement, we look at examples provided by hospitals, which have been affected by this pressure for some time, and by prisons, which have been more recently impacted. The market approach to reforming these two institutions has had its own problems. Some of these problems are especially disturbing if they predict how privatization eventually will play out in schools. By recognizing that privatization per se is not an answer, we set the stage for raising questions about the adequacy of our knowledge base for enhancing school performance and about the commitment of new resources needed to improve education.

It is important to realize that until educators and citizens begin to work for consensus on education, we are likely stalemated. Various writers have noted that without focused pressure, Democrats and Republicans are unlikely to agree on educational plans for many reasons.[1] Politicians want "their plan" for education to prevail, and too often the greater focus is on which party gets visible political credit, not on which plans are best for children. If the quality of education is to be enhanced with needed resources, bipartisan support for education must be garnered. It is time to attempt to think of education as we do foreign affairs—what is "best for our troops" thinking tends to provide at least a working consensus in government. We need to begin to find strategies for increasing "what is best for school children" thinking.

We examine President Clinton's education policy as another example of superficial recommendations that are popular with some public policy groups. Although we know that such lists are motivated by good intentions, we argue that these lists reflect a fundamental misunderstanding of the problems of American education generally and of inner city school settings specifically. Until informed citizens and professional educators are willing to identify the weaknesses of such lists (and willing to help others understand the triviality of such school-reform positions), school reform will remain at a largely superficial level. We need a larger, more informed group of citizens who are interested in students' educational programs if we are to achieve a consensus on education.

We end the chapter with comments on the paucity of research about why children fail generally and in inner-city schools specifically and with suggestions for what to do about it. Four reasons are presented to explain why policymakers are unwilling to invest in educational research, and we illustrate why these reasons are flawed. It is argued that politicians can help to reform education by funding educational research. We encourage informed citizens to urge politicians to provide funds for research to enhance the extant knowledge base.

A BRIEF REVIEW

Chapter 1 noted that education is a top political and social issue in America—everyone knows it is important—but there is no consensus about how good it is presently nor any agreement on how to begin to answer questions about quality. Consensus may become even harder to achieve, because in recent years both political parties increasingly have made education an election issue; hence, federal–state and state–local issues about the control of education (e.g., testing) are likely to intensify over the next few years. The fight for control of education, and credit for solving the so-called crisis of public education, is not just a battle between government units. It has also attracted the business community. Vast amounts of money have been contributed by the business community to both public schools and alternatives to public schools (e.g., vouchers). Many businesses also have argued for a reduced role of government in education, claiming that virtually anything government manages (e.g., the postal system) can be done better within the private sector. Citizens also are engaging in the war on public education. Some support public schools with considerable enthusiasm. Other citizens are voting with their feet and opening and sending their children to charter or private schools. Further, the judiciary is being called on increasingly to rule in various litigated educational disputes.

Chapter 2 discussed past reform efforts. The picture of reform in American education is akin to the fashion industry—some of the need for new approaches is artificially created by the people who sell the products and services. However, to complicate the issue, there are many real problems and concerns embedded in school reform efforts. Still, despite the important reform issues, we are amazed at the history of education in which simple—and false—dichotomous choices have been sold repeatedly to the American public as solutions (e.g., whole language or phonics). What appears to be new in this predictable movement of American education from one Zeitgeist to another and from one crisis to another is that the fight over educational reform now is as likely to be engaged in legislative chambers as in school board meeting rooms.

Chapter 3 examined the questions: How good are American schools? Were students better educated in 1960 than today? Are students in Bolivia or China outperforming our students? Given the political constraints we have identified, this debate is necessarily contentious, and much energy is spent making political arguments rather than examining evidence or improving procedures to gather useful evidence. However, despite the enormous complexity of the issue, we feel comfortable in advancing four conclusions. First, in terms of general achievement, today's students are more diverse, as more women, minorities, students from poorer homes, and students with disabilities are participating successfully at higher levels of education than ever before. Second, the general level of performance, as measured by conventional tests, is as high as ever. Hence, no argument for a general deterioration of the public school system can be made on the basis of available evidence. Third, given the extant research base, either American education is not generally in a state of crisis or, if one prefers, it is in a comparable state of crisis as in 1940, 1950, 1960, 1970, 1980, and 1990. Fourth, there is enormous variability in the funding and performance of American schools. We have some of the best and worst schools in the world.[2] Although there is not a general crisis in education, there is a crisis of schooling in many inner-city schools, and this crisis must be addressed.

Chapter 4 sketched the development of voucher plans, and chapter 5 the development of charter legislation. Importantly, discussions of the advantages for more choice were made at a general (and often polemical) level. Proponents argued that choice is good because it will make schools more competitive and reduce bloated bureaucracy. Although these arguments are written with a stirring ring, the key question, What does choice mean for students? is not addressed. Specifically, these general shibboleths do not tell us how greater competition will be manifested in classrooms or how children will benefit educationally from a smaller administrative staff. Further, we have seen that the form and, hence, the consequences of choice vary in important ways. On one hand, vouchers can be limited to students who come from families with an income level below a specified amount or can be authorized for use only at schools where at least one half the admission decisions are made by lottery. On the other hand, vouchers do not have to be restricted by conditions of income or admission practices. Many citizens were upset in Cleveland when they found out that students who were not from low-income families were included in the voucher program. However, students from higher income families were included because the voucher authorization only gave *preference* to low-income students. In contrast, some would argue that preferences not be given to any student and that individual choices equal social good.

We reported on the creation of charter schools and their enormous variability, some of which is the result of state law. Other differences flow from the relationship negotiated between the sponsoring agent and the charter school, and yet others are due to a charter school's own initiative and agenda. Some charter schools function as a comprehensive school and present a range of grade levels to a wide range of students (i.e., like public schools). Other charter schools serve primarily special populations (e.g., at-risk or college-bound students, or those with special interests in the arts, computers, or learning a specific trade). Further, there is marked variability in control and governance. Some are individual entities ("mom and pop" schools), whereas others are part of a chain (the "K-mart" group) or managed by professional for-profit companies. Some charter schools have considerable autonomy for program direction and use of finances, whereas programs and budgets in other charter schools are tightly controlled by sponsors. Finally we uncovered that some charter schools represent choice and freedom from bureaucracy, but others do not.

Chapters 6 and 7 reviewed the formal and informal research evidence on charter schools and presented instances of specific problems and successes. We acknowledged the difficulty of evaluating charter schools given the limited amount of data. With these important caveats in hand, we concluded that, in general, the charter school movement has replicated many aspects of the public school system. As with the regular school system, the range in quality is enormous. Moreover, as in public school districts, some schools have been closed due to reasons of poor performance,[3] and some have collapsed under their own financial weight without outside intervention. We graded charter schools in various areas and found their inability to deal with special education students a notable weakness.

Some of the many failures have resulted in wasted public funds, whereas the energy of creative individuals has sometimes created exciting educational venues for children in charter schools. Despite some successes, we concluded that overall the charter school investment has been a more wasteful than an informative experiment. In particular, charter schools as a group have failed to innovate and provide widely promised new approaches to classroom learning.

We cautioned parents that the variation of quality in charter schools is wide and offered questions that may help focus their attempt to see if a particular charter school is a good fit for their child. We also provided important recommendations for legislators that, if enacted, would provide a better balance between the rights of those who open charter schools and the rights of the citizens they serve.

Now chapter 8 turns to a discussion of the possibilities for increasing our ability to learn from the present reform effort and to structure actions so that in the future we might design better conditions for schooling and for assessing educational change.

PRIVATIZATION

School reform is embedded in a broader set of societal concerns and debate, especially the role of government in today's society. During the past 25 years many politicians and economists have increasingly argued the case for the virtues of privatization—turning over government business functions to private companies. The arguments are varied, but the basic assertions are that government workers have little incentive for improvement (products, services) and that private companies, because of competition and the profit motive, will make services both better and less expensive. Education represents one government institution being reformed through privatization. In this regard, education is part of a general culture that tends to mistrust governmental control and intervention. Many individuals who advocate more competition and choice in education are basically advocates for growth of the private sector—they want to reduce the role of government in all aspects of society.

In reviewing privatization efforts in other governmental institutions, we see that they do not provide compelling evidence that these institutions are better than the public institutions they supplemented or replaced. After reviewing these efforts, we note some of the possible lessons that can be drawn for public education.

Examples of Privatization

For-Profit Hospitals.   One example of privatization is the conversion of nonprofit hospitals to for-profit institutions. A well-documented effect has been that after gaining control, for-profit hospitals put into place a number of cost-reducing measures, including laying off employees, eliminating facilities or services that are unprofitable, increasing working hours, and reducing pay for medical personnel.[4] Importantly, related but lesser-known effects of such competition are that for-profit hospitals refuse to engage in expensive procedures for charity cases; eliminate research and teaching services; and redirect increased resources to advertising budgets designed to find attractive (i.e., insured) patients. Hence, many activities that have long-term returns on investments (training new doctors, researching new medicines) are reduced or eliminated because they have little short-run profit potential.[5]

Robert Kuttner noted that since 1970, the number of physicians has grown by roughly 60%; however, in contrast, the number of medical administrators has grown by 500%.[6] Despite the rise of medical managers, patients' reimbursement time has gone up as their benefits have gone down. The costs of time wasted in obtaining medical referrals and in justifying medical procedures, and the time that patients, doctors' offices, and insurance personnel spend on processing claims, are seldom included in the cost that market advocates calculate.

Another side effect of for-profit hospitals is that private insurers spend billions on advertising and market research, most of which is intended not to inform the consumer but rather to attack competitors and to identify the right type of patient. The industry has concluded that the least healthy 1% of Americans consumes roughly 28% of medical costs, and these patients need to be identified and screened out as effectively as possible.

Our major purpose in discussing health care is to illustrate that the move to reform existing practice is operating within several spheres. Will these same trends play out in education reform? On one hand, charter schools are dedicated to extending control and decision making to individual charter schools, but on the other hand, many of these schools are overwhelmed with so many management issues that they buy a standard packaged curriculum and are consumed in day-to-day problems that take time away from student care. Further, in a Michigan study of charter schools it was concluded that "mom and pop" charter schools were unlikely to survive and that only professionally managed chains would survive. Do we really want to leave the education of our children to the market place, or as Kuttner asked, "is everything for sale?"

For-Profit Prisons. The prison system offers another example of privatization efforts. How well have they worked? It is both ironic and instructive to note that although crime is down, private prisons flourish. Writing in 1998, Eric Schlosser noted that since 1991, the rate of violent crime had reduced 20%, but during the same time period, the number of individuals in jails or prisons had increased by 50%.[7] Although an increased prison population is due to numerous factors (e.g., less support for mental patients, and drug addicts), at least some of the growth in the prison population can be linked to the for-profit motive.

> The lure of big money is corrupting the nation's criminal-justice system, replacing notions of public service with a drive for higher profits. The eagerness of elected officials to pass "tough-on-crime" legislation—combined with their unwillingness to disclose the true costs of these laws—has encouraged all sorts of financial improprieties.[8]

Private prison companies are the most controversial and fastest growing member of the prison industrial complex. Prisons are a big business and offer many ways for profits to be made. For example, prisoners generate over a billion dollars in revenues on phone calls alone, and vast amounts of money are paid to food service companies, plumbing companies, and other suppliers of the prison system.[9] As Schlosser noted, the prison industry, given its mammoth growth, has come to share some of the attributes of the defense industry. For example, just as some admirals retire from public service and find appointments with defense contractors, prison officials are now often recruited for employment in those very firms that supply goods and services to prisons. The concern here is that an individual's long-term interest in personal profit may reduce the short-term competitiveness displayed toward prospective employers when today's contracts are signed.

Most disturbing is the willingness of some private prisons to cut costs in ways that generate more profit for themselves but result in increased public safety risks for citizens. Historically, prisoners who had to be picked up in one state and delivered to another were transported by sheriff's departments and U.S. marshals. Now, private companies offer the same transportation service for roughly half the cost. However, the way firms reduced costs was by cutting back on union employees and using personnel who were not only poorly trained but worked under more demanding and dangerous situations (e.g., driver guards are forced to make multiple pickups and deliveries on each trip such that on some occasions prisoners may spend a month on the road guarded only by those who are poorly trained).[10]

Perhaps the more invidious cost imposed by private prisons is that they create the illusion of handling the problem by providing for the demand for new prison capacity. This phenomenon diverts attention from other investments that could be made (better education, drug treatment, probation, and dealing with mental health issues in other more proactive and appropriate ways).

Privatization and Schooling. People have characterized privatization as a pressure that educators need to understand and deal with. Some educators have taken a more positive view about the potential of privatization than we have. For example, Joseph Murphy cited the 1988 President's Commission on Privatization, which noted that privatization "may well be seen by future historians as one of the most important developments in American political and economic life of the late 20th century."[11] Murphy agreed with the report and added:

The goal should be to find those forms of marketization that benefit society and minimize those that may harm youngsters and those who are responsible for their education. So, too, must we gain a better understanding of the implications of privatization for the educational industry as we know it—for our portrait of schooling.[12]

As we have said, clearly some of the factors that impact school reform are general societal issues (e.g., the belief in market forces) that affect other public institutions as well. We do not argue that all attempts at privatization are misguided; some forms of privatization have worked reasonably well, such as reducing the government's monopoly in the postal service. Still, one wonders if we would be pleased with the postal system today if the government were not a major player in mail services. Recall, as we noted in chapter 7, private companies should be seen as the lifeboats saving government-run institutions, not as the icebergs sinking them (i.e., some level of privatization may be useful, but not if it deteriorates the presence of government).[13] We stress that privatization per se is not an answer. We have seen that privatization of hospitals and prisons has led to problematic practices as well as to some arguable claims for success.[14]

Table 8.1 presents a list of issues acquired from the experiences of privatizing hospitals and prisons that should be avoided in charter school and other privatization attempts (e.g., vouchers). Some of the

TABLE 8.1
Problematic Effects of Privatization in Hospitals and Prisons

- The salaries for administrators increase substantially in comparison to the salaries of those who deal with clients (e.g., doctors, guards).
- The number of supervisors relative to direct-care providers increase.
- Administrators stress short-term practices that increase profits over long-term solutions.
- Administrators discourage certain types of clients, and seek attractive (easily managed) clients.*
- Research and development budgets decrease.*
- Advertising costs increase.*
- Administrators seek low-cost and minimally trained employees wherever possible to maximize profits.

Note. *These apply only to for-profit hospitals.

privatization issues described in Table 8.1 already have been identified as issues pertaining to public charter schools (e.g., more money going to management costs than to client services). Perhaps the biggest problem is the short-term illusion that privatization creates, that the problem is being addressed. As we saw in chapters 6 and 7, in many charter schools the problem is not well addressed: Data continue to illustrate that many charter schools are marked by low student scores.[15]

Privatization issues are especially salient today. An active debate is underway in the country about what to do with projected budget surpluses (lower taxes vs. increase social services, vs. lower the national debt, etc.). We agree with Robert Frank that it is time to consider that we may be better served as a public by considering the cost of not investing in public services:

> At a time when we are wealthier than ever, does it really make sense to be closing our public libraries on Sundays or cutting Federal inspections of meat-processing plants? Does it make sense not to have replaced antiquated water supply systems that deliver potentially dangerous levels of toxic metals, pesticides, and parasites to some 45 million of us? ... Paradoxically, a tax cut would actually leave Americans with less to spend on themselves. Money spent on a tax cut instead of repairing a road means not only having to spend two to five times as much to fix that same road in the near future, but also having to pay an average of $120 per car to repair the damage that bad roads inflict each year.[16]

Furthermore, he noted that the earlier drive to reduce the size of government in California (Proposition 13) was successful, but not without a cost. Californians who used to send their children to excellent schools now send them to some of the worst schools in the country.[17]

We return later to our suggestions for spending some of the "projected surplus" on educational programs. However, it is clear that privatization is not a panacea for education and if we are to improve education in inner cities an even larger role may be required for government.

POLITICALIZATION OF EDUCATION

Virtually every politician running in America, from the mayor's office to the White House, has a "strong" education plan, and each candidate is faced with an army of special interest lobbyists who constantly are trying to shift educational priorities in competitive ways. Given the contentious advocacy that has occurred, is consensus on education possible?

Is a Consensus on Education Possible?

There are some examples of bipartisan support. For example, Congress in 1998 passed funds of $120 million in grants under the Gear Up program that could be used by states and communities to prepare young people for college.[18] Still, in recent years bipartisan support for educational programs has been hard to obtain.

As noted in chapter 2, many prescriptions have been written for improving the educational system. We examined ideas from various groups, including *A Nation Still at Risk,* and we quarreled with their prescriptions, noting that "reformers" present sweeping and conflicting recommendations for reform. Table 8.2 presents items in President Clinton's call to action for American education in the 21st century from his 1997 State of the Union address. Given that the President has a Department of Education that reports to him and the resources of many concerned with educational policy, it seems reasonable to examine his plan for education.

President Clinton has long been concerned about education reform. Since his days as governor of Arkansas, he has been an avid supporter of education. He is clearly motivated to improve education for Amer-

TABLE 8.2
President Clinton's Call to Action for American Education in the 21st Century

- Set rigorous national standards, with national tests in fourth-grade reading and eighth-grade math to make sure our children master the basics.
- Make sure there is a talented and dedicated teacher in every classroom.
- Help every student to read independently and well by the end of the third grade.
- Expand Head Start and challenge parents to get involved early in their children's learning.
- Expand school choice and accountability in public education.
- Make sure our schools are safe, disciplined, and drug free and instill basic American values.
- Modernize school buildings and help support school construction.
- Open the doors of college to all who work hard and make the grade, and make the 13th and 14th, years of education as universal as high school.
- Help adults improve their education and skills by transforming the tangle of federal training programs into a simple skills grant.
- Connect every classroom and library to the Internet by the year 2000, and help all students become technologically literate.

ica's youth. And, indeed, at a general level, we concur with many of his recommendations, including the need for talented and dedicated teachers; that students should be reading by the end of third grade; that parents should be involved in children's education; that schools be modern, safe, and drug free; and that there should be help for improving adults' education. However, Clinton's overall plan is not impressive. Let's examine a few of the recommendations.

Standards

It is important that the call for rigorous national standards be seen as a shibboleth. Many would contend that the standards we have had historically would enable us to be number 1 in the world, if they were accomplished. Setting higher standards makes sense only if standards are currently too low. This is the case in some schools, but in many schools standards are already at a level that is sufficiently high to enable students to do well in college and to be productive citizens. Present school standards also allow students to function as social beings, without forcing them to be in school 6 days a week and to study until 11 o'clock at night as in some countries.[19] If we are going to improve education, we need to separate Zeitgeist notions from concrete plans.

Karen Wixson and Elizabeth Dutro have explored the relationship between educational standards and student performance.[20] In this research, they analyzed state standards for reading in primary grades within the backdrop of the literature about what is known about early reading. They examined the reading standards from 42 states and then focused on the 14 states that provided specific grade-level information for kindergarten through third grade.

The identification of standards did not ensure excellence in reading achievement. Wixson and Dutro advanced five conclusions about the establishment of state standards for primary-grade reading. First, the majority of states didn't provide specific grade-level standards, and the ones that did often missed important content specific to certain grade levels. Second, there was not a standard way in which reading instruction was organized. For example, reading and language arts were integrated to different degrees (if at all), resulting in differing uses of standards for curriculum development, assessment, and so forth. Third, objectives described in state standards varied notably in terms of specificity with some being so detailed as to represent specific instructional activities and others so general that they did not provide sufficient guidance for teachers or others developing curriculum. Fourth, the ways in which grade-level objectives were combined into a larger continuum of skills across grade levels was disjointed; many grade-level objectives did not "follow a logical developmental sequence."[21] Finally, some objectives were inappropriate to the grade level.

Simply developing standards does not ensure excellence. Standards must be well constructed, keeping in mind variables like setting, assessment, developmental level of the student, desired use, and instructional implementation. The movement to "chain store" schools and schools that buy packaged curriculums is not likely to yield teachers with sufficient curriculum development skills to adjust general curriculum goals to specific needs of students. Importantly, other researchers have also raised questions about the degree of relationship between high standards and improved student performance.[22] We are not against standards per se, because well conceptualized standards can be helpful in setting appropriate goals and in gauging progress. But a vacuous call for increasing standards without an explicit rationale and problem statement is simply counterproductive.

Good Teachers

We wholeheartedly concur with the goal that a talented and dedicated teacher should be present in every classroom. One way to provide high-quality teachers is to make policy recommendations and budget actions that increase teachers' salaries and make them as attractive as possible. Unfortunately, specific plans for increasing teachers' salaries were not included in the President's plan. Given the pending teacher shortage, it seems important to encourage college students to actively consider a career in teaching. Today, however, beginning teachers make, on average, $25,735, which pales in comparison with beginning engineer salaries at $42,862 and beginning computer science salaries at $40,920.[23]

As an example of the continuing political wrangling over educational issues, one can point to recent Republican action to prevent Clinton from funding his new teacher measure ($1.2 billion in the next fiscal year) to hire 100,000 teachers for reducing class size to 18. Republicans argued that rather than giving states money only to hire teachers, they should give options such as reducing class size, improving the quality of existing teachers, and obtaining more special education teachers. Political opposition has developed in part because Clinton's plan focused on low-income rural and inner-city school districts, whereas the Republican plan assures more dollars to affluent suburban school districts.[24] Stephen Holmes noted:

> In addition, the measure is caught up in Presidential politics, people from both sides acknowledge privately. The White House is hoping to make the teacher initiative a major theme in the coming campaign. The Republicans would like to deprive it of that theme in a way that shows that they care just as much about education.[25]

Modernizing School Buildings

In terms of the goal to modernize school buildings, we wholeheartedly agree, and having criticized the President previously for not being concerned about these conditions, we are encouraged by his current support.[26] However, as we have noted, the expansion into charter schools and the new facilities they require may leave communities struggling to maintain and renovate old school buildings while building new ones. If in fact the President wants charter schools to flourish, then perhaps we could have federal programs that provide ample amounts of money for the construction of school buildings when charters demonstrate rigorous and exciting programs of educational reform. However, in the rush to modernize school buildings, we must consider quality issues as well.

Many school buildings are improperly maintained, and the result is that instead of being candidates for renovation, they are having to be replaced. Contributing to this problem are maintenance schedules not being followed and less expensive materials replacing more expensive, longer lasting materials. This problem can only get worse with the advent of charter schools. Some charter schools are leasing buildings that are not handicap accessible and thus require renovation, whereas other charter schools are building new buildings, duplicating structures already in place. This causes a financial drain on existing public schools that leads to less money available for maintenance and building as well as for curriculum and instruction. As a result, many more schools are being created with lower costing and shorter-lived materials.

As noted in a report by 3D/International:

> Sometime during the 1960s budget pressures must have overwhelmed judgment and vision. Instead of terrazzo floors: vinyl tile. Instead of

polished block walls: sheetrock. These material substitutions may accommodate the current budget but they bring with them greater maintenance needs and shorter life cycles. Short-term fiscal limitations create long-term cost escalations.[27]

Admittedly, buildings created with a more extended life in mind also are less flexible in terms of classroom design and new teaching methods and strategies. However, 3/D International recommended, "In the future, we must look at the life cycle costs of school construction. Because the school was cheap to build does not mean the best buy was made. Decisions today must have recognizable consequences."[28]

Further, recent experiences in various cities, including Los Angeles and New York, have illustrated that children's safety is often ignored when repairs are made in public school buildings.[29] And, of course, as we argued in chapter 7, it does not make sense for states to waive (or reduce) facility requirements for charter schools.

School Choice and Enhanced Accountability

Expanding school choice and accountability is a reasonable goal, assuming that certain caveats are addressed, especially concerning quality issues. We have already argued that within the school choice movement, as it was applied to granting charter schools, there was virtually no accountability before these schools were opened. We would hope that, in the future, accountability is assessed at the chartering stage and after the schools have been in operation for a reasonable period of time.

Interestingly, in the OERI 1999 report, roughly 50% of charter schools indicated that they had submitted or intended to submit a report to their chartering agency. Less than 50% expressed those same intentions to the state department of education. It seems an understatement to suggest that charter schools are functioning with little monitoring from their charter agencies and the state departments of education. Given the potential of charter schools to reform education and the considerable amount of public monies that are being invested, it seems important that charter schools be more accountable to their immediate sponsors and, more broadly, to citizens.

Seymour Sarason reached a similar conclusion, that the quick and nonanalytical way in which charter schools are being created almost guarantees we will learn nothing from them about how to improve the present educational system. He advocated that from both success-ful and unsuccessful projects it is possible to learn a great deal (he cites the Manhattan Project as being useful) when people have made it their business to provide detailed, descriptive records of what occurred and why. Unfortunately, Sarason noted, "that kind of record would not be available to us in the case of charter schools. But, then again, the ab-sence of such a record is a feature of the history of educational reform as well as the history of the creation of settings. The more things change the more they remain the same, or get worse."[30]

Absent From the President's Plan

Missing from the President's list is any call for research and develop-ment. It is understood that research and development is necessary for the military and in fighting high-profile diseases; it would seem that attempts to deal meaningfully with understanding the complexity of teaching and learning situations is an equally important research area.

Unfortunately, such logic is not applied in the area of education. Rather, we see a marked capacity for leaders at the federal, state, and local levels to support and sponsor educational programs without even requiring that charter school directors have a coherent philo-sophical understanding of education and appropriate management and financial training to make a viable program work for children. Set-ting rigorous national standards may be an unobtainable goal. How-ever, being sure that those who open new charter schools have a coherent educational and financial plan seems to be reachable if only we have political resolve to do so.

Continue Scapegoating or Move Toward Consensus?

Without basic knowledge, we are likely to continue the blame cycle marked by moralizing about the deficiencies of others that have come to characterize the current war on education.[31] It is common to blame the poor conditions of urban education on parents, teachers, politi-cians, and so forth. We have become experts at blaming others. The media blames school officials and parents, administrators blame par-ents and teachers, parents blame others, and so it continues. Perhaps it is time to recognize that we all share in the educational disgrace that takes place in too many schools.

Oddly, even when schools do make progress in enhancing student performance on standardized tests, these improvements are often diminished by editorial assertions that the degree of progress is inadequate. If we can accept the premise that blame is widely shared, we may be able to secure a sufficiently broad citizen consensus necessary for securing the resources needed to develop strategies for strengthening our understanding of why students fail and what we can do about it. And, we must recognize that when schools achieve notable improvements, it should be an occasion for support and additional encouragement, not criticism.

Toward Consensus

Given the President's vague call for educational improvement, it is naive to think we can presently reach consensus on what is best for education. Politicians are guaranteed to fight over issues like national standards (e.g., federal vs. state vs. local control of curriculum) and the role of charters, vouchers, and privatization efforts. However, it seems that basic inquiry and solid information about educational progress is one area in which some degree of consensus may be possible. Researching information about the differential costs of type A and type B summer school and their comparative effects on different types of children would seem to represent an expenditure of funds that a wide variety of citizens could support, for instance. What are we spending our money on, and how are our children impacted? Perhaps a working consensus can be organized around designing needed programs for our children and finding out if they work and why.

BUILDING A KNOWLEDGE BASE

Why do policymakers not call for research and development funds for education as they do when the country faces a new medical issue, such as the research response to the AIDs virus?[32] First, their lack of enthusiasm for educational research may be because they believe that we currently have sufficient knowledge but lack the will to use it (thus, policymakers' calls to work harder and for market competition). The possibility of this view is strengthened by the fact that state legislatures have passed charter school legislation that has authorized charter schools to operate even if they are doing little, if anything, to create new knowledge. Second, it may be that state legislators, governors, senators, and others do not advocate for research funding because they believe that educating youth is a fairly easy task. Individuals with this view contend that maybe we don't have all the knowledge we need about how students learn but needed knowledge can be "picked up on the job" easily if teachers are willing to work harder. A third, and more disturbing, view is that children, or at least the ones who are failing in our schools, are not worth the investment of adequate resources. Since it is almost unthinkable that a majority of policymakers and legislators would deny research funds to support inner-city youth's educational development if they thought some children would gain educationally, we turn to the fourth possible explanation. A fourth reason is that policymakers do not think educators can conduct research that would yield a better knowledge base for enhancing students' education.

Current Knowledge Base

There is a rich professional knowledge base in the field that can be used in ways that enhance teachers' professional decision making and students' classroom learning.[33] Unfortunately, most of this knowledge has been developed in schools other than those in the most dire need—urban schools. There has been some informative research that has been conceptualized especially for inner-city schools,[34] but most typically the original research was conducted in other school settings and then transported and implemented in inner-city school settings.

Undoubtedly, there are schools in which teachers and administrators do not work hard enough. There are inner-city public schools that should be closed or taken into receivership.[35] As another example of the failure of public schools in some large urban settings, it is instructive to note that more than one-fifth of students in New Orleans are enrolled in private schools.[36] However, having acknowledged these conclusions—we do have some knowledge and we do have some incompetent or unmotivated teachers and administrators—we want to assert that typically they do not represent the problem at the most basic level.

One difficulty with improving student performance in schools with the greatest failure rates, is that we currently have an inadequate knowledge base. This fundamental problem could be improved by a rigorous research and development program. There are acute conceptual issues about learning and maturation in more advantaged schools as well; however, here we concentrate on the necessity for research to improve our knowledge of how to educate students in inner-city schools.

What We Cannot Know Without Research

Let's return to possible reasons why policymakers have been unwilling to fund education. Policymakers' views about the first two reasons for not calling for research—that we have sufficient knowledge and that any teacher can quickly find answers—are flatly wrong. Because we do not possess setting-specific, detailed information on many basic issues, answers to these questions are not obvious and cannot readily be found by teachers regardless of how hard they work.

If we are to improve urban schools, the most basic and most difficult step is to recognize that we do not know how to cure the serious learning problems and academic failures that afflict many of our students, particularly inner-city students. Students' failure cannot be explained by the polemical charges of lazy students or teachers and indifferent bureaucrats.

There is an arsenal of educational interventions, and for some students these treatments sometimes work. There are some examples of individual students who graduate from inner-city schools, matriculate from prestigious universities, and lead successful lives. Moreover, there are some inner-city schools that help a high percentage of their students to succeed academically. But the more frequent and tragic reality is that many students in inner-city schools are failing. What can we learn from this analysis?

Why is it that some schools have achieved high success rates with inner-city youth? Do students in these schools possess a rare blend of intelligence, motivation, and hardiness? Is it because of luck—a random event? Or is it because some adult(s) was there to provide support at critical moments?[37] Are students in these schools blessed with the presence of a number of unusually talented teachers and administrators who possess a rare blend of intelligence, knowledge of students (both as learners and as social beings), tremendous energy levels, and a strong work ethic? Are these talented teachers akin to talented surgeons in good, supportive hospitals who can respond to difficult cases in ways that less talented surgeons cannot? Or are the strategies used in these successful inner-city schools the types of actions and dispositions that could improve students' performance in other schools, where students are taught by ordinary teachers? The word *ordinary* is not used to demean teachers or teaching. The job of teaching in any setting is complex and requires capable and knowledgeable individuals.[38] However, within any profession, there are the ordinary or average and the exceptional. Can average teachers construct inner-city school programs that allow a significantly higher percent of students to succeed than is the case now? The answer to this question is unknown. There is reason to be somewhat hopeful, because some schools have been transformed into exciting learning centers.[39] It is time to face this extraordinary challenge of determining which programs and practices work and to see if it is possible to develop insights to help students generally to succeed in inner-city schools.

Unfortunately, most of the stories about school success are written after the success has occurred, not during or before. The stories of success are often told by competent authors who attempt to recapture and describe the steps that led to success. Although these accounts provide interesting descriptions of decisions, programs, and policies that took place, there is no way of knowing which of the many events reported, if any, were those actions and beliefs that helped students to learn. There are ample data to illustrate the fragile nature of human memory and our tendency to "find events and explanations" that fit into established cultural beliefs.[40] Further, without a working theory or understanding of why improvements occurred, it is unlikely that these descriptions can be used dependably in other settings.

Let's take an example. School A has made a comprehensive effort to increase homework for two years. The plan calls for five homework assignments a week, each taking about 90 minutes to complete, and doing homework really counts—40% of students' grades are based on homework assignments. After 2 years, student achievement scores have risen notably in the district. As attractive as this proposal might appear initially, without more specific knowledge an attempt to implement this homework policy in another school is as likely to worsen problems as to improve them.

When the "same" homework plan that worked well in school A is used in school B, it may have different effects for many reasons. Perhaps it wasn't the homework that made a difference in students' performance. Perhaps the way the policy was developed was endemic to its success (teachers visibly working together) or the way the policy was introduced by the school (it conveyed to students that teachers believed in their ability to master difficult material). Or perhaps homework was helpful because it emphasized key concepts that were similar to questions subsequently asked on classroom tests, such that students approached classroom tests with less anxiety. Further, the homework may have been important because it helped students to structure their after-school experiences more carefully, and this certainty of how to spend time led to renewed students'confidence in controlling their academic lives (i.e., enhanced efficacy and an internal sense of control). We could continue, but the point is that we don't know why it worked—even those who originally designed the homework policy cannot know why it worked without conducting carefully planned and controlled research studies.

Competence Reconsidered

Students can fail for many different reasons.[41] Often solutions for helping students to learn—especially those generated by policymakers—are generated without any consideration of the problem for particular students. It is exceedingly difficult to determine if a student's inability to apply a concept is because of a learning problem, memory problem, insufficient motivation, motivation that is different from the teacher's, or the interaction of all of these reasons. It is possible that students may start the year both motivated and learning but develop problems subsequently that may overwhelm them. Even seemingly minor events in students' lives may cause serious problems.

Let's consider Mary, a fifth-grade student who starts the school year strongly. After a month in class, she is consistently doing B work in a classroom where the teacher has appropriate standards. Mary becomes ill and misses school for the first 2 weeks in October. However, when Mary returns to school, she is determined to make good progress. This attitude is fortunate, because sometimes students who have missed a couple weeks of school return with a deep fear that they are hopelessly behind, or that classmates will not remember them. What happens to Mary when she returns? Her teacher has 27 students. On a given day, two students are absent; hence, in a given week, six to eight students miss at least 1 day of school. How does an ordinary teacher deal with finding the time necessary to help Mary and the other students who fall behind? Maybe there are teachers in inner-city settings who can do this routinely and well. If so, we need to identify them and learn from them.

But, let's look at a more difficult case. Consider Theresa, an eighth-grade student who starts the school year poorly in September. Her performance in all of her classes is at the D level. Theresa misses the first 2 weeks of October. Now, she returns to make up work with teachers who, on average, teach about 130 students a day and who have 40 or so pupils who miss at least 1 period a week. How do students and teachers deal with this issue? We can reasonably make the situation more difficult. In November, Theresa transfers to a new charter school in an adjoining school district. After 2 weeks, Theresa's school records still have not reached her new teacher. What do Theresa and her new teachers do to achieve academic success for her, especially when it is likely that Theresa's new teachers will receive other new transfer students that also have problems? Some transfer students may have learning difficulties that are similar to Theresa's (they have fallen behind); however, some of the transfer students who come to Theresa's room will be ahead of her class. How does the teacher accommodate these students (who may quickly develop a motivational problem if they perceive that the curriculum is being "dummied down" for them)? Teachers who must resolve these issues also have their own personal lives, which are sometimes exceedingly difficult as well.[42]

Too often those who recommend school reform policies have only a competency model in mind. However, the causes of failure are varied, and student ability (and the competency of their teachers) is only one reason. Students fail for reasons other than personal ability and effort, and it is difficult to identify and remediate these reasons for failure without appropriate, setting-specific research. Much more research is needed on the "nonability" reasons for failure, and what to do to resolve such reasons.

Competent Environment

Sadly, we know that there are many other problems that teachers and students face in school situations. Students attend schools where there are puddles on the floor and inadequate heating in the winter.[43] They attend schools that are physically unattractive and unsafe. Students who share classrooms with roaches are more likely to remember the roaches than their algebra assignments. Further, in those inner-city schools that do have adequate physical plants, students and teachers often suffer the consequences of inadequate libraries, laboratories, and technology. What do inner-city youth think adults believe about them and their potential when they compare their school to others?

Given the circumstances in which many students are schooled, we find recommendations like those advanced by *A Nation Still at Risk*—market competition, accountability, and higher standards—to be a cruel prescription for youth. What these shibboleths represent in too many cases is simply social Darwinism at school. We now have a small percentage of talented youth emerging from schools successfully. Why make the competition even more rigorous so that even fewer students survive? It seems that we should demand a better return on our investments in inner-city schools for reasons of both morality and self-survival. Too many students are educated in incompetent environments.

As Smrekar and Goldring noted:

> Children in neglected and isolated urban areas are vulnerable to the pathologies of rootlessness, hopelessness, and violence in the absence of a set of organizational and institutional affiliations (e.g., civic, recreational, religious, professional) that bind families in stable, predictable, and enduring social ties. The challenge rests with crafting public policies that reconstitute school–community linkages in ways that help promote school achievement, neighborhood and family stability, and economic revitalization (Wehlage, 1993[44]).[45]

Some Examples of Important Questions

It is time to document with research the types of programs that work for particular students and problems.

Summer School. If, for example, second-grade students go to summer school because they are deficient in reading, math, and writing, how to structure the summer experience is problematic. This is especially the case if students are under pressure—if they must pass a test at the end of summer school in order to be promoted to third grade.[46] Should students go to summer school for 12 weeks and spend a third of the time on each of three subjects daily? Or would students benefit from a massive review and opportunity to think about one subject for only 4 weeks, take the test, and then move on to the second subject? Should students start with the subject in which they are least far behind or the one in which the gap between their current and expected level of performance is greatest? What is the maximum number of students a given teacher can work with intensively but successfully? If we place 15 students in a remedial summer program, have we guaranteed failure for all because of class size? Given that many students will be going to summer school the next few years, it seems important to begin to build a knowledge base that documents successes and failures of various approaches to summer school.

Attendance. To give another example, if students are attending school regularly, they are more likely to do well than if they are frequently absent. Thus, one way to prevent some achievement problems is to be sure that students are routinely in school. Further, we know that some schools are better at attendance than others, and we know that some interventions have proven to be successful in increasing attendance in ways that are both practically important as well as significantly important.

For example, DeWayne Mason, Assistant Superintendent of Education Services for Jurupa Unified School District in Southern California implemented practices that led to increased student attendance and an additional $1,000,000 in state funds for the district. To accomplish this, he made attendance a district priority and developed a rewards' program to reinforce schools and principals with increased attendance. In those schools that demonstrated .50 of 1% increase in attendance over the previous year, the principal received a gift certificate for dinner at a local restaurant and the school teachers and staff a luncheon delivered by Dr. Mason. If the district's attendance rate increased by .22 of 1% , then all schools whose attendance increased received 15% of the additional monies the district received from the increased attendance. In addition, trophies and prizes were awarded to the schools with the best attendance rates. These practices led the district to achieve 13-year highs for attendance in 20 of the 23 schools (records were only available for 13 years). Dr. Mason commented, "notably, 17 of the schools improved their attendance by over one-half of one percent, and 11 schools by .93 of one percent or better."[47] During the second year in which increased attendance occurred there were increases in achievement in 20 of the 23 schools. For example, two elementary schools that had the highest attendance gains increased their total achievement (reading, mathematics, and English) on the Stanford-9 by 10 percentile points.

Although some may raise an eyebrow about using economic incentives to encourage extra efforts from school principals, we should recognize that incentives are used successfully in the corporate world to positively encourage performance and loyalty to the company rather than to punitively coerce them. Some have even given employees leased BMWs as long as they remain in the firm and others have provided $1,200 a year vacation allowances.[48]

Dealing With Absences.   Even with good attendance policies in hand, there are important knowledge gaps. We know that many urban students, given their poor life conditions, are going to miss school, and in some cases extended absences will occur. Consider the brief student illness vignette presented earlier in the chapter. It may be that when students miss a specific number of days it is simply counterproductive for teachers to continue to work with them. These students don't recover, and valuable time is taken away from other students. Perhaps students who have extensive absences need to go to specifically designed programs that specialize in catching students up.

On the other hand, a better way to proceed could be to attract the best teachers possible and to keep class sizes to a maximum of 10 (or even 18 as President Clinton is trying to achieve) in K–3 classrooms. Such a plan would enable teachers to work with students who are absent and to maximize other goals and possibilities as well (e.g., most students read at grade level when they graduate from third grade). Yet another approach might be to develop major forms of software that deal with key grade-level concepts in creative and interesting ways so that technology becomes a better tutor for students who have excessive absences. However, for various reasons, this strategy probably still would not be a good idea for certain types of students who do not do well when they learn in isolation from others. It may also encourage absentees in the first place.

Certainly, we can do a better job of sharing information about students who transfer from one school to another; too many students are simply lost in the process. It is unacceptable that a country that has developed the capacity for discovering new objects in deep space cannot keep track of students who move across district or state lines. It is time to develop information exchange procedures that are easily transferable (e.g., computer disk) when a student moves from one school to another.

Fourth-Grade Decline.   We know that some inner-city students get off to a good start but begin to falter in the fourth grade. There are many hypotheses for this occurrence, but the most frequent argument is that the curriculum changes cognitively such that more abstract thinking is required. Unfortunately, this observation is typically followed by the inference that many students aren't up to the increasingly difficult cognitive tasks. Importantly, there are many competing explanations for why students' failure rates might go up at this time other than reasons related to student competence. As students move through school, much is changing other than curriculum. For example, students are social beings as well as academic learners, and increasingly these needs become important (balancing friends and scholarship).[49]

It is well known, especially by students, that around fourth grade, effort is not enough. In fact, it is clear that when students take longer to learn—effort takes time—many students (and adults) infer that students are less competent. In reality, students' academic difficulty as they move into the fourth grade simply may be because a subtle difference in assigned work is not adequately explained to them or because the task features of the new work are not as motivationally salient as were tasks in earlier grades or that earlier well-learned strategies are no longer useful (asking quickly for help).

Case study work conducted by Mary McCaslin and Tamara Murdock illustrated other nonability determinants that may explain student failure.[50] For example, beliefs instilled at home by parents are related to motivation and the value of achievement. McCaslin and Murdock's work illustrated that metacognitive skills of students who start school similarly may develop differentially not because of the school curriculum but because of the match of school and home expectations.

We could continue to cite areas of needed research, but the point has been made. We need to better coordinate working definitions of problems and possible solutions and to study those implemented strategies in ways that allow us to understand when we have made progress and when we haven't so that in time more dependable sets of strategies are developed.

Summary

It is time to bring serious research and development efforts to inner-city schools. It is important to invest funds in talented researchers who are charged with the task of conceptualizing inner-city educational problems in sophisticated ways that ultimately yield detailed problem statements that are meshed with particular types of solutions. In the best spirit of market competition and accountability, funds should only go to those who have solid plans.

If we want to improve education, we need to understand why students fail. Different reasons for failure undoubtedly require different types of solutions. For example, a child who has a learning disability in reading and a child who is undernourished and has not eaten since lunch the day before may have similar difficulties concentrating during reading; however, the solutions for these two children vary dramatically. One needs regular well-balanced meals and the other needs special help with his or her reading skills.

It is wasteful to invest vast amounts of funds in school programs when we have no idea of what we are trying to do with those funds. As a case in point, summer programs and retention policies (i.e., get tough on social promotion) require large resources, and typically such programs are designed to respond to a range of problems; which problem is of the highest priority is seldom specified let alone adequately defined. On those occasions when programs work generally well, we do not know why they do.

MAKE SCHOOLS WORK BY INCREASING GENERAL SUPPORT AND THE KNOWLEDGE BASE

In this section we argue the need for building community support for increasing our knowledge about student learning in schools. We start by arguing that charter schools become sites for experimentation and innovation and, hence, contributors to the knowledge base. We then turn to the general issue of trying to capture societal interest and support for research.

Unique Possibilities for Charter Schools

Policymakers who believe in market competition are in an excellent position to reward innovative thinking and research and development in the area of education, especially in inner-city schools. It is important to begin to take actions that could conceivably present workable strategies to help more of our students succeed in urban schools. These efforts and funds are ill spent on developing charter schools that replicate many of the facility costs of existing public schools without adding replicable research knowledge. Policymakers need to recast legislation to improve the possibility that charter schools will fulfill a research function.

George García and Mary García, two public school superintendents, expressed guarded optimism about the potential for charter schools as a basis for contributing to research and development ideas in public education.[51] Writing in 1996, they indicated:

> Critics and supporters alike will be watching charter schools to see whether these schools are models for improving achievement for all students. As noted above, the possibility may be the idea that charters serve a specific function within the public school. With the adaptability of small size, charter schools could pilot new teaching strategies, curriculum offerings, and organizational structures where best practices can be studied, validated, and replicated in traditional schools.[52]

Despite the passage of time and the lack of generalizable information from charter schools, we too remain guardedly optimistic that charter schools might play a role in research and development. However, this can happen only if policymakers and especially legislators are willing to design practices and laws that encourage charter schools to fulfill a research and development role.

Charter schools, if properly established and evaluated, could add increased information to our knowledge base about what works in schools generally and in specific types of environments for specific types of students. Although charter school enthusiasts have made promises about innovation, these promises have seldom been fulfilled in practice. As we pointed out in chapter 7, the cause for this is that charters largely have been granted without requiring charter schools to compete. Further, charter schools have not had to illustrate that they are using sufficiently interesting practices that afford some opportunity to develop, implement, and assess new strategies for helping students learn particular content or for developing particular attitudes toward school. If the recommendations we advanced in chapter 7 can be enacted even partially, the potential for improving the knowledge base through a careful exploration of charter schools can be enhanced substantially.

Although most states allow charter schools to operate generally, some states are so concerned about inner-city schools that they have limited charter school operations to those settings (e.g., Missouri). Philosophically we are not opposed to the notion that charter schools might operate in some suburban settings, but we feel strongly that if charters as experimental agencies are to be granted, a problem statement needs to be spelled out. When charters are granted, there should be explicit, compelling reasons for doing so, so that citizens and policymakers can be assured that charter schools that operate in noncrisis situations are more than simply an opportunity for entrepreneurs to make money. There should be a legitimate educational issue being addressed and assessed so that those experiments and attempts at innovation can be examined for information about new strategies and tasks that might work in other settings.

Societal Recognition and Economic Incentives

There is presently a national debate about how best to use projected federal budget surpluses. Should they be used for social programs? Reducing the national debt? Tax cuts? Given the possibility that large budget surpluses may be realized in the next few years, it is important for interested citizens to mobilize to secure more resources for research in education and more direct support for our schools.

Economic and social incentives are sufficient that medical researchers will work tirelessly for decades for cures (or even relief of symptoms) for life-threatening diseases: When advances are made researchers receive tremendous social and financial rewards. Why not target some revenues to encourage engineers and software computer specialists, among others, to design systems that enable students to do catch-up work while still in the hospital and to make up for lost opportunities in well-designed and effective summer programs? Why not provide incentives for educational researchers to collaborate with professionals in other fields? For example, educators' understanding of students as social learners could be combined with others' expert knowledge of organizational planning, technology, and so forth.

If a team of experts addresses specific issues successfully, the rewards to society would be large. For example, wouldn't it be exciting if the number of students who begin a downward educational spiral in fourth grade were cut in half? Wouldn't it be an incredible service to society if the number of successful readers at the end of third grade were increased by 20 percent? Yet, the federal government does little to define realistic goals or to structure focused research programs with sufficient funding to attract talented and motivated researchers to help meet these goals.

We recognize the work of talented and productive citizens in many areas of society (Pulitzer Prize, Nobel Prize, etc.). Why not have an award sponsored by federal or state government—or by private foundations or the business community—to recognize citizens and researchers who make thoughtful contributions to education? It is not surprising to see that many high paying jobs (e.g., principals) in education do not attract many applicants, because the jobs involve incredibly long hours, conflict, and often public indifference or, worse, public abasement.[53]

Newspapers routinely publish test scores. Why not also do more developmental reporting to represent more generally the difficult issues that education addresses? Certainly newspapers should report the failures of schools, but why not also notice progress?[54]

Some students may simply claim that no matter how hard they work, they will not have the resources to go to college. At some point, students who are consistently getting A's and B's may recognize that the social contract implicitly offered them—work hard and do well in school and you will have a future—is simply not the case. If we are trying to design competent environments, perhaps part of those environments should be an awareness that if students truly do well in school, their motivation and hard work will be recognized, and they will receive either financial aid or scholarships to pay for their college education.

Why not consider the use of new revenues—especially if projected surpluses materialize—to make inner cities more attractive to homeowners and the business community? Why not reduce property taxes and use other incentives to attract new businesses and homeowners to our inner cities? Why not add school and community recreational and educational programs, so that various after-school programs are available for youth? If we want talented teachers in the inner city, why not provide forgiveness loans for college debts for capable students who are willing to teach in inner-city schools for some minimum time period.

As a case in point, in May 1999 the Missouri legislature announced its intentions to provide incentives for helping to attract teachers. Beginning in 2000 the state plans to forgive $8,000 for 2 years of undergraduate work and $8,000 for students in graduate school. Further, an additional $8,000 is forgivable for every year a student works in an urban or rural school district.[55] As an example of local school districts attempting to use incentives to encourage teachers to accept positions in low performing schools, a new program in New York City offers a

15% salary increase and a $2,500 reimbursement for teachers who are pursuing master's degrees.[56]

CONCLUSION: A GENERAL CALL FOR RESEARCH AND DEVELOPMENT IN URBAN SCHOOLS

Certainly a country that has sufficient strength, courage, and resources to help reduce atrocities throughout the world has the capacity to affect the tragedies that are occurring in some of our own school settings. A society that could develop a Marshall Plan to save Europe after World War II can certainly develop a Marshall Plan to save inner-city schools—if it chooses to do so.[57] In recent times, some political and military strategists have admitted that they were unaware of the problems that our troops would face in Vietnam. Now that President Clinton has admitted that he underestimated the magnitude of the problems our forces would encounter in Kosovo, perhaps he and other politicians and reformers, with similar honesty, can admit that they have underestimated the diverse forms of help our school children need if they are to thrive educationally. Research on these problems is needed

Researchers who seek funding should be held accountable for developing coherent descriptions of why students fail and hypotheses about plausible strategies for intervening. Useful data will not be obtained collecting pre- and posttest data on students who are held back, students who receive summer programs versus those who do not, or students who participate in uncontrolled educational experiments (e.g., charter schools). We know that some students who are retained will do well and that many who are socially promoted will be okay. Studies are needed to help determine *why* some students benefit from a summer program and others don't and what we can do to *improve* the program for students who do not benefit initially.

Researchers and program developers need to work with specific students in longitudinal research that enables them to talk to students, their parents, and their teachers and to understand the multiple conceptions of what is taking place and how students are reacting to strategies presumably designed to benefit them. Such work has the potential for identifying different types of failure and sophisticated strategies for intervening. Effective intervention will require quantitative and qualitative research that carefully documents what happens in the classroom and at home and attempts to understand participants' beliefs and feelings.[58]

Although surveys can provide some useful information about what teachers report they are doing inside classrooms,[59] there is no substitute for observational research that actually attempts to document practices and to relate them to achievement. For example, in a recent federal study it was reported that "more than half the teachers surveyed were using portfolios to assess students in some area of learning."[60] Our reaction to such information is "so what?" Is the use of portfolios related to improved student attitudes or to improved student performance or to improved home-school communication and is this practice more likely to be seen in high versus low performing urban schools?[61]

In particular, we should place more emphasis on getting students to discuss their beliefs and needs. Obviously, if students alone could solve their problems, many would. We do not suggest that students can give answers but that understanding their beliefs is part of the solution. Advertisers are wise enough to talk to children about their beliefs to more effectively sell them products. Indeed, in recent years advertisers have invaded classroom materials (e.g., textbooks) to enhance their marketing to students.[62] Students in Florida have shown the capacity to design helpful advertising approaches about how to stop teen smoking.[63] It stands to reason that policymakers and researchers who want to improve schools should seek advice from students.

We hope that these arguments are sufficiently persuasive to induce policymakers and citizens to agree that some educational answers are not obvious and that education has some fundamental gaps in its knowledge base. Further, we hope that needed social and economic incentives will be enhanced to retain and attract additional talent to the field of educational research.

Earlier in the chapter we voiced the possibility that perhaps policymakers do not think educators have the ability or willingness to conduct competent research.[64] If this is the case, the issue can easily be resolved. Create open competitions for conducting research so that individuals from any occupation (physicians, lawyers, engineers, politicians, journalists, teachers, educational psychologists, and so forth) can compete. Award grants only for well-thought-out and promising proposals. Governors, citizens, committees, legislators, and members of the professional and business community should be involved in developing lists of valued research questions and solicit legislative funds to support this needed research.

Clearly, left to their own devices, it seems that politicians are unlikely to move toward finding consensus positions on education. If the current politicalization of education is to be altered, it will be because citizens and organized groups push for political consensus and a focus on improving life conditions, especially for children. To move politicians from conceptualizing educational issues as political footballs to an area of personal morality and professional accountability requires the involvement of many professional groups working in concert to bring about this change. Certainly the media (e.g., Educational Writers Association), various professional groups (American Nurses Association, American Psychological Association, American Educational Research Association, American Medical Association, National Education Association), and various community groups interested in children (Casey Foundation, Girl Scouts, and others) need to find broader coalitions for working together to stimulate educational research and development.

Citizens can continue to blame teacher educators, teachers, parents, and students for educational failure. Or, we can begin to take steps to reverse this destructive blame cycle. We can move toward finding consensus in funding and developing stronger programs for children through various collective acts, including research and program development. To do so, we must put the needs of children ahead of politics and begin documenting what educational practices work for our children.

Endnotes

1. Associated Press. (1999, August 8). Clinton says GOP budget plan imperils education programs. *The New York Times*, p. 14.
2. Berliner, D., & Biddle, B. (1995). *The manufactured crisis: Myths, fraud, and the attack on America's public schools*. New York: Addison-Wesley.
   Rose, M. (1995). *The promise of possible lives: The promise of public education in America*. Boston, MA: Houghlin Mifflin.
3. Hartocollis, A. (1999, June 24). Crew to close 13 poorly performing schools and take control of 43 others. *The New York Times*, p. A29.
4. Kuttner, R. (1997). *Everything for sale: The virtues and limits of markets*. New York: Knopf.
5. Ibid.
6. Ibid.
7. Schlosser, E. (1998). The prison-industrial complex. *Atlantic Monthly, 282*(6), 51–77.
8. Ibid., p. 55.
9. Ibid.
10. Ibid.
11. Murphy, J. (1996, October). Why privatization signals a sea of change in schooling. *Educational Leadership*, 62.

12. Ibid.

13. Wildavsky, B. (1999, June 28). Why charter schools make Inkster nervous. *U.S. News Online*. Available: http://www.usnews.com/usnews/issue/990628/charter.htm

14. From *A NewsHour* with Jim Lehrer. (1999, June 24). *Doctors vote to unionize* [Online]. Available: http://www.pbs.org/newshour/bb/health/jan-june99/doctors_6-24.html

15. Fisher, H. (1999, June 25). Charter schools say state rules put undue weight on low marks. *Arizona Daily Star,* pp. 3A, 3B.
Hornbeck, M. (1999, June 6). Charter schools fall short of expectations. *The Detroit News*. Available online [http://detnews.com/specialreports/1999/schools/990606main/990606main.htm]

16. Frank, R. H. (1999, July 31). Which do we need more, bigger cars or better schools? *The New York Times*, p. A27.

17. Ibid.

18. Associated Press. (1999, August 8). Clinton says GOP budget plan imperils education programs. *New York Times*, p. 14.

19. McCaslin, M., & Good, T. (1996). *Listening in classrooms*. New York: Harper Collins.

20. Wixson, K. K., & Dutro, E. (In press). Standards for primary-grade reading: An analysis of state frameworks. *The Elementary School Journal*.

21. Ibid, ms. p. 31.

22. Boser, U. (1999, June 23). Study finds mismatch between California standards and assessments. *Education Week, 18*(41) 10.

23. American Federation of Teachers. (1999, June 21). *Teacher salary boost is one way to stem teacher shortages*. Press release [Online]. Available: http://aft.org/press/index.html

24. Holmes, S. A. (1999, July 2). Republicans thwart Clinton on new teachers, *The New York Times*, p. A14.

25. Ibid.

26. Good, T. (1997). Educational researchers comment on the Education Summit and other policy proclamations from 1983–1996. *Educational Researcher, 25*, 4–6.

27. 3D/International. (1999, March). *Problems of underfunded maintenance are being compounded by the lack of capital renewal plans*. White paper, p. 4.

28. Ibid., p. 5.

29. Sullivan, J., Drew, C., & Steinberg, J. (1999, July 26). Careless risks in fixing New York city schools. *The New York Times*, pp. A1, A16.
Purdum, T. (1999, July 28). A $200 million school that may never open. *The New York Times,* pp. A1, A17.

30. Sarason, S. (1998). *Charter schools: Another flawed educational reform*. New York: Teachers College Record.

31. Applebome, P. (1999, September 14). Scold war: Yelling at the little red menace. *The New York Times,* sec. 4, 1,5.

32. Shavelson, R., & Berliner, D. (1988). Erosion of the education research infrastructure: A reply to Finn. *Educational Researcher, 17*, 9–12.

33. Good, T., & Brophy, J. (2000). *Looking in classrooms* (8th ed.). New York: Longman.

Biddle, B., Good, T., & Goodson, I. (1997). *International handbook of teachers and teaching* (Vols. 1–2). Boston, MA: Kluwer.

Dworkin, A. G. (1997). Coping with reform: The intermix of teacher morale, teacher burnout, and teacher accountability. In B. Biddle, T. Good, & I. Goodson. (Eds.), *International handbook of teachers and teaching* (Vol. 1, pp. 459–498). Boston, MA: Kluwer.

Biddle, B. J. (1997). Recent research on the role of the teacher. In B. Biddle, T. Good, & I. Goodson (Eds.), *International handbook of teachers and teaching* (Vol. 1, pp. 499–520). Boston, MA: Kluwer.

Smylie, M. A. (1997). Research on teacher leadership: Assessing the state of the art. In B. Biddle, T. Good, & I. Goodson (Eds.), *International handbook of teachers and teaching* (Vol. 1, pp. 521–592). Boston, MA: Kluwer.

House, E. R., & Laplan, S. D. (1997). Policy, productivity, and teacher evaluation. In B. Biddle, T. Good, & I. Goodson (Eds.), *International handbook of teachers and teaching* (Vol. 1, pp. 593–620). Boston, MA: Kluwer.

Nuthall, G. (1997). Understanding student thinking and learning in the classroom. In B. Biddle, T. Good, & I. Goodson (Eds.), *International handbook of teachers and teaching* (Vol. 2, pp. 681–768). Boston, MA: Kluwer.

Randi, J., & Corno, L. (1997). Teachers as innovators. In B. Biddle, T. Good, & I. Goodson (Eds.), *International Handbook of teachers and teaching* (Vol. 1, pp. 1163–1221). Boston, MA: Kluwer.

Putnam, R. T., & Borko, H. (1997). Teacher learning: Implications of new views of cognition. In B. Biddle, T. Good, & I. Goodson (Eds.), *International handbook of teachers and teaching* (Vol. 2, pp. 1223–1296). Boston, MA Kluwer.

34. Mehan, H. (1997). Tracking untracking: The consequences of placing low-track students in high-track classes. In P. Hall (Ed.), *Race, ethnicity, and multiculturalism: Policy and practice* (pp. 115–150). New York: Garland.

Weinstein, R., & McKown, C. (1998). Expectancy effects in context: Listening to the voices of students and teachers. In J. Brophy (Ed.), *Advances in research on teaching* (Vol. 7, pp. 215–242). Greenwich, CT: JAI Press.

35. Hartocollis, A. (1999, June 24). Crew to close 13 poorly performing schools and take control of 43 others. *The New York Times*, p. A29.

36. Associated Press. (1999, August 8). Ex-marine with ideas not degrees tries to save New Orleans schools. *Arizona Daily Star*, A4.

37. Michael Rose, the author of various books on public education (e.g., *Possible lives,* (1995, Boston, MA: Houghton Mifflin), has noted that as an individual who, himself, has escaped from inner-city life the presence of mentors was extremely important in his development in terms of the capacity and the perspective for continuing to move forward even when things got difficult.

38. Good, T., & Brophy, J. (2000). *Looking in classrooms* (8th ed). New York: Longman.

39. Meier, D. (1995). *The power of their ideas: Lessons for America from a small school in Harlem*. Boston, MA: Beacon Press.

40. Bartlett, F. C. (1932). *Remembering*. Cambridge: Cambridge University Press.

41. The authors acknowledge Mary McCaslin in the Department of Educational Psychology at the University of Arizona for helping us to strengthen the points

made in this section and the one that follows, entitled "Competent Environment."

42. Spencer, D. (1986). *Contemporary women teachers: Balancing school and home*. New York: Longman.
    Spencer, D. (1997). Teaching as woman's work. B. Biddle, T. Good, & I. Goodson (Eds.) *International handbook of teachers and teaching* (Vol. 1, pp. 153–198). Boston, MA: Kluwer.

43. Hayden, J. (Producer and Director), & Cauthen, C. (Director). (1996). *Children in America's schools with Bill Moyers* [film]. (Available from South Carolina ETV).

44. Wehlage, G. (1993). Social capital and the rebuilding of communities. In *Issues in restructuring schools* (pp. 3–5). Madison, WI: Center on Organization and Restructuring of Schools.

45. Smrekar, C., & Goldring, E. (1999). *School choice in urban America: Magnet schools and the pursuit of equity*. New York: Teachers College Press, pp. 119–120.

46. Archibold, R. C. (1999, July 18). In season of play, daunting struggle to learn. *The New York Times*, pp. 1, 38.

47. Mason, D. (1999, July 9). Personal communication.

48. Garrigan, L. M. (1999, August 8). Work hard. You might win a prize. *The New York Times*, 11.

49. McCaslin, M., & Good, T. (1996). *Listening in classrooms*. New York: Harper Collins.

50. McCaslin, M., & Murdock, T. (1991). The emergent interaction of home and school in the development of students' adaptive learning. In M. Maehr & P. Bintrich (Eds.), *Advances in motivation and achievement* (Vol. 7, pp. 213–259). Greenwich, CT: JAI Press.

51. García, G., & García, M. (1996). Charter schools: Another top-down innovation. *Educational Research, 25*, 34–36.

52. Ibid., p. 34.

53. Editorial. (1999, July 21). No time to crow. *Arizona Daily Star*, A10.

54. For example, an examination of materials from the Educational Writers Association often have a "gotcha" mentality about how to find problems in schools and not to be snowed by school administrators, but comparatively rarely have ideas about promising interesting ways to do news coverage about positive events. As a case in point, in a recent issue of the *Education Reporter, 33(4)* Deb Kollars in the lead article entitled "A case of missing dropouts" offered the following strategy "If you have ever had doubts about the accuracy of high school dropout rates, trust your instincts and take a look at high school graduation rates as well. If you see a big gap in the numbers, you probably have an important story to tell" (p. 1).

55. Blair, J. (1999, August 4) MO. Lawmakers OK sweeping K-12 reform package. *Education Week*, 22, 28.

56. Steinberg, J. (1999, June 25). Advancing an agenda. *The New York Times*, p. A23.

57. The Marshall Plan was proposed by Secretary of State George Marshall and aided European nations in economic recovery following World War II.

58. McCaslin M., & Good, T. (1996). *Listening in classrooms*. New York: Harper Collins.

59. Henke, R., Chen, X., & Goldman, G. (1999, July 7). *What happens in classrooms? Instructional practices in elementary and secondary schools, 1994–98* [Online]. Available: http://www.nces.ed.gov/pubsearch/pubsinfo.asp?pubid=199348.

60. Viadero, D. (1999, August 4). Broad federal study of teachers looks inside classrooms. *Education Week*, 18.

61. Ibid.

62. Manning, S. (1999, March 24). Classrooms for sale. *The New York Times,* A27.

63. Portner, J. (1999, June 23). Florida's four-pronged attack on teen smoking pays off. *Education Week, 18*(41), 7.

64. For example, Chester Finn, a leading advocate for vouchers and charter schools, likes to describe his experience when he was in charge of OERI. In particular, he has noted that the proposals he received from researchers were poorly written, unimaginative, and most of them unworthy of consideration. However, what Finn fails to report is that the amount of money being offered in the competition was so low that many competent researchers decided more time and energy would be expended in competing than the funds warranted. Further, given the way in which OERI was politicized at the time, many researchers concluded that the competition was more about political fit than about interest in serious basic research.

Epilogue

Presidential Election 2000 and Beyond

As we finalize this book in October 1999, the political hunting season on public schools has started once again. President Clinton has just released $100 million in new money for charter schools.[1] And although the 2000 year election is still 13 months away, both Governor George W. Bush and Vice President Albert Gore have issued statements about their positions on public education. Bush has indicated a willingness to remove federal funding from inner-city schools whose students test poorly and to provide parents with as much as $1,500 to help send their children to private schools (including religious schools). Furthermore, Bush expressed interest in guaranteeing $3 billion worth of private loans for new charter schools.[2] Gore has promised to bring about a "revolution in education." Among his proposals are reducing public school class sizes, making sure students develop basic computer competency by the end of eighth grade, encouraging parents to save for college, and testing teachers to certify their competency.[3]

In Cleveland, parents planning to transfer their children into private schools (using vouchers) were told on August 26, 1999 by Federal Judge Solomon Oliver, Jr. that the voucher program was suspended because it had the "primary effect of advancing religion."[4] The next day, he modified his ruling by allowing students previously enrolled in the program to use their vouchers in private schools. However, he denied students who had not already been in the program the right to transfer.[5]

Many educators and politicians at the state and local levels are encouraging school improvement efforts. For example, New York City schools are requiring more than 14,000 students to repeat a grade because they failed a proficiency exam last spring and either did not enroll in mandatory summer school or failed to take the test.[6]

Furthermore, in the spring of 1999 it was reported that only 7% of Virginia's schools passed the state's achievement test (Standards of Living Test).[7] The other 93% face sanctions in the future if the test performance of their students does not improve. Although it is certainly possible to believe that 93% of Virginia schools' students failed to achieve a 70% passing score on the Standards of Living Test, it is difficult to believe that 93% of the schools in Virginia are inadequate. Yet these conceptions of failing public schools are being increasingly disseminated by politicians. Under the guise of standards and cracking down on unmotivated youth and their teachers, too many politicians seem motivated to describe American schools in sweepingly negative ways.

More than 50 years ago, the widely respected sociologist, Robert Merton, coined the expression "self-fulfilling prophecy"—a false belief that fulfills itself because many people believe the premise is true.[8] Merton used the hypothetical example of a run on a bank to represent the concept of a self-fulfilling prophecy. The bank was solvent but it collapsed because many people believed it was insolvent. Customers guaranteed the bank's failure by demanding the immediate return of all of their assets. What is the value, not to mention the ethics, of creating a run on a bank or a run on the public school system? The evidence presented in this book strongly suggests that such a run must be avoided and that monies should be transferred cautiously from public to charter schools on a very selective basis. Fortunately, some citizens are attempting to avoid a "run on the bank" by making massive gifts to public schools.[9]

Charter schools, as one mechanism encouraging innovation, especially in inner-city schools, are a good idea. Unfortunately, the political process that regulates charter schools needs to hold them accountable for innovation and for assessing the effects of that innovation on student development. Otherwise we won't learn from this educational experiment. As they listen to informed citizens in the coming months, we hope that politicians' educational perspectives will become more differentiated and that issues of quality, not just form, will become more prevalent in the great school debate.

Endnotes

1. National News Brief. (1999, August 29). Praising charter schools, Clinton announces aid. *The New York Times*, p. A16.

2. Sterngold, J. (1999, September 3). Bush would deny money to schools judged as failing. *The New York Times*, pp. A1, A12.
   Bruni, F. (1999, October 6). Bush says G.O.P. stresses wealth at expense of social ills. *The New York Times*, pp. A1, A14.
3. Ibid.
4. Johnson, D. (1999, August 26). Many Cleveland parents frantic as voucher ruling limits choice. *The New York Times*, pp. A1, A11.
5. Belluck, P. (1999, August 27). Federal judge revises order, allowing vouchers for now. *The New York Times*, pp. A1, A6.
6. Hartocollis, A. (1999, September 2). Most assigned to summer school, will not be promoted. *The New York Times*, p. A16.
7. Lewin, T. (1999, September 6). Schools taking tougher stance with standards. *The New York Times*, pp. A1, A11.
8. Merton, R. (1948). The self-fulfilling prophecy. *Antioch Review, 8*, 193–210.
9. Steinberg, J. (1999, September 23). Nation's wealthy, seeing a void, take steps to aid public schools. *The New York Times*, pp. A1, A19.
   Steinberg noted that Mr. Gates has recently announced $1 billion in college scholarships to support low-income high school students. Mr. Annenberg has contributed more than $800 million to public schools since 1993, and as another example, Mr. Board recently donated $100 million to public schools.

Author Index

Subject Index